UNIVERSITY GHAM

WITHDRAWN

Business and Politics in Britain

FROM THE LIBRARY

DATE DUE FOR RETURN

UNIVERSITY LIBRARY

1 7 AUG 2007

SEM BUS 03

This book may be recalled before the above date.

Also by Wyn Grant

Government and Industry: a Comparative Analysis of the US, Canada and the UK
Pressure Groups, Politics and Democracy in Britain
The Political Economy of Industrial Policy
Independent Local Politics in England and Wales
The Dairy Industry: an International Comparison
The CBI (with David Marsh)
The Politics of Economic Policy Making (with Shiv Nath)
Government and the Chemical Industry (with William Paterson and Colin Whitston)
The Political Economy of Corporatism (edited)

Business and Politics in Britain

Second Edition

Wyn Grant

NOTTINGHAM UNIVERSITY LIBRARY

MACMILLAN

© Wynford P. Grant 1987, 1993

All rights reserved. No reproduction, copy or transmission of
this publication may be made without written permission.

No paragraph of this publication may be reproduced, copied or
transmitted save with written permission or in accordance with
the provisions of the Copyright, Designs and Patents Act 1988,
or under the terms of any licence permitting limited copying
issued by the Copyright Licensing Agency, 90 Tottenham Court
Road, London W1P 9HE.

Any person who does any unauthorised act in relation to this
publication may be liable to criminal prosecution and civil
claims for damages.

First published 1987 by
THE MACMILLAN PRESS LTD
Houndmills, Basingstoke, Hampshire RG21 2XS
and London
Companies and representatives
throughout the world

ISBN 0–333–59330–8 hardcover
ISBN 0–333–59331–6 paperback

A catalogue record for this book is available
from the British Library.

First edition reprinted 1991
Second edition 1993

8   7   6   5   4   3   2
03 02 01 00 99 98 97

Printed in Hong Kong

For Sophia, Rosalind and Amelia

Contents

Contents

ix

Preface

It is now over twenty years since David Marsh and I travelled as postgraduate students from Exeter to Bristol to interview the regional office of the Confederation of British Industry for an article on that organisation we were writing to fill a puzzling gap in the political science literature. That was the start of what has proved to be an enduring interest in the relationship between business and politics, most recently extended to Russia and East-Central Europe. Over the past twenty years, I have acquired so many intellectual debts that it would be impossible to acknowledge them all. For the second edition of this book, the Nuffield Foundation awarded me a grant to conduct further interviews with business persons, business association officials, civil servants and others in London and Brussels. It was pleasant to meet some long established contacts again, some now in much more senior positions than when I first interviewed them, but also to meet some of the new participants in the world of business–government relations.

The first edition of this book was stimulated by my participation in a major international comparative project, co-ordinated by Wolfgang Streeck and Philippe Schmitter, on the organisation of business interests. I have continued to keep in contact with many of the participants in this project who have formed an informal network of individuals with broad interests in the area of the relationship between business and government. The study of business–government relations is a growing subject all over the world, and I am grateful to the academics and business persons who have sent me books, articles and papers they have written in the area.

The whole book has been thoroughly revised, but one of the chapters in the book that has required particularly extensive re-writing is that on the European Community, and I am grateful to Mike Cockburn and Jane Sargent for their extensive and helpful comments on earlier versions of this chapter. They bear no responsibility for its contents.

The University of Warwick has continued to provide an excellent intellectual environment for work concerned with business and government. I am particularly grateful to my colleagues in the Department of Politics and International Studies for their support and encouragement which has enabled me to combine continuing to research and write with my role as departmental chair. Special thanks are due to Professor Barry Buzan for his good advice and to the department's secretaries: Iris Host, Dorothy Foster and Linda Freeman.

Last but not least, thanks are due to my wife, Maggie, and to Sophia, Rosalind and Amelia for their tolerance, common sense and good humour. It is easy to become too preoccupied with large firms, and Ros's job as a junior manager in a small business has helped me to keep in mind the special challenges and problems facing smaller businesses.

WYN GRANT

Leamington Spa

1 Introduction

The 1980s were characterised by the retreat of the state. Privatisation and deregulation in Britain was part of a global trend, eclipsed in significance by the collapse of the old Communist states in the Soviet Union and Eastern Europe. The old orthodoxy of the mixed economy, and speculation about the benefits of a planned economy, collapsed in the face of a widespread acceptance of the supremacy of the market mechanism as the only sound basis for an economy.

Does this mean that government is no longer a significant factor in the decision-making environment of businesses, and that business–government relations are no longer a subject worthy of study? Far from it. It is true that old forms of government involvement with the economy have decayed. Nationalised industries have largely disappeared from Britain, and industrial policy is a shadow of its former self. However, the high priority of environmental issues on the political agenda has created a new form of politics which affects the operations of business. Deregulation has been accompanied by reregulation, and the emergence of a 'regulatory state' (see Chapter 3).

It was evident at the beginning of the 1990s that the advocacy of a pure market economy, in which government would simply provide the framework for economic activity, was being replaced by a new emphasis on a social market economy. Government should not seek to run the economy, but it should take action to cope with some of the less pleasant consequences of a market economy. In particular, government was seen as having a responsibility to safeguard the quality of life enjoyed by citizens. The emphasis on the term 'citizenship', if sometimes apparently used in a cosmetic fashion, itself reflected a shift away from the self-aggrandising agenda of the 1980s. Government action in areas such as the protection of the environment, or food safety, necessarily affects the commercial operations of firms. The treaty responsibilities to protect the environment given to the European Community under the Single European Act have increased its activity in this area,

1

ensuring that environmental protection issues are not dependent on the vagaries of domestic politics.

Government retains a responsibility for the general management of the economy, for example, the management of the exchange rate, even though for two years the options open to the British Government were constrained by membership of the Exchange Rate Mechanism of the EMS. It seeks to ensure that monopoly powers are not abused, that cartels are not allowed to operate, and that mergers which will significantly undermine competition do not go ahead; these are also areas in which the EC is assuming an increasing responsibility. Government's interest in restraining the harmful social consequences of the market mechanism is not limited to the environment and health and safety, important though these areas are. Other examples are interventions to prevent discrimination against women and ethnic minority groups. Government remains a major customer for some industries, such as pharmaceuticals and construction. Above all, government decisions about the level of taxation it needs to raise to fund its policies, and the ways in which it is going to raise taxes, have a profound impact on business.

Government, then, continues to significantly affect the operating environment of businesses ranging from the corner shop to the multinational enterprise. But government also depends on business. Electorates judge the success of modern governments to a considerable extent in economic terms, and such success often depends on business cooperation. For example, in 1991 the Conservative Government successfully pressurised leading building societies to pass on interest rate reductions to their customers as quickly as possible. The effectiveness of government policies in areas such as training depend considerably on business cooperation. Indeed, the dismantling of many quasi-governmental agencies has increased government dependence on business cooperation.

Business and government, then, need each other. However, the relationship between the two in Britain has not been one between two partners pursuing generally shared goals, as could be said to be the case in Japan. Rather, it has often been characterised by mutual mistrust and misunderstanding. Government's withdrawal from some of its relationships with business has not solved this problem. Indeed, in some respects, it may have compounded it by undermining some of the mechanisms which had been developed to improve contacts between business and government.

Questions of definition

A business is a company, public corporation, partnership or individual which sells goods and/or services with the intention of generating a surplus from its trading activities for its owners. This book is concerned with businesses of all kinds: manufacturing, distributive and commercial. It excludes non-profit-making organisations of various kinds which simply seek to cover their (long run) costs so that they can provide and develop a particular activity (e.g. a museum) and charities which intend to make a surplus on their fund-raising activities, but apply that surplus to a designated group of beneficiaries who do not 'own' the charity. Clearly, there are marginal cases. For example, consider a privately-owned steam railway which devotes most of its income to the task of preservation, but pays a deliberately restricted dividend to its shareholders. Unlike a preserved railway which ploughed all its surplus back into the activity, the former case would be counted a business. However, these marginal cases represent a very small portion of the whole range of analysis. The main focus here is on the large companies which dominate the highly-concentrated British economy, although attention is paid to smaller businesses and the particular problems they encounter in securing business representation.

This book's concern with business and politics is not focussed on the internal politics of businesses, although some references to decision-making processes within firms are necessary. Rather, the focus is on the interaction between business (as an aggregate of businesses) and political institutions: ministers and civil servants; Parliament; the European Community; and, to a lesser extent, local government. The term 'European Community' (EC) is used throughout to refer to the European Economic Community, the European Coal and Steel Community, Euratom, and their common institutions. When the term 'government' is used in this book (with a lower case 'g' and without any reference to a particular administration), it means ministers of the crown and the civil servants who advise them and execute their policies. The term 'state' is used sparingly to avoid depicting the apparatus of government as more monolithic that it actually is. When the term 'state' is used it is intended to refer to purposive, strategic actions by government with enduring consequences.

Reference will be made throughout the book to various types of associations representing business interests. Their nomenclature often gives rise to confusion. A 'trade association' seeks to defend and promote the common commercial interests of business enterprises operating in a particular sector of the economy. An 'employers' *organisation*' is an association concerned with collective bargaining and related industrial relations questions, but not with commercial matters. In many sectors, merged associations perform both functions; they may then be referred to as 'employers' *associations*'. This term also encompasses the business interest associations whose memberships are not confined to a particular sector of industry. These include the chambers of commerce serving all business enterprises in a city or town, and the 'peak' or 'umbrella' associations such as the Confederation of British Industry (CBI) which claim to speak for business as a whole at the national level.

Economic globalisation

Economic globalisation refers to a process whereby transactions across national borders become more important than those within nation-states, and whereby national borders cease to offer significant impediments to the movement of goods and services. This second condition is far from being fulfilled. Although economic interdependence between states has increased and is likely to increase further, it is easy to exaggerate the extent of the globalisation process. One constraint is the short supply of managers with a truly global perspective (Reich, 1991; Taylor 1991).

Even so, there are a number of changes taking place in the international economy which point to increasing globalisation. International trade continues to grow faster than national levels of output. 'Since the middle of 1980s, the volume of merchandise trade has expanded at significantly higher rates than world production. The growth rate of world trade in real terms was about 7 per cent, compared to an expansion of world production of 3 per cent' (Smeets, 1990, p. 60). Second, there has been a substantial internationalisation of world financial markets. For example, global turnover in the foreign exchange market more than doubled to 650 billion dollars a day in the three years to April 1989 (*Financial Times*, 29 April 1991). There has also been a marked increase in the creation of new financial instruments through what is known as 'financial engineering', the creation of customised products for borrowers and investors. Third, while world trade has been increasing more quickly than national output, foreign direct investment has been increasing even faster. 'While world trade volumes grew at a compound annual rate of 5 per cent between 1983 and 1988, global FDI increased by over 20 per cent in real terms over that period' (Julius, 1990, p. 14).

These developments have a number of implications for the subject matter of this book. One consequence of the continuing growth of foreign direct investment has been the emergence of a new type of international company, the 'stateless company'. Unlike the conventional multinational company, which has a home base in one state, and branch plants elsewhere, the 'stateless company' sets out to become a truly internationalised entity in terms of its ownership, management and operations. This phenomenon is discussed further in Chapter 5. One consequence that needs to be noted is that this development further increases the potential significance of the large firm as a political actor in its own right.

The internationalisation of financial markets in particular creates a more unstable decision-making environment for national governments. It becomes more difficult for a national government to follow a distinctive national economic strategy, as both France and New Zealand discovered in the 1980s (Hall, 1986; Jesson, 1987, 1989). Even so, one must be careful about an increasingly fashionable orthodoxy of simultaneous globalisation and localisation which argues that the nation-state is becoming irrelevant, with power shifting upwards to supranational bodies like the European Community, and downwards to local and regional authorities who are able to be more responsive to community problems. The nation-state still possesses considerable bureaucratic resources and the ability to enact and implement authoritative decisions. Local government in Britain has become more constrained in the 1980s.

Even so, the European Community is gradually acquiring more statelike characteristics, and more decisions that affect British business are being taken in Brussels. Its major limitation, and an important opportunity from the perspective of business lobbyists, is that it is still largely dependent on national governments for the implementation of its decisions. Even so, the period since the publication of the first edition of this book has seen the passage and implementation of the EC treaty revision known as the Single European Act. This has both enlarged the powers and responsibilities of the EC (e.g., in environmental protection), and increased the use of majority voting in the Council of Ministers. It is clear that the EC dimension has become increasingly

important for business, an importance that is reflected not only in a
separate chapter on business representation at the EC level (Chapter 9),
but also in a consideration of the EC dimension throughout the book.

The politics of production and of collective consumption

The 1980s have seen a shift from what may be termed a 'politics of
production' towards a 'politics of collective consumption'. In more
general terms, this could be viewed as a shift from a modernist to a
postmodernist form of politics. Thus, there has been a 'gradual
weakening ... of a politics based ... on class interests and class perceptions' (Heller and Fehér, 1988, p. 3). What takes its place is more
heterodox, and has no room for grand theories. Rather, one sees 'the
continuous creation of brand-new, and highly diverse, social issues'
(ibid., p. 10). The shopping mall replaces the factory as a central source
of activity and identity.

Although set against the background of this transformation, the terms
used here have a more precise meaning in the context of the discussions
of the politics of business. A politics of production is centred around a
struggle between management and labour over the distribution of the
fruits of the productive process. It focusses on such issues as wages
and conditions; the rights of trade unions; industrial relations law;
arrangements for worker participation in decision-making; and attempts
by government to intervene in collective bargaining through incomes
policies. Such issues, not least incomes policies, were at the centre of
political debate in Britain and most other western states in the 1970s.
They gave rise to a form of politics that has often been termed neo-
corporatist (see Chapter 2).

The politics of collective consumption is concerned with the outcomes
of the production process, rather than what happens within the process
itself. It focusses on the externalities of the production process. It is
termed a politics of *collective* consumption because at its core is a
concern with public goods, or at least goods which have some of the
characteristics of public goods (or public bads). Examples would include
the quality of the area we breathe, the quality of the sea water we bathe
in, or the contamination of the soil by toxic substances. It generates a
form of politics which is far less amenable to corporatist solutions.

This political agenda needs to be distinguished from the older social
agenda concerned with such questions as health policy and pensions

policy, issues which social democratic parties and labour movements historically saw as one of their central concerns, and which could form part of corporatist trade offs on that favourite term of the centre left in the 1970s, 'the social wage'. Although such rights may have been collectively pursued, they were individually consumed in a way which is not true of the atmosphere or weather systems influenced by global warming.

It is not implied that the politics of production has disappeared from the political agenda, or that the politics of collective consumption will necessarily dominate. Indeed, there are some signs that the trend towards a politics of collective consumption may have been halted. California is often seen as a harbinger of political trends elsewhere, and has been in the forefront of the environmental movement. In November 1990, California electors voted down by a majority of nearly two to one the so-called 'Big Green' referendum initiative. In Germany, the West German Greens have lost their seats in the Bundestag, although they continue to be influential at Land level.

To some extent, these setbacks for the environmental movement may be a cyclical response to economic recession. There has been a lasting shift in the direction of an increased importance for quality of life issues on the political agenda, perhaps part of a more general trend in the direction of a post-modern form of politics. The increased attention given to environmental issues in primary and secondary education may help to ensure that future generations of voters give a higher priority to environmental issues.

Changes in the politics of food in Britain provide an illustration of the way in which the political agenda has been changing. Smith notes (1991, p. 235), 'In the last two years food and, in particular, the production and quality of food has become a political issue.' New and radical pressure groups, and substantial media interest, have forced food safety issues to the centre of the political stage, removing them from what had been a closed policy community. In the early years of the postwar period, scarcity of food was the central issue, a problem which required technical solutions by industry, government and various experts. Once people have enough food to eat, however, they develop new priorities. Smith observes (ibid., p. 253), 'with adequate supplies of food, interest in healthier eating rather than the provision of food has developed.' A politics of production has been partially displaced by a politics of collective consumption.

This shift in the political agenda has a number of implications for business. It increases political uncertainty. When the main antagonist of business was organised labour, the battle was conducted on familiar territory and in accordance with some basic rules of the game. Industrial disputes could be settled by adjustments at the margin in the employer's offer. Both employers and workers had an ultimate interest in a settlement which would allow the enterprise to continue in production. Indeed, trade unions have often supported employers in disputes with environmentalists. Environmentalists may be less easy to satisfy with particular concessions. They may not be interested in whether a particular firm continues in production; indeed, in many cases, they would be happier if it ceased production. Moreover, quality of life issues are often conducted in the full glare of media publicity. Environmental disasters provide compelling pictures for television and the press, while food scares can be the main news story for days on end.

Even so, the change in the balance of power must not be exaggerated. Business interest associations remain better resourced than their environmental counterparts. The environmental movement is divided over objectives and methods. Many environmental groups have very specific concerns. For example, the largest mass membership environmental group in Britain is the Royal Society for the Protection of Birds. Some groups favour radical tactics, while others prefer to use more conventional methods of exerting pressure. Diversity can, however, be an asset. Drawing on Canadian experience, J. Wilson notes (1990, p. 150), 'It means that the movement as a whole is able to cover a range of tactical bases, and that some segment of the movement can usually be counted on to gravitate quickly to the approach deemed most appropriate in a particular circumstance. The movement's opponents have found it to be something of a hydra.' It should be noted, however, that some of the more radical anti-growth groups have disappeared or been seriously weakened. Apart from the radical fringe of the animal rights movement, business now has responsible environmental groups it can negotiate with.

Business is itself ambivalent about environmentalism. The environmental concerns of consumers may provide an opportunity to launch new products which can be priced higher than conventional products. Retail stores have been at the forefront of 'green consumerism', seeking to identify with what they see as the new quality of life concerns of their customers. This may amount to little more than a symbolic form of niche marketing, but it also may represent an opportunity for consumers, in conjunction with large scale retailers, to bring about changes in products and their packaging not through politics, but through the exercise of market power. There is also a substantial and growing market for environmental control devices and systems, even if this 'end of pipe technology' often only converts one waste stream into another. The Swiss-Swedish multinational ABB received over four billion dollars worth of orders in its environmental control business in 1991, and expects strong growth to double the size of this business segment by the mid-1990s.

The balance of business interests on environmental issues may, therefore, change. While a 'dark green' position is difficult to reconcile with present methods of industrial production, business may be able to accommodate environmental and consumer groups with more specific demands. What is clear is that the political agenda which business faces in the 1990s is very different from that of the 1970s. A senior government relations manager commented in an interview in 1992, 'The impact of environmental questions is far greater than five years ago. I spend more time talking to civil servants and MPs about environmental matters than any other subject.' In the 1970s, government seemed to be increasingly intervening in the key investment and pricing decisions of business, leading some analysts to predict an economic system of private ownership and state control achieved through 'imposing intensive state control in all major areas of private economic activity' (Pahl and Winkler, 1975, p. 29). Such predictions at the time seemed to be a reasonable echo of contemporary fears. In the 1990s, the politics of collective consumption is creating more indirect but nevertheless influential forms of government intervention which may be summarised through the concept of 'the regulatory state' (see Chapter 3).

The comparative context

This book is about business–government relations in Britain, but an attempt is made to place the findings within an internationally comparative context, a theme that is returned to in the conclusion. It is important to ask whether there is anything that is distinctive about business–government relations in Britain from the patterns to be found in other advanced western countries.

Relations between business and government do not occur within a vacuum: they occur within the context of a set of shared (or different) values, mutual understandings (or misunderstandings), and uncodified, but nevertheless significant 'rules of the game'. Mutual but unstated

understandings between, for example, civil servants and business association officials about how relations should be conducted are generally
of greater importance than formally stated rules in the British case. In
particular, specific legal provisions play a relatively unimportant part in
shaping business–government relations in Britain compared, for
example, with countries such as France and West Germany where
chambers of commerce enjoy public law status. In the United States,
where adversarial legal proceedings play an important role in defining
and enforcing the conditions under which business operates, regulation
through the courts is much more important than in the United
Kingdom. In countries such as Britain the general 'tone of the
relationship is more consensual and less confrontational' (Calingaert,
1992, p. 30). The British emphasis is on the mutual search for
pragmatic, 'common sense' compromises, a search aided by the
existence of a common language code shared by civil servants, business
association officials, and even some business persons, particularly those
'industrial politicians' who regularly interact with government. This
language code is characteristically one of understatement. Where there
are conflicts of interest or value, they are hidden in the thickets of long
sentences, hedged round with qualifying clauses.

Nevertheless, it is important to be cautious about cultural explanations. They can seem to explain everything, and yet explain nothing. It
is too easy to assume shared values where they do not exist, or to
accumulate evidence which appears to sustain a particular interpretation, without looking at conflicting evidence or alternative interpretations of the evidence used (see Grant, 1982). Used improperly, culture
can easily become a garbage can variable, to which everything that
cannot be explained in other ways is too readily assigned.

Even so, there is some value in cultural explanations, particularly
when they are applied to elite groups that interact frequently with one
another, and often have shared backgrounds, as is the case with business persons, their representatives and civil servants in Britain. Dyson
draws an interesting distinction between industrial cultures which stress
a 'private' concept of the autonomy of action and self-sufficiency of
the firm (as in Britain) and those which emphasise a 'public' conception of the firm seen as intermeshed within a network of institutional
interests based on an acceptance of the central role of the state (Dyson,
1983). Self-organisation of industry can give business associations an
ability to coordinate intra-industry adjustment. However, in the British
and American cases, the cultural tradition of the self-sufficient firm

meant that 'industrial associations did not acquire the wide range of functions and the integrative role that would have enabled them to preside over an intra-industry adjustment' (Dyson, 1983, p. 56).

It is certainly the case that industrial policy in Britain has been premised on the autonomy of the firm, and it also true that one can find many descriptions in the literature about the 'arms length' relationship between government and business. Equally, business persons frequently complain that government does not really understand industry's needs and priorities. However, it is easy to fall into the trap of exaggerating the gap between government and business. There is, after all, a long established tradition in Britain, reinforced by civil service rules, of consulting with affected interests (see Jordan and Richardson, 1982, p. 87). Business cannot complain that it does not have ample opportunities to put its point of view across to government. Vogel's comparative study of environmental regulation in Britain and the United States suggests that business is much more of an 'insider' in the policy-making process in Britain. His study shows that in the United States business participation in policy making largely involves lobbying, an activity directed from outside the place where policy decisions are made. In Britain, on the other hand, industry is an active and officially recognised participant in the policy process itself (see Vogel, 1986).

It could be, however, that the elaborate processes of consultation are simply a courtly dance designed to entice business into the arms of government. This is the view taken by writers such as Nettl (1965) who see business persons as lacking a social identity of their own, and as having been emasculated through being drawn into a consensus that emanates from Whitehall. In many respects, this view is shared by business persons. In his study of the British business elite, Fidler summarises the view of business power in Britain as follows: 'the government that is, in practice, the cabinet plus senior civil servants, controls business, not business the government' (Fidler, 1981, p. 231). In particular, British business persons 'drew unfavourable contrasts between their position and that of their French, German or even American equivalents. A particular complaint was of the enormous volume of legislation aimed at industry' (Fidler, 1981, p. 231).

The idea that business in Britain is more harshly treated by government than business in France or the United States, however firmly such view is adhered to by business persons, is scarcely credible, and it does not square with most of the available evidence. In particular, the notion of a lack of trust and understanding between business and government in Britain is inconsistent with statements that have been made by business association leaders and officials comparing their relationships with the civil service with those enjoyed by their counterparts in other western countries. For example, one official of a chemical industry association commented in an interview: 'when I talk to other associations in Europe and outside Europe, perhaps there is a closer relationship between our association and government than other industries experience'.

How can this somewhat contradictory evidence about the closeness or otherwise of business and government in Britain be reconciled? First, it should be pointed out that business association officials may be closer to government than to business persons. After all, it is the job of business association officials to maintain close and regular contacts with government, and some of them are former civil servants themselves. Second, business persons in very large companies are likely to have regular contacts with government, whereas smaller businesses will not usually enjoy such contacts. Indeed, they are likely to be ideologically suspicious of government (see Scase and Goffee, 1980). Third, the existence of contacts does not mean that the form and nature of such contacts is determined by business; indeed, they are much more likely to take place on government's terms.

Are government–business relations in Britain more distant and more adversarial than in most other countries? There are plenty of mechanisms for contact which, on the whole, work well; there is much familiarity, in the sense that business association officials, leading business persons and civil servants know each other well; but there is much less mutual understanding than all this contact and familiarity would suggest. On the part of business, there is a persistent individualistic ethic which dates back to the origins of industrialisation in Britain and which is difficult to adjust in changed circumstances to engender effective collective action. On the part of government, there is a tendency to see business association as 'lobbies', legitimate interlocutors with government, but not part of the system of governance itself. The growth in the numbers of political consultants (see Chapter 5) and the employment of some individuals with such a background in trade associations had, by the early 1990s, encouraged more emphasis on a 'strategic lobbying' rather than an 'intermediation' role in some business associations.

A typology of business–government relations

The typology sets up a series of ideal types characterising the *predominant* form of business–government interaction. The framework of analysis is built on the answers to two simple but fundamental questions. First, are government–business relations mediated or unmediated? In other words, is the preferred form of business–government contact direct between firms and government, or does it take place through an intermediary? If the answer is through an intermediary, then a second question is whether the principal intermediary is a political party or a system of business associations. The answers to these questions lead to the identification of three basic types: the company state (e.g., the United States); the associative state (e.g., Germany) and the party state (e.g., Italy). These terms are not intended to characterise the form of the state entirely in terms of its pattern of business–government relations. The labels are simply terms of convenience.

In practice, all three types of government–business interaction will be found in any one country. There will always be some direct government–business contacts; there will always be some use of business associations; and political parties will always play some part in government–business relationships. However, by identifying and analysing the predominant mode of interaction, it may be possible to make some useful general statements about business–government relationships in different societies. It should be noted that it is not pretended that the nature of these relationships does not change over time. The form taken by business–government relationships will be affected by important changes elsewhere in the political system such as changes in the party system. For example, business–government relations in Japan would be profoundly affected if the Liberal Democratic Party ever lost its dominant status.

'The state' is regarded in this analysis as a variable rather than a constant, i.e. its role in relation to the character of business–government relationships may vary from country to country, and over time within one country. Thus, for example, Italy is characterised by an incoherent state, one in which civil society penetrates the state, which has the effect of increasing the political space in which the parties, and factions within them, may manoeuvre for advantage. In Britain, a supposedly 'weak' state, the Thatcher Government changed political structures and the 'rules of the game' in such a way as to bring about significant changes in the form of business–government relations. One prediction that can be derived from the typology is that each form of business–government relations identified has implications for public policy implementation (see Chapter 8).

Britain displays many of the characteristics of a company state. In a company state the most important form of business–state contact is the direct one between company and government. Government prioritises such forms of contact over associative intermediation. Government relations divisions form within large companies to handle relations with government.

The development of a company state in Britain is relatively recent, dating form the mid-1970s, and accelerating over the last few years. For much of the twentieth century, attempts were made to invigorate business associations in Britain, but these attempts largely ended in failure. The reasons for these failures are complex, but they include a persistent individualism which considered that the best way that government could help industry was to keep out of its affairs, and the absence of a developmental state engaged in a catching-up activity of the kind found in Germany and Japan (Marquand, 1988). Judge (1990, pp. 3–4) observes:

> Industrial development ... occurred within a context of ideas and social and political relations which all stressed the separation of enterprise from government. British success was ... believed to emanate from individual initiative, the self-sufficiency of the firm and resolute leadership of individual entrepreneurs.

By the Second World War, if not before, it was evident that 'British trade associations had proved largely ineffective because of the suicidal individualism of the British manufacturer' (Barnett, 1986, p. 269). Any action that involved compulsion rather than the customary voluntary approach was, however, avoided as much as possible, and such interventions as government did make by forming new associations increased the complexity and incoherence of the 'system' of associations (Grant, 1991a). The Second World War did, however, draw industry and government closer together, and the more interventionist postwar policies necessitated by the adoption of a full employment commitment meant that a closer continuing relationship was unavoidable. What emerged as a response to the evident deficiencies of British trade associations was an ersatz associative state, in which to some extent the aggregation and representation of business interests had to take place within the state apparatus itself through sponsorship divisions in ministries dealing with industry.

Direct contact with business has always been an attractive option in Britain because the economy is so highly concentrated. Grove (1962, p. 157) noted, 'The largest firms are so large they can deal with Government departments direct.' This trend accelerated in the 1970s, a period which saw the formation of government relations divisions in many of the largest firms. From the mid-1970s onwards, civil servants put increasing emphasis on direct contacts with firms (Mueller, 1985, p. 105). In 1988, the then Secretary of State for Trade and Industry, Lord Young, abolished the sponsorship divisions which had been a key element in fostering government contact with trade associations. Lord Young denounced trade associations as 'the lowest common denominator, producing mutual dependency between sectors and sponsoring civil servants' (*Financial Times*, 16 January 1988).

Germany offers a good example of the associative state in which business associations play a key role as intermediaries between business and the state (Sweden is another example). Peak associations in Germany do represent the summit of a hierarchically integrated system of associations, rather than being umbrella associations as in Britain. The BDI and BDA are associations of associations, with a measure of authority over their member associations. The sectoral and subsectoral associations are well-resourced, have high membership densities, have clearly demarcated areas of responsibility, and provide a wide range of services to their members. In addition to this well-resourced and vertically integrated system of business associations, there is obligatory membership of the chambers of commerce and of Handwerk (*artisan*) organisations. The 'characteristics of British and German subnational [business interest associations] suggest clear differences in their respective capacities to represent and to act upon the territorial interests of their members' (Anderson, 1991, p. 73). Government relations divisions are relatively unknown in Germany.

German business associations exhibit an ability to substitute self-regulation for intended regulation by the state. Analysis of comparative data on British and German business associations shows that the German associations are more likely to provide exclusive services to their members which have state backing or support (Grant, 1986). In every category analysed except one (which related to a peculiarity of

British competition law), German associations had a higher level of supply of such special services to members. They were particularly active in the administration of public policy programmes in the area of vocational training.

Italy offers a good example of business–government mediation through a political party or, more precisely, through factions within a dominant political party. The parties have tended 'to control sectors of civil society, and colonize state institutions' (Martinelli and Grant, 1991, p. 278). The state apparatus in Italy is poorly developed, with civil society penetrating the state as much as the state has penetrated civil society. Employers associations developed later than in other countries, and territorial forms of organisation remain important.

In the 1950s there were well developed bilateral links between the employers organised in Confindustria and the politically dominant Christian Democratic Party (DC). However, successful industrialisation produced new lines of division. 'The once close link between a unified party and a rather homogeneous business class became instead a fragmented network of influences in which different party factions were allied to different centres of economic power' (Martinelli and Treu, 1984, p. 284). The relationship between business and the political sphere fragmented, with major firms developing their own lobbying capabilities, and funding several factions within the DC simultaneously.

Since the late 1970s, there have been a number of changes in the Italian economy and political system. The centre-left parties have become more significant, although business seems in part to have used this new situation to bring about changes within the DC. Management of the major state firms has been depoliticised. Multinational technocrats who live by the rules of the game of the international business community, rather than domestic Italian rules, have become more significant. There has been some modernisation of business associations.

The evidence suggests that the influence of parties in Italy in diminishing, although it is still greater than in other western countries. The party state model, in which party factions receive donations in return for political support and financial favours from government, is incompatible with a modern economy run by technocratic managers. Under a party state arrangement, 'the style of managers was political, not entrepreneurial, the criterion for evaluating performance was party allegiance rather than professional achievements, and corporate strategies were more important to political competition than to market competition' (Grant and Martinelli, 1991, p. 87).

There are some interesting parallels between Italy and Japan, notably in terms of the key role of a factionalised hegemonic party, and the extensive if controversial involvement of organised criminals in business transactions. Despite these interesting similarities, the Japanese case is an exceptional one in terms of the typology because it manages to combine elements of the company state, the associative state and the party state. Large Japanese companies have direct contacts with ministries such as the Ministry of International Trade and Industry, and their own equivalents of government relations divisions. The system of business associations in Japan is well-developed, and performs a range of functions on behalf of government in such areas as export promotion. Dore notes (1987, p. 15) that industry associations are 'the vehicle for a wide range of concerted activities, frequently conducted under the guidance, surveillance, covert condoning, or subsidization of their sponsoring ministry'.

There is a close relationship between business and particular factions within the governing LDP. Much business activity is directed at the Policy Affairs Research Councils which draft laws for the LDP. However, 'so long as MITI and industry can work together to achieve common goals that advance private and public interests, there is little reason for either side to involve the LDP. It is only when industry feels that it cannot work out mutually acceptable industrial policies with MITI ... that incentives arise to turn to the LDP for political assistance' (Okimoto, 1989, pp. 181–2).

All these relationships add up to a political economy in which 'the relationship between the bureaucratic and industrial bodies of Japan remains close to a degree without parallel in the western world' (van Wolferen, 1989, p. 45). Samuels characterises the Japanese state in terms of a negotiated politics of reciprocal consent which produces a series of shifting compacts between business and government (Samuels 1987). This is very different from the British experience, and it would be foolish to suppose that the Japanese system, even less parts of it, could be transposed elsewhere. 'The adoption of parts of the System is not likely to work without the rest of the Japanese package, and the costs of that package cannot be paid by the West' (van Wolferen, 1989, p. 16).

It is predicted that party state forms of government–business relationship are likely to become less important in the future. It is increasingly unacceptable in a modern state for the benefits of public policy programmes to be dispensed as favours, as part of a network of mutual reciprocity in which, for example, donations to party funds lead to public contracts. In a party state, publicly appointed offices may be dispensed on a patronage basis rather than in accordance with criteria of competence and, in the worst possible outcome, criminal organisations may be able to derive substantial sums from public funds. All these dysfunctional aspects of a party state are apparent in Italy, with third world public services being delivered in a first world society. Even in Japan, where the party state is complemented by other forms of business–government relations, there may eventually be less tolerance in the future of relationships that would be regarded as corrupt in other advanced industrial countries.

The long run prediction that is offered on the basis of the typology is that the company state model of business–government relations will tend to become more important in the long run. Business associations will continue to be important as intermediaries, particularly in those countries where they have been historically strong. The trend towards a greater emphasis on direct relationships between business and government will be a very long drawn-out one, not least because there are many variables which influence the form of relationships between business and government. One important factor, however, is the emergence of the 'stateless' corporation referred to earlier in the chapter. Such international companies are in the vanguard of developing highly-sophisticated government relations functions in each of the countries in which they operate. They are likely to place a considerable emphasis on direct, high-level contacts with governments. 'Although there is some evidence that trade associations are themselves becoming international in scope ... their response lags a long way behind that of the leading transnational firms' (Cawson *et al.*, 1990, p. 32).

The political weakness of business

The central argument of this book is that Britain has a business sector in which there is an increasing concentration of economic power, but that business remains politically weak, making it difficult for government to enter into a partnership relationship with business even if it wanted to. This imbalance is debilitating, and potentially dangerous.

It is not easy for business in Britain either to define its interests or to select the best political strategy for pursuing them, in part because there are important divisions of interest between different sectors of business (and not just between financiers and industrialists), in part because the optimal strategy to secure a desired end is not always readily apparent or, at any rate, is the subject of dispute. The business community in Britain is capable of acting politically in a cohesive fashion if the perceived level of threat is sufficiently high, as was the case with the Bullock Report on industrial democracy in the late 1970s. In general, however, 'For more than a century and a half British capital has been weakly represented both politically and bureaucratically' (Leys, 1985, p. 14; see also Nettl, 1965; Brown, 1981; Tylecote, 1981). Business in Britain has not been able to get its political act together. As Leys convincingly shows, an effort was made by the CBI to get business leaders to think strategically in political terms, but this met with little response. Only two of the twenty business leaders interviewed by Leys in 1983 'saw the direction of the state, the definition of national goals and of strategies for achieving them, as natural concerns of business-men, and neither of these had ever sought a major role in leading or forming business opinion' (Leys, 1985, p. 19).

Business has not been without political influence. However, at times of crisis for the economy, leadership in the sense of developing and articulating an overall strategy has not been provided by business persons and their representatives, but by politicians with their own vision of what business needs (see Chapter 7). This was particularly true of the Thatcher Government which represented a departure from the historical relationship between business and the state in Britain of 'bargaining between two weak entities which often did not know their own minds' (Turner, 1984, p. 3). The Thatcher Government had a clear view of what was needed to secure a revival of business enterprise, although the question remains whether what British business needs is not so much freedom from the shackles of the state, but a mutually supportive relationship with government. At the end of the Thatcher decade, the British economy still displayed fundamental weaknesses in areas such as vocational and technical education and management skills, suggesting that there are deep-seated economic problems which cannot simply be resolved by the actions of autonomous firms freed from the shackles of government.

The political weakness of British business makes it difficult to implement any concertative approach to the country's problem, such as might be favoured by a broad spectrum of opinion, ranging from Tory moderates to the mainstream of the Labour Party. The absence of 'employer solidarity' in Britain compared with countries such as Germany (for an analysis of this contrast, see Tylecote 1981) is a continuing problem. Ineffective employer organisation is as much an obstacle to developing a concertative approach to economic policy problems as the deficient trade union organisation which is more usually blamed. The political weakness of business is therefore a rarely acknowledged indirect cause of relative economic decline.

Proposals for a more effective relationship between business and government are often dismissed as an attempt to resurrect the nightmare of corporatism. The Thatcher Government took the view that 'The ability of the economy to change and adapt was hampered by the combination of corporatism and powerful unions. Corporatism limited competition and the birth of new firms, while at the same time, encouraging protectionism and restrictions designed to help existing firms' (Cm. 278, 1988, p. 1). It is questionable whether Britain has ever really had arrangements that can properly be termed corporatist. In any event, countries such as Japan have managed to develop partnership relationships between business and government without corporatism (van Wolferen, 1989, p. 81). A balance has to be drawn between necessary cooperation and desirable competition. In his analysis of the factors affecting competitive advantage, Porter (1990, p. 594) notes how the efforts of firms can be complemented by trade associations upgrading the pool of factors from which all the firms in an industry draw. When trade associations are primarily lobbying organisations, their most important potential benefit is squandered.

It has long been recognised that business–government relationships in Britain are far from satisfactory. As is often the case in Britain, the capacity for analysis is not often matched by an ability to bring about change. This problem is returned to in the conclusion, but if this book helps to bring about a realisation that there is a problem that needs addressing, it will have achieved its purpose.

2 The Power of Business

In this chapter, alternative perspectives on the power of business are reviewed. 'Business' is no more of a monolith than the state, but before attempting to consider distinctions between, for example, large firms and small firms, a general overview of its power potential will be offered. In particular, the nature and extent of differences in the power position of manufacturing industry and the financial sector will be considered more fully in Chapter 4.

In providing an overview of the power of business, a distinction will be drawn between three different perspectives: pluralist perspectives, corporatist perspectives, and those which emphasise the privileged position of business in society. Limiting the discussion to three main perspectives does conflate a variety of viewpoints. For example, those analysts who consider that capital is a privileged interest may arrive at that conclusion from a perspective based on a model of society dominated by elite groups for whom ownership and control of the means of production is just one resource, or they may stress the central importance of patterns of ownership and control. Those influenced by the neo-Marxist tradition adopt a variety of views about the role of the state in protecting the interests of capital. However, as will be suggested later, although the three main perspectives may appear to be highly divergent both between and within themselves, there are also elements of convergence in their interpretation.

Pluralism

With its emphasis on the dispersal of power in society, the non-cumulative character of any inequalities in its distribution, and the way in which the exercise of power is supposedly checked by the activities of countervailing groups, pluralism remains a highly influential perspective. Indeed, given what must be regarded as the failure of the

21

project to establish corporatism as a distinct model, and the weakening of the neo-Marxist tradition, pluralism has re-established itself as the most acceptable model of political analysis, even if in the British case this acceptance is tempered by a scepticism about the realities of political power (Jordan, 1990a, p. 471).

Some defenders of the Marxist tradition would like to claim that it has been strengthened rather than weakened by the collapse of state socialist regimes in Eastern Europe and the Soviet Union, because the situation is no longer confused by the existence of a debased form of socialism. This is not a very credible argument, but perhaps an even more serious problem has been the diversion of Marxist analysis into debates which may be less useful than the participants in them would claim. The debate about the supposed transition from Fordist to post-Fordist modes of production and consumption has preoccupied many analysts influenced by a Marxist tradition, but the value added by this debate provides is open to question. Fordism refers to a system of assembly line standardised production for a mass market, post-Fordism to the use of information technology for new forms of more specialised production. Numerous forms of 'prefix Fordism' have been identified (neo, flexi, flawed, peripheral to name but a few), but even those sympathetic to this approach are obliged to admit that 'a lot of speculative "newspeak" ... uses this increasingly popular heading' (Nielsen, 1991, p. 27).

Pluralism has itself been seen as highly congruent with post-modernist analyses of politics. It has been claimed that 'Pluralism (of various kinds) is implicit in postmodernity as a project' (Heller and Fehér, 1988, p. 5) and that postmodernism as a cultural movement can be seen as a 'boundless pluralism' (ibid., p. 138). Yet before we celebrate too enthusiastically the extent to which pluralism is in tune with the postmodernist times, it is worth pausing for reflection. The very elasticity of pluralism that makes it attractive to so many is also a central weakness. A wide variety of power distributions and policy outcomes can be accommodated within a pluralist model, an outcome which is, of course, perfectly consistent with the assumption that there are dispersed inequalities of power. It should be emphasised that the criticism sometimes made of pluralism that it assumes an equal dispersal of influence is misplaced. As Williamson (1989, p. 53) emphasises, 'the pluralist argument is that *influence is widely, not equally, dispersed*. Pluralists do recognise that there are inequalities in influence among different interests.' Similarly, pluralist assumptions about the ease with which interest groups can be formed have also been caricatured. Rather than assuming that groups find it equally easy to organise and acquire political influence, 'pluralist empirical studies display a realistic understanding of the influences which pattern groups' success or failure' (Dunleavy, 1988, p. 23).

Although some analytical developments within the pluralist tradition, such as the idea of policy communities, have been helpful, the predictive power of the pluralist approach remains weak. Jordan complains (1990b, p. 286), 'Since pluralism is so vague a set of ideas it is difficult to understand how opponents can have rejected it with such confidence.' It is this very vagueness which is being objected to. Pluralism covers most eventualities, yet explains less than one might hope. While accepting Jordan's argument that any single model is likely to be inadequate, political science's claims as a discipline must rest on more than a model that offers vagueness and variety.

One of the difficulties that immediately arises in using pluralism as an analytical perspective is that there is a wide variety of pluralist interpretations which could be deployed to analyse the power of business. Lively (1978, p. 191) develops a useful distinction between 'arena' and 'arbiter' pluralist approaches:

> The arbiter theory envisages government as standing above the group battle, settling the ground rules for the conflict (particularly those determining what groups and what modes of action are legitimate), ensuring the enforcement of those rules, and perhaps correcting imbalances if there is danger of particular groups growing into overmighty subjects. The arena theory, in contrast, sees politicians merely as co-equal participants in the group battle.

This distinction does help us to make sense of the diversity of approach that characterises pluralist thinking. As Lively points out, the arena theory assumes 'that the given distribution of power is generally acceptable' (ibid., p. 200). The arbiter theory could be said to assume a more interventionist state which determines 'what groups are legitimate, how they may legitimately act, and what is a proper balance between their powers ' (ibid, p. 192). Such a state might, therefore, be concerned that groups such as unions and consumers had an adequate hearing as well as business. However, neither of these approaches requires the state to take any attitude towards the influence of business, although the arena approach effectively rules out governmental challenges to the existing distribution of power. Pluralist writers have, however, pronounced on the role of business in the political process. In particular, one of the classic works of pluralism, David Truman's *The Governmental Process* may be taken as setting out the conventional pluralist position on business as an interest.

Truman maintains that 'inequalities in the opportunities open to groups, of course, depend in large part on the structure and values of a given society' (Truman, 1951, p. 248). Critics of this position would argue that it begs the question of how that structure and those values arose in the first place and were then perpetuated. Truman's view is that the highest status in society is given to those groups whose achievements are particularly valued. The achievements of business in the United States have been such as to give it 'a status of the highest order' (ibid., p. 249).

Truman, then, does not deny that business is a privileged interest, but maintains that that position of privilege has been earned through the efforts of business in bringing about the prosperity of American society. However, this does not mean 'that in the United States and similar societies "business" groups always enjoy a controlling advantage as interest groups' (ibid., p. 253). Business groups have difficulty in maintaining internal cohesion and hence engaging in unified action. Moreover, 'economic power can be converted into political power only at a discount, variable in size' (ibid., p. 258). It could be argued that the distinction between economic and political power is a misleading one, although Truman maintains that what is different about political power is that it involves eliciting consent from a heterogeneous mass of people. Truman therefore concludes that although '"business" groups in the United States currently enjoy special advantages in the use of propaganda and in other political efforts, it does not follow that they are or must be dominant or exclusive or unchanging' (ibid., p. 259).

More recent accounts based on a pluralist perspective may be termed neo-pluralist in so far as they have moved away from the emphasis of some of the earlier discussions on interest group activity and the consequent neglect of the various interlocutors with which groups interacted, not least the state. In particular, the 'policy community' approach provides a framework for examining the behaviour of a whole range of actors within a particular political arena. Jordan and Richardson argue that within the setting of sectors based on government departments, 'there is a tendency for policy communities to emerge. The policy community in any area is an imprecise sector likely to alter from time to time and from particular issue to issue, yet it is worth identifying as a community: in other words, it has continuity, implicit authority structures' (Jordan and Richardson, 1982, p. 94). A policy community has a history, and an anticipation that it will provide the context for tackling further issues in the future, thus placing some constraints on the way in which current issues are processed (Jordan, 1990c, p. 326). 'The policy community is thus a special type of *stable* network which has advantages in encouraging bargaining in policy resolution' (ibid., p. 327). The policy community concept has become increasingly influential and has been used in a number of studies in a variety of contexts (for example, see Rhodes 1986).

This emphasis on the division of the policy-making map into 'a series of vertical compartments and segments' (Richardson and Jordan, 1979, p. 174) is perfectly consistent with the earlier pluralist contention that policy-making is carried out in a series of largely insulated issue arenas, with those actors who are influential in one issue arena generally being unable to exert a similar influence in other issue arenas. This vertical division of policy making could be seen as a inbuilt safeguard against undue concentrations of power, although as Richardson and Jordan comment (ibid., p. 174), 'One cost involved in the increasingly close relationship between groups and government is that the policy process has if anything excluded the general public from any effective influence.' Pluralism thus starts to degenerate into something that resembles an elite political cartel.

The 'policy community' approach has the merit of providing a basis for examining a wider range of actors in the policy-making process than more traditional versions of pluralism. It also offers the *potential* for examining the common values and shared assumptions which underpin the procedural values which regulate interaction in a policy community and which thus bind potentially opposed actors more closely together. However, even this does not really take account of the objection that particular interests may best be served not by overt political action, but by the unstated and hence unquestioned assumption of certain beliefs about what is and what is not politically possible. Thus, Blank's analysis of postwar British economic policy emphasises 'the creation of an interlocking network of policies which related to the preservation of Britain's role as a world power' (Blank, 1978, p. 102). These included such policies as the restoration of sterling's international reserve role, and fixed exchange rates. Despite the importance of such policies which, for example, could be argued to have damaged manufacturing industry, there was 'little debate and little discussion' (ibid., p. 103) about them.

As Coates observes, 'The power relationship of capital to govern-ment is of a subtler kind, less visible and more potent than simply the interaction of lobbyist and lobbied' (Coates, David, 1984, p. 77). However, it is this interaction which forms the focus of pluralist analyses. Moreover, pluralism has been criticised not just for providing an inadequate account of the political process by confusing the defence of interests with their organisation, but also on the grounds that the encouragement of pluralist forms of decision-making has pathological consequences for the political system as a whole.

This attack comes from two directions and leads to rather different prescriptions. On the one hand, there are those who argue that an encouragement of group activity leads such groups to dominate the political process to the detriment of more general interests. Monopoly rights are sought from the state by groups, and 'the resulting market privileges impose a welfare loss on consumers and taxpayers' (Mitchell, William, 1990, p. 95). Olson claims that special interests are 'harmful to economic growth, full employment, coherent government, equal opportunity and social mobility' (Olson, 1982, p. 237). In the British case in particular, 'society has acquired so many strong organ-isations and collusions that it suffers from an institutional sclerosis that slows its adaptation to changing circumstances and technologies' (ibid., p. 78). Such an analysis leads to the advocacy of neo-liberal solutions based on the repeal of all legislation that favours special interests and the application of rigorous anti-trust laws (ibid., p. 236). Olson does not believe that such a policy would be enforced, but it is worth noting that neo-liberals differ from pluralists in that they regard organised interests as a sign of democratic pathology rather than health. In particular, Mrs Thatcher was eager to condemn the influence of 'vested interests'.

Goldthorpe's analysis of the limitations of pluralism shares some common ground with Olson, although it leads to rather different con-clusions. He points to the 'generally damaging effects of interest group activity on the operation of market mechanisms' (Goldthorpe, 1984, p. 322). In particular, the power of organised labour makes standard techniques of macroeconomic management inoperable. One response is to transcend pluralism institutionally through corporatism which seeks to introduce a greater degree of order and predictability into relations between government and organised interests and also between those interests (ibid., p. 324). The other alternative is to limit the beneficiaries of pluralism through 'the widening of those sectors of production in which market forces and managerial authority are relatively unimpeded' (ibid., p. 338). Goldthorpe refers to this exclusion of a substantial part of the workforce from certain apparently well-established protections (such as the promise of full employment) as 'dualism'. Unlike Olson, his analysis of the spread of neo-liberalism draws attention to the losses incurred by particular sectors of the population, as distinct from the benefits supposedly accruing to the population at large as a resulting of the curbing of special interests.

Sociological analyses of business have often seen business as a key part of a ruling class or elite in society. The analytical task is then to tear away the veil which hides the dominant position of business, and to explain how conflicts between different 'fractions' of capital are mediated (see, for example, Overbeek 1986). Economists claim that the explanations they offer are 'invariably more rigorously deductive, and abstract than that of a political scientist' (Mitchell, William, 1990, p. 86). The elegance and explanatory power of the models developed may, however, offer a less good fit with the messy realities of the empirical world than some of the inductive efforts of political analysts. Political scientists realise that interests are not simply evident, but have to be identified; they then have to be organised, a process fraught with pitfalls and difficulties; and, once they have been organised, they have to engage in complex interactions with the state which often have unpredictable and unexpected outcomes.

That does not mean that political scientists have abandoned the central task of the social scientist, developing models which help us to understand a very complex reality without distorting it beyond recognition. One effort to explain the changing role of interest organisations that some political scientists advanced in the 1970s and 1980s was the corporatist model. Sociologists were sceptical about its explanatory power (Panitch, 1980) and economists could dismiss it as yet another shrine to producer interests, but some political scientists attacked it with a vehemence that was surprising unless one realised just how many political scientists felt comfortable only if they could go on using their well-worn pluralist slippers. At its worst, this degenerated into a veneration of the supposed eternal verities revealed by the well-known (and less well-known) pluralist writers of the 1950s, a kind of political science equivalent of the cult of morbid nostalgic voyeurism which has developed around Marilyn Monroe. It is, however, evident that the corporatist project was defective in a number of important respects.

Corporatism

Cox has claimed (1988, p. 27) that 'despite the claims made for it, neo-corporatism has not led to any significantly new insights into how policy is made or implemented.' If that is the case, then it need not detain us further. However, corporatism's presence of absence, and its desirability or potential for harm, have been such central themes in the debate about government–business relations in Britain that it requires further consideration.

There have certainly been many difficulties with the corporatist debate. Williamson observes (1989, p. 5) that 'the cumulative picture presented over the years is one of a rather elastic concept with a some-what uncertain central core.' Yet this is the very criticism that was levelled against pluralism in the last section. This is not so surprising, however, when 'Pluralism and corporatism share a number of basic assumptions' (Schmitter, 1979, p. 15). Corporatism incorporates many of the flaws of pluralism, and indeed some writers have claimed that it is nothing more than a subtype of pluralism (Almond, 1983).

Another difficulty is that there has been little agreement about the definition of corporatism, for example, do corporatist arrangements have to be tripartite (employers, unions and government) or can they be bilateral? The essence of corporatism can, however, be captured in terms of three concepts: intervention, intermediation and incorporation. One might add to these a belief in social partnership as the ideological cement which bonds the disparate elements together (see Katzenstein, 1984, 1985). Of these three, intermediation could be claimed to be the most distinctive, although it is important to remember that 'Corpora-tism involves the organisational link between intermediation and policy formation, not one or the other' (Cawson, 1986, p. 71). As far as intervention is concerned, Cawson (1982, p. 66) distinguishes corpora-tism as a mode of state intervention in which 'the state is neither directive nor coupled to an autonomous private sphere, but is inter-meshed in a complex way which undermines the traditional distinction between public and private.' Incorporation refers to the fact that interest organisations involved in corporatist arrangements are necessarily drawn closer to the state; the price of partnership is some loss of autonomy.

Although intervention and incorporation (and the tensions it can generate) are relevant to an understanding of corporatism, 'The concept of corporatism is most usefully used in a restricted sense to refer to a distinctive style of interest intermediation' (Cox, Lowe and Winter, 1990, p. 191). Intermediation refers to the particular kind of relationship that develops between the state and organised interests operating corporatist arrangements. The organised interests do not simply negotiate agreements with the state, they try to ensure that their members comply with the terms of those agreements. The state shares some of its authority with organised interests, but in return the interest groups are expected to regulate as well as represent their members. As Cawson notes (1985, p. 9), 'nowhere in the literature on interest groups written from a pluralist standpoint is stressed the reciprocity of the relationship between interest groups and the state'.

Intermediation has not, however, been an uncontested concept. 'Intermediation has perhaps caused more dispute amongst scholars working in this field than any other concept' (Lewis, 1990, p. 65). Cox and O'Sullivan (1988, p. x) argue that its application has involved oversimplification because interest intermediation as 'postulated by the corporatist model does not correspond to the variety of complex conditions that surround policy-making'. This is not surprising, as one is dealing with an 'ideal type', the function of which is to highlight certain factors as an aid to explanation, not to provide a complete description of reality in all its complexity. Indeed, one can expect a combination of different types in any empirical case (Cawson, 1988, p. 311).

Cox does not rest his case there, however, but also criticises the distinction between direct and indirect state intervention made by this writer (Grant, 1985, p. 8). 'Unfortunately, the distinction between "direct" and "indirect" state action is often too vague for this to be a very helpful observation' (Cox, 1988, p. 12). Direct state intervention involves the use of ownership, management or direction by the state to achieve a given objective without an intermediary. Indirect intervention involves working through an intermediary (which could be a quasi-governmental agency, an association or a specially created private body) to achieve government objectives. There are many examples from the wartime period. The government sometimes directly controlled raw materials, but in other cases left the management of controls to special wartime associations or to existing business associations (Grant, 1991a). The way in which matters were handled did make a difference. Business associations often had difficulty in controlling their members even though it was wartime. Government sometimes made mistakes because it did not understand the industry (as when a requisitioned food factory was then used to store prams) or became entangled in very complex procedures in an attempt to be fair in response to public pressures (as over the distribution of breakfast cereals with laxative properties). Each mode of intervention had its particular advantages and disadvantages.

One of the most careful evaluations of intermediation is to be found in Williamson (1989, Chapter 5). He accepts that it is an essential element of the corporatist model and that it is doubtful whether pluralism can be described as a theory of interest intermediation; he is less certain that it is a distinguishing feature of corporatism. He reasonably points out that empirically there may be borderline cases between pluralist and corporatist regulation, and suggests that intermediation needs to be divided into a number of types. He also argues that 'it does appear rather arbitrary to exclude pluralism from covering a role in overseeing the compliance to interventionist policies by its members' (Williamson, 1989, p. 104). The difficulty is that the alternative to drawing rather arbitrary divisions may be to concede the elasticity of pluralism, and hence to undermine its explanatory value.

In any event, the problem of compliance helps to illuminate the failure of the rather hesitant experiments in macro-corporatism in the form of tripartite economic management that took place in Britain between the 'Brighton Revolution' of 1960 (a conference at Brighton organised by the Federation of British Industries which prompted a change of direction in British economic policy) and the election of the Thatcher Government in 1979. The failure of these experiments is hailed as the end of a corporatist nightmare by some, and a missed opportunity by others. One of the problems with the corporatist debate has always been the confusion of prescription and analysis. From an analytical standpoint, this writer's perspective has been that, however well it might have worked elsewhere (and that of itself is contentious), corporatism faced insuperable obstacles in Britain (Marsh and Grant, 1977). One was organisational, the weakness of the organised employers and unions in terms of their ability to control their membership. The CBI voluntary price restraint initiative of 1971–2 was one of the most ambitious attempts at self-regulation by an interest organisation, but ultimately ended in failure and the imposition of statutory controls (Grant and Marsh, 1977, pp. 192–7). If one asks why governments, or the associations themselves did not do something about these organisational weaknesses, the answer is that they tried to (Middlemas, 1986, pp. 346–7) and failed. The reasons for this failure are complex, but are essentially related to the other main obstacle to corporatism, a set of attitudes among employers and organised labour which emphasised voluntarism, including a pluralist model of industrial relations. As noted earlier, this voluntarism had deep historical roots.

Whatever terminology one wants to use, there was a clear distinction between the political style of the 1970s (under both Conservative and Labour governments) and that of the 1980s. There is a world of difference between the statement in the 1978 Queen's Speech, 'In all these matters [government economic policies] my ministers will cooperate closely with the Trades Union Congress and the Confederation of British Industry' and Lord Young's claim that 'we have rejected the TUC; we have rejected the CBI. We do not see them coming back again. We gave up the corporate state' (*Financial Times*, 9 November 1988). The 1990s may see a more pragmatic style of government, in which close contacts with the employers and the unions are seen as an aid to effective policy-making and implementation, rather than a cornerstone on which an economic strategy can be built.

There has certainly been an erosion of intermediary institutions in the 1980s (Grant, 1989), and most of the tripartite bodies created in the 1960s or 1970s have been abolished, although some long established forms of meso-corporatism (corporatist arrangements at the sectoral level) survived into the 1990s, as in the dairy industry (see Chapter 8). On the other hand, the retreat of the state has created new forms of private interest government involving individual business persons, business interest associations, or specially-created institutions. Policy implementation has come to 'involve state agencies and private associations working together in some relatively complex implementation networks' (Williamson, 1989, p. 114). The interdependence of government and business is a pervasive reality. 'In the economic sphere, no clear dividing line can be drawn between those organizations of a private nature and those entitled to the exclusive exercise of public authority' (Hancher and Moran, 1989b, p. 275).

These issues are pursued further in Chapter 8. Many of these arrangements can best be characterised as 'private interest government', a concept that emerged out of the corporatist debate, (Streeck and Schmitter, 1985) but may be regarded as a distinct model from meso or sectoral corporatism. One of the unfortunate deficiencies of the corporatist debate is that it has attracted so much partisan and academic controversy as to undermine its usefulness, so that analysts are driven towards alternative, less contentious terminology. Indeed, Middlemas suggests that one of the ways of escaping 'the rather sterile later stages' of the corporatist debate is to engate in a more general and less restricted debate about the nature of modern states (Middlemas, 1991, p. 479).

Much of the corporatist debate has been about increasing policy effectiveness by converting a zero-sum game into a non-zero game in which cooperative strategies make all participants better off. It does, however, have implications for the debate about business power. Corporatism is a model of inclusion, which also implies exclusion. In general terms, it usually privileges business over consumers. In the business sector, it focuses attention on big rather than small business because big business can deliver more in the short run in terms of desired economic outcomes (e.g., higher investment), and is better organised politically. Corporatism also tends to freeze existing power structures, and makes non-incremental change more difficult. This is an important consideration when viewed in the context of the shift towards greater economic globalisation. As Traxler notes (1990, p. 26):

> Overall, since internationalization has become an indispensable element of economic restructuring, there is a self-destructive tendency inherent in the corporatist mode of modernization. Its dilemma is that it will simply grow obsolete if it fails to modernize the economy; and if it succeeds in this task, this will contribute to undermining its own base.

Business as a privileged interest

Any analysis of the position of business as a privileged interest has to start from a recognition of the fact that 'Capital is different from other interests because it exercises power or influence in two ways — directly through interest groups and structurally because of the crucial role boards and managers exercise over the production, investment and employment decisions which shape the economic and political environment within which Governments make policy' (Marsh and Locksley, 1983, p. 59). Business can exert power in at least four ways (see Figure 2.1): through decisions made at the level of the individual enterprise, through cartel-like collective economic action (cartels may be less blatant than in the interwar period, but as a series of successful prosecutions by the EC shows they have not entirely disappeared); through political action by the firm; and through collective political action by business through a variety of business interest associations.

Figure 2.1   *Mechanisms through which a profit-seeking business can pursue its objectives*

	Economic mechanisms	Political mechanisms
Action by the individual enterprise	Purchase and sale of goods and services; acquisition and sale of assets; internal financial discipline, management of financial paper	Use of government relations divisions; contacts with individual politicians and civil servants; donations to political parties
Collective action by business enterprises	Cartels and cartel-like activities, e.g. control of prices, allocation of raw materials, market sharing, control of tendering	Participation in business interest associations – peak associations, trade associations, employers' organisations, territorial associations, propaganda organisations

Moreover, trade union power is limited in ways that casts doubt on the pluralist account of countervailing groups. As Offe and Wiesenthal have emphasised, whereas capital can exert power even if it is not collectively organised, labour can exercise power only through collective organisation. Capital can to some extent release itself from its dependency on labour through technical change, but labour cannot release itself from its dependency on capital for employment. The union movement is involved in pursuing interests which are based both on individualistic rationality and a collective identity, whereas 'business organisations represent a pure form of individualistic rationality' (Offe and Wiesenthal, 1985, p. 205). The combination of different logics of collective action in union organisations 'leads to an on-going contradiction between bureaucracy and internal democracy, aggregation of individual interests and formation of a collective identity' (ibid., pp. 205–6).

In so far as labour is dependent on collective organisation for the exercise of influence, the trade union movement has been weakened in Britain in the 1980s. This is a result of a combination of circumstances, encompassing structural changes in the composition of the workforce, including a decline in the size of the manufacturing sector and growth of temporary and part-time work, and labour laws opening up new forms of legal action which place limitations on the use of the strike weapon. One might add that the unions have also been weakened by the way in which such power as the unions have has been used on some occasions in the past (as in the 'Winter of Discontent'). By 1992 the trend towards a smaller number of large unions in Britain was raising questions about the future of the TUC's coordinating function.

It could be argued that the real countervailing power to business today is not the trade unions but the environmental and consumer movement. In the United States, 'the environmental movement has established an alternative standard by which significant numbers of Americans, most of whom do not consider themselves environmentalists, now evaluate the performance of both business and government' (Vogel, 1989, p. 294). However, the environmental movement is fragmented and consumers are difficult to organise.

Lindblom's analysis of business privilege

One of the most influential studies of the privileged position of business has been Lindblom's *Politics and Markets*. Lindblom (1977, p. 200) finds classical liberal and pluralist thought to be grossly defective. As far as business is concerned, he states:

> Who are the main leaders in the market? Businessmen. Who are the main leaders in the exercise of privileged business controls? Businessmen, of course. Who are the main leaders in polyarchal politics? Businessmen are influential in enormous disproportion.

How is this position of privilege maintained and exercised? In Lindblom's view, fundamental issues such as private property and enterprise autonomy are kept off the political agenda. Disagreements between business and government are confined to 'an ever-shifting category of secondary issues — such as tax rates and particulars of regulation and promotion of business' (ibid., p. 180).

How, then, are certain issues such as private property and the distribution of wealth kept off the political agenda in supposedly free and democratic societies? According to Lindblom, there is 'Early, persuasive, unconscious conditioning ... to believe in the fundamental politico-economic institutions of one's society', although he acknowledges that such conditioning 'is ubiquitous in every society' (ibid., 1977, p. 207). Moreover, businessmen 'simply try to indoctrinate citizens to overlook their privileged position' (ibid., p. 203). In particular, Lindblom argues that businessmen use the media to associate private enterprise with political democracy. Business, however, often sees the media as unsympathetic to private enterprise in contemporary Britain. Certainly, in Britain, the media has given a considerable amount of often favourable publicity to the environmental movement. This is partly because environmental disasters provide strong visual images for television, and partly because newspapers, just like retailers, have responded to a growing public interest in 'green' issues.

Questions about whether the position of business in society is maintained because values favourable to it are perpetuated through socialisation and the media are difficult to resolve through the consideration of empirical evidence. A counter argument to the view that government is dependent on business to deliver economic success, and is therefore inextricably tied to its defence is 'that government is impelled to maintain economic performance due to citizen demand and employs business enterprises as the socially accepted instrument for this purpose' (Windsor, 1989, p. 10).

Vogel has argued (1989, p. 7) that 'There is no need to choose between the depictions of business power offered by the pluralists and their critics. The accuracy of each perspective depends on the period in which one is interested.' Vogel identifies the period from the late 1960s to the late 1970s as one when business was on the defensive through a combination of the rise of 'public interest' groups, stagflation, and a liberal Democratic Congress. It was also a difficult period for business in Britain. Vogel argues that (ibid., pp. 7–8) 'While it is true that during this century the years when business has been relatively powerful have been more numerous than those when it has not, it does not necessarily follow that the former state of affairs is the normal one.'

Vogel may have successfully identified cyclical variations in the level of business influence, although these cyclical variations may take place on top of a bedrock of underlying structural power Windsor argues, however, that there has been a secular change in American government, the main features of which are a sophisticated and independent media, 'and a complex web of pressure groups and lobbyists combined with an enormous growth in government's size, importance and functions' (Windsor, 1989, p. 13). Against that, Vogel notes an increase in the political sophistication of business with government relations becoming an integral feature of corporate planning. 'Business is unlikely to be caught off guard again' (Vogel, 1989, p. 296).

Concentration and economic power

Much of the American debate is relevant to Britain, but any analysis of the power position of business in Britain must take account of the high degree of concentration in the British economy. This increases the significance of decisions taken by individual firms about investment, production, employment, etc. (the top left-hand box of Figure 2.1).

As Marsh and Locksley observe (1983, p. 38), 'There are almost as many figures on concentration as there are authors on the subject.' However, the evidence reviewed by them suggests that the top hundred private manufacturing firms account for around forty per cent of net manufacturing output, paralleled by a high degree of concentration in the financial sector. A report jointly authored by the Cabinet Office claims that 'Manufacturing enterprise in Britain is highly concentrated, one hundred firms controlling over 70 per cent of output' (Cabinet Office, 1978, p. 16). This higher figure probably takes account of the fact that it is possible to control a business whilst owning a minority of the shares, and also of the dependence of many smaller companies on larger companies which they supply with components and services. Whatever the precise measure used, the important point is that 'the great increase in the relative growth of the largest enterprises in the UK in the last twenty-five years has produced a manufacturing sector which is one of the most highly concentrated (if not *the* most highly concentrated in the world' (Utton, 1982, p. 22).

There was undoubtedly a further increase in concentration as a result of a takeover boom in the mid-1980s. One development, connected with the so-called 'Big Bang' in the City of London, was the emergence of multi-purpose financial conglomerates which transcended the traditional barriers between different kinds of financial services (see Chapter 4 for a fuller discussion). However, there was also a substantial growth in concentration in the retail sector, as well as a number of bitterly-fought takeover bids in manufacturing industry.

This takeover boom should not be seen as 'accidental'. Its timing was related to such factors as a recovery in profits from the low point of the early 1980s, the development of new mechanisms for financing takeovers, and probably an element of imitation, fuelled by the perception that it was better to take over than be taken over. The boom faded away in the recessionary conditions of the late 1980s and early 1990s, but it could easily revive in better economic conditions. The general importance of mergers and takeovers in the UK is related to underlying structural factors. As an experienced businessman, Sir Hector Laing, has commented:

> Because institutional shareholders predominate in the securities markets, many managements have little real sense of identification with the objectives of their shareholders. Nor do fund managers have the expertise to solve problems of undeperformance by the companies in which they hold shares so they resort to selling out. The takeover bid has thus become a widely used device to cure corporate woes. (House of Lords, 1985, p. 69)

There can be little doubt that the UK has a less effective anti-trust policy than the United States or West Germany. From time to time, there are reviews of competition policy, but the results are usually limited in terms of any impact on the trend towards greater concentration. This is not a simple matter of a lack of political 'will', although it is arguable that Conservative Governments have not been as vigorous in these matters as they might have been. Very large scale mergers are now the responsibility of the European Community, although not to the exclusion of domestic competition authorities. However, although the EC may be able to prevent excessive concentration in the Community as a whole, its actions are unlikely to modify the level of concentration in the UK economy.

Globalisation and business power

The phenomenon of globalisation has already been discussed in Chapter 1. The internationalisation of business is not something that just affects Britain, although there are a number of specific features of the British economy which make it particularly exposed to such a development. Among these are the 'openness' of the British economy in terms of the proportion of output that is exported, and the proportion of domestic demand that is met by imports; the role of London as an international financial centre; and Britain's role as both a host country and a base country for major transnational companies.

The growth of stateless companies, and the globalisation of financial markets, is bound to weaken the control capacity of national governments. The main political responses to globalisation take either the form of regional confederations like the European Community or *ad hoc* cooperation arrangements at the international level, notably G-7 which has helped to stabilise international currency markets. Britain is a G-7 country, but often the greatest influence is exerted by the G-3 countries (Germany, Japan and the United States) (Dobson, 1991).

Globalisation has been particularly marked in the financial sector, with London operating as one of the three leading international financial centres. One theme that has been pursued by analysts who view capital as a privileged interest is that a particular feature of the organisation of business in Britain is the dominant position of finance capital, to the detriment of both manufacturing industry and the broader public interest. For example, Coates argues 'the political power of the City stands as the first major blockage to any successful strategy of industrial regeneration, let alone of socialist transformation' (Coates, David, 1984, p. 67).

These issues will be discussed more fully in Chapter 4. The general position to be taken will be that analysts have often failed to understand the diversity of the financial sector, and the alliances that exist between certain parts of the City and large-scale industry. However, the transformation of the financial services sector in the mid-1980s is leading to a form of organisation which is more unified and closer to what might be termed 'finance capital'.

The perspectives: an assessment

Elements of convergence

Despite their very different emphases, there are quite considerable elements of convergence between the three broad approaches discussed. For example, the neo-pluralist notion of 'policy communities' could be applied to what Lindblom terms 'secondary issues', leaving grand majority issues to be resolved in a different way by key actors with considerable power resources at their disposal. Although, as Marsh points out (1983, p. 7) Lindblom's distinction is somewhat imprecise, one could maintain, as Westergaard and Resler do, that there are two levels to the study of power. One level is that of the core assumptions of society, such as private property, which largely go unquestioned. These core assumptions set the terms of reference for conflicts and outcomes at the lower level where 'the picture will look something like the polygon of forces found by pluralist analysis' (Westergaard and Resler, 1976, p. 248).

There is also broad agreement that neither the state nor capital are monolithic entities, but are composed of a variety of conflicting interests and perspectives, some of which are more influential at particular times than others. As Coates notes from his perspective, the 'basic unity of class interests should not blind us to the fact that, more normally, politicians operate within a plurality of pressures from the world of capital, and accordingly face a multiplicity of potentially conflicting demands from it' (Coates, David, 1984, p. 59). As a consequence, 'The state ... is the focus of various, often conflicting, pressures that do not resolve easily into policies functional for capitalist interests' (Batstone, Ferner and Terry, 1984, p. 8).

The nature and limitations of business power

Despite the existence of elements of agreement between the three perspectives identified, there are evident disparities between them. Pluralists take a relatively benign and generally non-interventionist view of business power, although, as has been noted, there are significant differences of view among pluralist writers; corporatists consider that business can be harnessed to the pursuit of public policy objectives through collaboration with the state; whereas those who see business as a privileged interest see its power as potentially threatening to democracy and the ability of a democratic government to achieve its goals. 'The principal factor in the switch of former pluralists such as Dahl and Lindblom ... is the perceived incompatibility of large business corporations with democratic philosophy' (Windsor, 1989, p. 15).

It is evident that business has considerable economic power, that this power is enhanced by the level of concentration in the British economy, and that opportunities for government control of business activity are undermined by its increasing internationalisation. Moreover, as suggested in Chapter 1, the combination of economic power and relatively poor political organisation of business makes it difficult for government and business to enter into a mutually beneficial partnership relationship. Pluralist writers do not really address these issues; in particular, they have little to say about questions of ownership and control.

However, any general picture of business as a privileged interest must be qualified in three important ways. First, it is evident that many issues are resolved in particular policy arenas or 'communities'. Although the economic power of business may be relatively constant from one sector to another, the political power of business may vary significantly. In particular, the strength of countervailing groups may vary from one policy community to another, and over time. For example, farmers have generally faced relatively weak countervailing groups, although environmental groups have started to exert a greater influence on agricultural policy. At the other end of the spectrum, 'The activities of Lynx [a campaigning organisation] have helped to decimate the fur trade in this country by making it socially unacceptable to wear fur' (Garner, 1991, p. 291).

Second, business persons are not able to determine by themselves which matters should remain in the market place and which should be taken into the political sphere. In modern conditions, this is not so much a matter of public or private ownership, as of which activities should be regulated, in what ways, and how the regulations should be enforced. Reviewing Lindblom's ideas in the context of banking regulation in Britain and the United States, Moran concludes that bankers are able to make important discretionary decisions in markets, but the range of such decisions at their command varies greatly over time. Regulators are neither passive nor marginal and 'to treat markets as arenas where business takes untrammelled decisions is thus to neglect the shaping power of regulation' (Moran, 1984a, p. 189).

Matters which business might like to keep in the market sphere are nevertheless brought on to the political agenda as a consequence of the democratic pressures which exist in western societies. The capacity of democratic socialist and trade union parties to influence the political agenda declined in the 1980s, but there has been a general growth of environmental, consumer, feminist and animal welfare movements in western societies in the 1970s and 1980s, none of which align themselves with the values of business. Indeed, these groups arising from a postmodernist politics may pose more difficulties for business than traditional groups arising from the politics of production such as trade unions. It is at least possible to construct production coalitions with trade unions.

Once a matter is subject to political decision, the outcome for business is uncertain. This is not only because other interests come into play, but because business often has considerable difficulty in deciding what its interests are and, having made such a choice, in choosing a strategy to pursue those interests. This is in part a reflection of the simple fact that each profit-maximising firm has its own particular set of interests. It also reflects genuine uncertainty among many business persons about what is in the best interests of business, doubts made more difficult to resolve by the fact that most of them are so busy running their businesses that they have little time to think about wider issues (see Leys, 1985). It is not difficult for a business person to suggest what objectively would assist in profit maximisation, but a realistic business politician must consider the background against which he or she is working. He or she has to balance the long-range task of changing the background against the short run task of optimising in a given situation at a given time.

The third qualification that needs to be introduced is that any remarks about business privilege really only apply to big business. Small businesses operate in a completely different environment from big businesses (it is difficult to offer a precise definition of what constitutes a small business, but this difficulty should not be allowed to obscure the force of the general argument). For example, they generally find it more difficult to secure access to capital than larger businesses, and when they do the form in which the capital is provided may be less favourable (e.g., bank overdrafts secured on the personal assets of the small-scale entrepreneur). Indeed, a recurrent complaint of small businesses is that they suffer cash flow problems because of the tardiness of their large-scale customers in settling their bills. Government regulations which can be easily handled by a large business may impose a real burden on smaller businesses run by owner-managers, even allowing for the exemption from some regulations. If they have a grievance, small-scale businesses cannot generally secure direct access to a minister or relevant civil servant. Small-scale businesses also lack the degree of market protection which is provided by *Handwerk* system in Germany (see Grant and Streeck, 1985).

These qualifications aside, is business a privileged interest? In seeking to answer this question, it is necessary to be clear about what is meant by 'privilege'. Even the most primitive versions of pluralism did not pretend that all interests or potential interests in a society are able to exert an equal amount of influence on the decision-making process. In economies organised on free enterprise, capitalist lines, it should not surprise us that business is one of the most important interests.

In lexicographical terms, privilege refers to an advantage of some kind, although it also implies an advantage which is more durable than most. In modern usages, 'privilege' has come to carry the connotation of unjustified or illegitimate advantage. Historically, however, privileges were granted to parts of society which were thought to make a special contribution to its well-being, and therefore deserved special rights and privileges of some kind.

It is also important to bear in mind that even if it could be established that business in some sense occupied a 'privileged' position in the political process, this would not necessarily be undesirable. A distinction should be made between the empirical question of whether or nor business does have special advantages compared to other interests, and the subsequent value judgement about whether or nor this is desirable.

Often, in contemporary discussions, it is assumed that the mere demonstration of 'privilege' is enough to condemn it. However, interpretations of the economic power of capital depend on the political perspective adopted. A devotee of the free market would argue that the economic power of business is both necessary and desirable. Entrepreneurs can assemble factors of production so as to make goods that people want, and hence are able to contribute to national prosperity through creating jobs, exports etc. Freedom of action is necessary if an entrepreneurial system is to work properly; if the consequence is some concentration of wealth and power, so be it (although genuine economic liberals might take a different view on this point). In any case, free marketeers would argue, the most successful entrepreneurs often come from humble backgrounds. In so far as employees are disadvantaged by such a system, they have the option of exit through becoming self-employed and hence small entrepreneurs in their own right, or they could be given a stake in their firms through share ownership schemes and the creation of a relationship between their earnings and the profit level of the enterprise.

Free marketeers would go on to argue that, in so far as the free enterprise system does not work as it is supposed to, this is the result of externally-imposed constraints. Politicians impose regulations on entrepreneurs in such areas as employment law which inhibit the free movement of labour and drive up its price. Governments extract taxes which reduce the incentive to the entrepreneur, and the revenue thus obtained is diverted to less desirable, and often parasitical, activities such as levels of social security support which, it is claimed, discourage people from seeking work. An anti-entrepreneurial culture, fostered by an educational system hostile to business activity, reduces the number of individuals willing to create and maintain new enterprises. The trade unions limit the freedom to act of employers, slowing down or preventing the introduction of new technology and the shedding of surplus labour.

A socialist would see things very differently. He or she would argue that employers use their control of capital to extract surplus value from the labour of workers which they expropriate as profits. Success has more to with access to finance than genuine entrepreneurial skills. Increasingly, profits accrue to those skilled in the manipulation of financial paper, rather than to genuine innovators in the sphere of production. Examples of entrepreneurs from humble backgrounds can be found, but they are the exception rather than the rule. Workers have little interest in share ownership, and tend to dispose of shares made available to them as soon as they can realise a profit. Any scheme to relate earnings to the profits of the employing firm fails to take account of the tenuous relationship between the worker's own efforts and the success or otherwise of the enterprise.

The externally-imposed constraints on employers, a socialist would argue, are in reality very limited and can simply be used as an excuse for failings in their own performance. Taxes spent on services such as education and health are providing an infrastructure of support for capital in the form of a skilled and healthy workforce. Social security only seems generous in the context of the very low wages paid by some employers. The educational system is, in general, highly supportive of existing values. Trade unions are the only line of defence that workers have. They may appear to act irrationally on occasions, but this is only to be expected in a capitalist society which is not itself run on value lines.

It may seem difficult to bridge these conflicting perspectives or to resolve the issues raised by them through reference to relevant evidence. Indeed, many issues that arise from the role of business in society can only be resolved through a value judgement. For example, the argument that citizens are encased in a set of values favourable to business can not be resolved by producing evidence about what the values of citizens actually are, for such evidence would not tell us how they arrived at their preferences. Even a thought experiment would not resolve the problem. For example, supposing that a society which had previously espoused capitalist, free enterprise values, decided to persuade its citizens, through the educational system, and the media, that socialist values were preferable. Depending on the efficiency of the techniques used, such an experiment in re-education might ultimately be successful, although even in highly-controlled state socialist societies there have been dissidents who questioned the teachings of the state. However, all that such an experiment would prove is that indoctrination is possible. It would not tell us anything about the 'real' preferences of individuals.

The use of the power of business

It is important to consider not only where power is concentrated, but also *how* that power is used. That is not to say that one should not be concerned about increasing concentrations of economic power in the hands of a relatively small number of businesses. In particular, the international financial system is developing in such a way as to place it beyond the reach of any countervailing power, whether governmental or supranational. It has so many inherent instabilities (see Grant and Nath, 1984, pp. 191–9) that it could experience a major crisis that inflicted severe damage on the whole system of business enterprise.

A central problem is whether business is able to make a constructive response to the problems facing modern western societies, not least the emergence of an 'under class' afflicted by high levels of unemployment and other severe difficulties. Reference is not being made here to individual efforts by particular firms who aspire to be 'good corporate citizens', worthy though such efforts are. The concern is with a strategic response by business as a whole to these problems, acting through its collective organisations in concert with government. Unfortunately, business in the 1980s seems to have been willing to abdicate political leadership to neo-liberals whose policies were arguably not in the long-run interest of business or, in so far as they do not provide a solution to serious social problems, of society as a whole. Individual business persons, and individual businesses display socially responsible attitudes, and a concern for the general condition of the society in which they operate. In general, however, business in Britain is open to the charge of not matching its considerable economic power with a discharge of its social responsibilities through a constructive political partnership with government.

Readers must make their own judgements about the role of business in society and whether, for example, they would agree that it is 'undeniable that in an advanced democratic country citizens would place the question of governing economic enterprises high on the agenda of important issues' (Dahl, 1989, p. 331). The general perspective adopted in this book is what has been referred to as 'statist' theory (Elkin, 1989). 'In statist theory, business and government are both independently powerful [but] related through a system of mutual control that functions within a weak popular sovereignty ... Statist theory is in effect a compromise position midway between the dominancy and competing interest views' (Windsor, 1989, p. 3).

Such a perspective should incorporate Vogel's insight that business power is not a constant, but waxes and wanes. Of course, if one accepts that the market mechanism is the preferable general, although not exclusive, organising principle for an economy, an inevitable consequence is that business values and priorities will always have a high priority in the decision-making process. This does not mean that business values should exclude all other values. In the 1980s in Britain it often seemed that business values were becoming not just central but dominant. One of the tasks of the 1990s is to redress the balance. The voice of business should always be heard, and always considered seriously, but not to the exclusion of alternative perspectives.

3   Government and Business

A large firm will have extensive contacts with government every day at a variety of levels and in relation to a variety of tasks. Members of the main board may be engaged in confidential discussions with a minister and his advisers about whether a new plant could be located in Britain rather than overseas. Elsewhere in the same government building, members of the firm's technical staff may be part of a trade association delegation discussing a draft EC directive on a particular product with civil servants. Members of the firm's financial staff may be holding a meeting to discuss the implications of proposed changes in tax law. Commercial staff may be discussing the categorisation of machinery imported from a closed foreign plant with Customs and Excise. At one of the plants, the safety arrangements for a new piece of machinery may be under discussion with the Factories Inspectorate. The personnel manager at the plant may be discussing the possibility of vacancies with the local Job Centre. A planning application for a plant extension may require a site visit from the local authority.

One way of making sense of this variety of interactions (and many more could be added) is to define the main roles that government has in relation to business. There has been a major transformation in this respect since the early 1980s. One of government's most important roles in relation to business has largely disappeared: its role as an owner of key industries. Its role as a sponsor of industry, exercised through the sponsorship divisions which were abolished in 1988, has significantly diminished. Government subsidies to industry were reduced sharply during the 1980s. On the other hand, government's role as a regulator has increased in importance, in part because the privatised public utilities are supervised by specially created regulatory bodies, and also because of the increased importance of environmental regulation. It might even be possible to talk of a 'regulatory state'. Government's other roles in relation to business are as a customer, although this role is diminishing, and as a policy-maker.

As a maker of economic policy, government substantially influences the context in which enterprises make decisions. For example, government's exchange rate policy or its stance on interest rates, can have a significant influence on the profitability of a company and even its ability to survive. Decisions by government on corporate taxation, or on industrial relations law, or on public sector borrowing, all influence what enterprises can do and how they do it. This area of broad policy is, in general, the most politicised arena in which government interacts with business. Because it is so politicised, and because of publicly-made policy commitments by government, it is difficult for business to change economic policies in the short run, although they can be modified beyond recognition by a 'drip, drip, drip' process of extracting concessions from government on particular points. General economic policy of this kind is shifting to some extent to the EC level, although the pace at which this happens is likely to be slow and uneven, particularly after the events of September 1992.

The policy relationship

It would be misleading to portray the relationship between business and government in terms of a political struggle between lobbiers and lobbied. There is an exchange relationship from which government secures three types of benefit: information for policy design; consent for policy clearance; and cooperation for policy implementation.

As far as the first of these is concerned, information for policy design, the government machine in Britain operates on the basis of the collation, internal dissemination, and political use of information. Information is its raw material; hence the importance of debates over the extent of official secrecy. Information is a key bureaucratic power resource, and particular pieces of information may be hoarded by parts of the machine to be used at the most politically-appropriate time.

Information is a crucial resource in the inter-departmental discussions that play a central role in the process of governmental decision-making. Departments may be able to make use of the information garnered from firms and business associations with which they are in contact to press the departmental point of view with other parts of the government machine. For example, departments concerned with particular industries may use such information to counteract arguments advanced by the Treasury. One large firm that was interviewed recalled that they had been asked by the former Department of Industry to provide papers on such subjects as the impact of exchange rate policy on industry, and the erosion of the industrial base.

Government is, of course, able to generate a considerable amount of information on its own behalf. It employs every conceivable kind of expert from vets to psychologists to marine biologists. Nevertheless, trade associations and firms have a mass of information at their disposal which may, on the one hand, forewarn government of impending political danger and, on the other, assist in the routine conduct of the policy-making process. For example, a firm may warn government that it is planning to close a plant in an area of high unemployment. A trade association can provide government with statistical information which is essential to policy-making, but which firms might be reluctant to provide direct to government. In the event of an emergency such as a strike in a crucial industry or service, trade associations will be able to advise government on the impact on their members. Assistance from trade associations may be particularly useful when government has to deal with highly technical proposals emanating from the EC. More generally, associations may be able to advise on the design of a policy so as to appeal to those affected or to minimise obstacles to its successful implementation, although this can also be a subtle means of changing policy content.

Although firms and associations undoubtedly gain some benefits from exchanging information with government, they are able to assist policy-makers by advising on the design of government measures so that they are most likely to achieve their stated objectives. Miller notes that a proposal for a 10 per cent levy on audio recording tape by officials who did not understand the mechanics of retail pricing 'failed to appreciate the difference between making manufacturers or consumers pay the levy ... Officials expect technical guidance from outsiders in order to prevent such errors' (Miller, 1990, p. 94).

Consent for policy clearance

The notion of policy clearance refers to securing the consent, or at least the acquiesence, of affected publics to policy proposals that a government wishes to put into effect. If an affected interest group strongly opposes a particular measure, they may be able to obstruct its implementation in a number of ways. Of course, there may be occasions when a government considers that it has to push ahead with a policy proposal in the face of organised opposition, because it is of such importance to its overall strategy. Such occasions were more frequent under the Thatcher Government than they were before its formation or have been since its replacement.

The Thatcher period did not change the fundamental character of the British system of government in which extensive and intensive consultation with affected interests, not least business interests, is a basic operational principle. 'It is routine for government departments to consult groups in the preparation of proposals. For example, the Scottish Development Department maintains a list of 309 names interested in building control alone' (Jordan and Richardson, 1987, pp. 4–5). In some cases, a duty to consult with appropriate organisations is imposed on the responsible minister by law, but the real basis of the system is not law, but custom and practice.

The basic principle is to make the consultative process as wide-ranging as is practicable, although many of the letters that are sent out receive no response. In the case of the EC's proposed jams directive, the Commission's proposal was sent out to about one hundred organisations for comment: twenty-four replied, of which six did not offer substantive comments; and meetings during the development of the directive were confined to two food processors' associations (Coates, Dudley, 1984). As Richardson notes, what consultation often means is negotiation, a process in which certain key groups really matter. 'For example, several hundred groups were involved in discussions relating to the reform of the engineering profession in the 1970s but the *real* decision-making process finally centred on less than half-a-dozen key groups' (Richardson, 1990, p. 5). Nevertheless, it is considered better to over-consult rather than to under-consult. As a senior civil servant explained to the House of Lords:

> We consult on any proposal those organisations which seem to be representative of the subject or interests under discussion. It is a subjective judgement on every occasion but we work on the basis that we would sooner over-consult rather than under-consult because you cannot from our position judge the importance on occasions of a particular proposal to a particular group of people. (Quoted in Coates, Dudley, 1984, pp. 146–7)

British government is characterised by highly routinised policy-making processes in which there is a close working relationship between civil servants and interest groups operating within small and relatively closed policy communities. These relationships can, however, be disturbed by the pressures introduced by a new generation of consumer groups operating through a sympathetic media. Food safety questions once offered a classic example of a small and closed policy community of civil servants, business association officials and experts (Coates, Dudley, 1984). Smith (1991) shows how changing public attitudes but, more important, a changing balance of power between food producers and food retailers, opened up the policy community. 'What was once a closed and united policy community dealing with what were seen as technical issues had changed into a wider policy network' (Smith, 1991, p. 250).

Although in some respects this offers a good example of the impact of a shift from the politics of production to the politics of collective consumption on the policy clearance process, one of the most important factors has been a division within the business community. 'The retailers have to an extent undermined the policy community partly through representing interests in conflict with those of farmers and the food manufacturers but more importantly through by-passing the community completely' (Smith, 1991, p. 248). Consumers are still largely excluded from the policy formation process, often only being consulted after decisions had been made (Smith, 1991, p. 252).

Cooperation in policy implementation

Business associations and firms can cooperate with the implementation of government policy in a variety of ways. An association may be able to assist government in making a policy effective at the level of the firm by disseminating information about the policy and its applicability to members. An employers' association may not only be able to publicise, for example, a training policy initiative to its members, but also explain its relevance to their particular needs through seminars or direct contacts with member firms.

A more active form of cooperation arises when an association assumes responsibility for a task would otherwise have to be discharged by government. For instance, an association may devise a self-regulating code of conduct in a particular problem area that obviates the need for direct government regulation. In a review of food legislation, the Ministry of Agriculture, Fisheries and Food discusses how, in some cases, the production of codes of conduct by trade associations has removed the need for statutory measures and suggests that this practice should continue to be encouraged (MAFF, 1984).

It is sometimes assumed that the involvement of business associations in policy implementation is associated with an expanding state, but this is not necessarily the case. Smith (1990, p. 132) notes that in agriculture, 'As the wartime controls lapsed, the [National Farmers Union] was expected to take on more functions to govern the industry.' A retreating state may prefer to devolve existing functions to business associations or bodies created by them, or to create new bodies run by business to cope with any unavoidable new functions such as the expansion of regulation of financial services. These themes are explored further in Chapter 8.

The structure of government

All government departments take decisions which have implications for business, but some departments are of more importance to business than others. Potentially the most important is the Department of Trade and Industry (DTI) which might be thought to act as the voice of business within Whitehall. However, the Thatcher years saw a diminution of the role of the Department of Trade and Industry, not helped by the fact that there were nine Secretaries of State for Trade and Industry (formerly Industry) during Mrs Thatcher's premiership.

Some analysts would like to see the Department of Trade and Industry become an equivalent of Japan's Ministry of International Trade and Industry (MITI). Such accounts overlook the importance of the Ministry of Finance in Japan, and the extent to which MITI has to engage in turf fights with other ministries responsible for industry such as Posts and Telecommunications, Construction and Transport. 'The level of coherence ascribed to Japanese industrial policy tends to be overstated' (Okimoto, 1989, p. 3). Even so, the DTI has increasingly failed to undertake the basic task of ensuring that the needs and views of business are taken into account elsewhere in Whitehall. A source 'close to the Confederation of British Industry' is quoted as saying:

> The DTI needs to be a powerful voice for business in Whitehall and Westminster. But it has not been powerful enough, so ministers have been able to secure things like high electricity prices and the uniform business rate because the DTI has not stood up in Cabinet. (*The Observer*, 5 May 1991)

A report issued before the CBI's 1991 conference was critical of the DTI. One of the authors of the report, Sir Colin Chandler, commented, 'We need a powerful voice sitting around the cabinet table speaking up for industry' (*Financial Times*, 22 October 1991). [Sir] John Banham, then the CBI's director-general, subsequently called for the DTI to be split in two, with a department of enterprise to promote the interests of business and a department of commerce to take on the role of regulation. It was evident from speeches at the 1991 CBI conference that dissatisfaction among CBI members with the DTI was at a high level. In interviews conducted for this book, industrialists complained about the 'dismemberment' of the DTI under Nicholas Ridley and Peter Lilley, and of a complete reliance on the market mechanism, except in competition policy.

The appointment of Michael Heseltine as Trade and Industry Secretary (or President of the Board of Trade as he decided to style himself) after the 1992 Election brought a minister to Victoria Street who had frequently called for a more prominent and central role for the DTI, particularly in ensuring that the views of manufacturing industry were in the mainstream of policy-making. He made it clear that he intended to build up a closer relationship between government and industry, to build up over time a collection of policies amounting to an industrial strategy, although this did not mean that government would be a 'fairy godmother' offering instant solutions to long-standing problems. He commented that he had always believed that government departments 'should talk and listen carefully to the industries, to the companies, which you sponsor' (*Financial Times*, 6 May 1992). Mr Heseltine's approach to his job in his first six months was notably cautious. Public expenditure constraints made it difficult for him to take major new initiatives even if he had wanted to, although a clear interest was shown in the structure of government–industry relations in Britain. A new division was set up to look at the problem of industrial competitiveness. Within industry, however, there was some scepticism about how much he would be able to achieve. A senior manager in a major British company commented in interview six months after Mr Heseltine had moved to the DTI:

> Can Michael Heseltine be influential in himself, do they want to keep him in there? There is a cabal against Michael Heseltine deliberately keeping him out. ... Nothing has shown yet. There is a lot of hot air at the moment. I'll believe it when I see it.

The abolition and replacement of the sponsorship function

For much of the postwar period, government conducted its relationship with industry through 'sponsorship' divisions which were responsible for particular sectors of industry. Most of these divisions were in DTI, although some industries were covered elsewhere, e.g., pharmaceuticals in the Department of Health and construction in the Department of the Environment. A typical example of a sponsorship division in the mid-1980s was the DTI's Chemicals and Textiles Division, headed by an under secretary. Because of regulatory and support policies, textiles took up much of the division's work, but chemicals had its own branch headed by an assistant secretary with a total of fourteen staff above executive officer rank. Each subdivision of the industry, e.g., paints, fertilisers, would have a civil servant concerned with its affairs. Sponsorship divisions thus gave not only every industry, but virtually every product, a principal point of contact somewhere in Whitehall. As a booklet issued by the CBI explained:

> The most important relationship that the majority of businessmen will ever have with government is with their sponsor department, and specifically with those officials who are responsible generally for communicating with, and keeping an eye on, and looking after the well-being of ... the sector or sectors of industry and commerce in which their business operates ... Everybody is loved, in other words, by someone — or at least is regarded as an object of concern, and as a possible partner. (Coffin, 1987, p. 12)

Sponsorship had a special importance for the nationalised industries. A privatised utility manager commented in interview in 1992 that before privatisation, almost all relations were with the sponsoring department. Although the Treasury would sometimes try and circumvent them, the relationship was essentially a T-shaped one, with the sponsoring department dealing with all other government departments.

Sponsorship divisions dealing with sectors outside government ownership had three main functions: to act as representatives of their industries within government; to explain government policies to their industries; and to act as a source of specialised advice and expertise within government. The first function, that of representation, was emphasised in government accounts of sponsorship:

The basic aim of sponsorship is to help the industries to be successful, and to this end to ensure that in the formulation of policies by
Government (and by international organisations such as the EEC and
GATT) the particular interests of the industries sponsored are
identified in consultation with them; and that these policies so far as
possible support and promote these interests. (Industry Committee,
1980, p. 55)

In an interview at the beginning of the 1980s, one civil servant
described sponsorship as acting as an 'internal lobbyist for industry in
Whitehall. If industry has problems of a governmental nature, we try to
take an interest and where appropriate act as a lobby within the
Whitehall machine.' It must emphasised that this aspect of the sponsorship function did not simply involve acting as a 'mouthpiece' for
industry. Civil servants emphasised that departments with sponsorship
responsibilities needed to be 'critical lobbyists' (Mueller, 1985, p. 101).
Sponsorship involved pooling the views of the industry and placing
them in the context of government policy. The sponsorship division
thus compensated for the inadequacies of an often incoherent system of
business representation by aggregating the views emerging from an
industry. Rather than being evidence of the structural power of capital
(Cowling, 1982), the sponsorship divisions were evidence of its political weakness. The sponsorship divisions did not necessarily compen-
sate for these weaknesses. Wilks (1984, p. 194) argued that 'the whole
concept of sponsorship is to some extent a pretence'. Sponsorship was
'a passive, best-endeavour sort of relationship, it involves no planning
and little policy-implementation capability.'

When Mrs Thatcher placed Sir Keith Joseph with his pronounced
social market views in the Department of Industry in 1979, it might
have appeared that the sponsorship function was in danger. However,
Sir Keith asserted their value in terms of the standard civil service
script: 'Industry needs to identify somewhere in Whitehall where its
problems can be understood, because its problems have to be taken
account of by the Chancellor and other Departments; so the sponsorship function involves understanding and will survive if the grant
function diminishes' (Industry Committee, 1980, p. 87). By the mid-
1980s, however, there were indications from interviews with industrialists that the sponsorship function was being undermined. One business
person commented, 'The sponsoring department concept has been
substantially weakened in recent years ... there is no specialization

now, they are trying to keep a relationship with many industries and failing.' Another respondent saw the decline of sponsorship as part of a more general decline of DTI's role within government: 'The advocacy role of the DTI is unquestionably diminishing and it is Government's desire that it should diminish' (quoted from Grant, Paterson and Whitston, 1988, pp. 78–9).

As part of his efforts to remould the DTI as a 'department for enterprise' in 1988, Lord Young abolished the sponsorship divisions. It was argued that the whole idea of sponsorship was out of tune with the government's market-orientated philosophy, although this had been the case since 1979. Lord Young considered that the divisions did not help ministers and civil servants to know what was going on:

> The reality was quite different: often quite junior civil servants would be given a sector for a three-year term, and then have to learn as much as they could about the business. This almost inevitably led them into the clutches of the relevant trade association and they ended up as a conduit for the industry to dun ministers for more money and more support. (Young, 1990, p. 240)

The sponsorship divisions were replaced by market divisions 'which will focus on the markets for particular goods and services rather than particular supplier industries. Market divisions ... will tackle broad policy issues affecting all the suppliers and customers to the market in question rather than dealing with particular industries' (Cm. 278, p. 39). Thus, for example, the Consumer Market Division had branches dealing with market assessment and technology transfer; international markets; the Single European Market; and consumer services. Underlying the whole exercise was an attempt to move away from the industrial policy ethos of the 1970s.

These changes reflected a further shift towards a company state model of government–business relations with market divisions at DTI's head offices maintaining direct contact with the largest companies, whilst regional and satellite offices, often located in chambers of commerce, responsible for direct contact with smaller companies. The view was taken that there would still be a role for trade associations but, given their variability in quality, the new arrangements would give DTI more scope to decide where the weaknesses were and act accordingly.

However, the market divisions never settled down as effectively as was hoped for. There was certainly still a strand of thinking in the department that supported the idea of sponsorship, and market divisions did not represent a complete break with the old ethos. There were practical problems as well. The market divisions were asked to be expert in a wide range of the department's activities and to offer a specialism in explaining the policies of other parts of the department. Expertise was thus spread too thinly.

Given these difficulties, Lord Young initiated a review of the market divisions before he left the DTI. The outcome of this review was not a foregone conclusion, because the market division structure had its supporters within the department. However, Nicholas Ridley, who succeeded Lord Young as Secretary of State in 1989, took an even more restricted view of the role of the DTI, believing that it 'should revert to doing little more than the pre-war Board of Trade' (*Financial Times*, 1 May 1991). He criticised other government departments based on sponsoring sectors of the economy such as agriculture or energy as a symptom of the past (*Financial Times*, 13 October 1989).

The results of the review of market divisions announced in February 1990 concluded that 'market divisions had to promote too wide a range of issues and policies handled by others in the Department, and lacked a clear role or set of objectives' (DTI Press Notice 90/82, p. 1). They were replaced by divisions concentrating on a set of policies or programmes such as information technology, manufacturing technology, and the environment and business. Continuing government responsibilities towards specific industrial sectors such as aerospace and shipbuilding were handed over to 'task forces', a name chosen to reflect their possibly temporary character. These task forces were clearly technology and market-oriented, with only the Vehicles Task Force bearing even a slight resemblance to an old-style sponsorship division.

The loss of the sponsorship function did make some difference to the quality of business–government relations. One senior trade association official complained in interview in 1991 that in the absence of a sponsorship division ministers could set priorities, but this could lead to product sectors in particular losing out. The DTI received a trickle of complaints from trade associations that didn't know where to go, who maintained that there was no one to talk to regularly, and that the department was not listening to industry. These complaints no doubt arose in part because of concern about high interest rates, complaints which would have arisen whatever structure had been adopted by the department.

As part of the changes he introduced when he became minister in charge of the DTI in 1992, Michael Heseltine re-established fifteen sectoral divisions reflecting 'the adoption of a sectoral approach to the industries for which the DTI is responsible' and 'assigning to all sectoral divisions, both new and existing, an explicit role to sponsor their industries ... as a basis for an informed dialogue and a constructive partnership between Government and business' (DTI Press Notice P/92/440). The extent to which sectoral boundaries still matter in terms of economic structure, technology and product markets was thus once again recognised within government.

The Treasury

Advocates of a reinvigorated Department of Trade and Industry often regard it as a necessary counterweight to the Treasury within the government machine. Industrialists frequently complain about the Treasury's lack of understanding of their problems and needs. The chairman of British Aerospace has commented, 'The real problem is the Treasury. The Treasury happens to operate on a one-year basis, and our twenty-five year programme is something that is very difficult to bridge' (quoted in Heller, 1987, p. 120). The authors of a CBI report commented in 1991 that the Treasury and the Bank of England were handicapped 'by a combination of poor information, lack of first-hand understanding of the realities of manufacturing, and an apparent mistrust of outsiders' (*Financial Times*, 22 October 1991). These comments reflect those of a broader literature which portray the Treasury and its attitudes as a major cause of poor British economic performance (Ham, 1981; Pollard, 1982).

What these criticisms often overlook is that the central finance ministry is going to be powerful in any advanced industrial country, and that one of its tasks will be to reject projects which are favoured by industrialists but place a burden on public expenditure. Its general management of the economy, along with the central bank, will have a significant impact on the climate in which business operates. Thus, even in Japan, 'Because authority over monetary policy is vested in the [Ministry of Finance] and the Bank of Japan, Japanese industrial policy must be conducted within the broad, macroeconomic parameters set forth by these two financial agencies' (Okimoto, 1989, p. 20).

The Treasury does have direct contacts with the largest firms and leading business associations. When ICI was aggrieved by a clause in the Finance Bill which directly affected its interests, its Chairman met the Chancellor, the Chief Secretary of the Treasury, other ministers, and senior Inland Revenue officials (Grant, Paterson and Whitston, 1988, p. 106). One Treasury official has commented that the CBI 'seems to be in and out of the Treasury every week.' (Young and Sloman, 1984, p. 73). They may have had a less sympathetic reception in the Thatcher years than hitherto (Bruce-Gardyne, 1986, p. 150), although Denis Healey considered the CBI too weighted towards international big business, and therefore consulted the chambers of commerce as a means of keeping in touch with smaller firms (Healey, 1990, p. 382).

Tensions between the Treasury and the industry department sometimes come to the surface, as in 1979 when *The Guardian* carried a leak of a letter from the permanent secretary of the Treasury to his opposite number at the Industry Department, complaining about losses calculated at £800 million on seven investment programmes, and suggesting 'we must try to find some means of influencing the decision-making process so as to ensure a higher rejection rate in the future' (Browning, 1986, p. 119). It is also open to question whether the Treasury understands industry as well as it sometimes claims. Even so, some of the more exaggerated criticisms of the Treasury by business may reflect a failure to understand that the requirements of business are only one consideration that government has to balance in arriving at policy decisions.

Government as a regulator

The impact of government's role as a regulator increased rather than diminished during the Thatcher years, in spite of efforts to promote deregulation. The then head of the government's deregulation unit identified obstacles such as conflicts with other policy objectives, for example, environmental protection; lack of awareness among civil servants of the importance of the problems caused by regulation, and the limited ability of business persons to communicate their case to government; and the slow build-up of regulatory impact. The achievements of the deregulation unit had been 'numerous but small' (Ashmore, 1988, p. 78).

Apart from the difficulties of securing deregulation, and the pressure for reregulation in areas such as financial services and the environment, the policies of the Thatcher Government created a need for more rather than less regulation. Hancher and Moran observe (1989, p. 2) that 'Regulation is a feature of all economies, but as the American case graphically illustrates it is peculiarly important in economic systems marked by the predominance of private ownership and the allocation of resources through markets.' For example, the privatisation of public utilities in Britain led to the creation of a new family of regulatory agencies designed to ensure that a potential monopoly position was not abused.

'"Regulation" is a contested concept' (Hancher and Moran, 1989a, p. 3) which is not easy to define. Rule-making and enforcement is at its heart, but it is a process of rule application that generally involves an element of discretion on the part of the regulating agency. In defining the term, it is easier to specify what it isn't than what it is:

> It is generally agreed that the term is confined to statute law and the associated delegated legislation which enables departments or agencies to constrain the activities of firms and individuals in the private sector within the framework of the policies pursued by the government in power. It follows that regulation does not embrace fiscal measures that are designed to influence the flows of revenue and expenditure of firms and individuals through grants and subsidies, and through taxation. (Peacock, 1984, pp. 24–5)

One could make a further distinction between the exercise of regulatory powers which confer benefits, and those which impose penalties. The idea of conferring benefits might seem at odds with the idea of constraint in regulation, but American analysts include within their understanding of regulation 'franchising or licensing ... by which regulatory agencies permit or deny an individual the right to do business in a specified occupation or industry' (Meier, 1985, p. 1). In Britain, the classic examples of conferring benefits have been the allocation of television franchises or air routes, although the introduction of an auction mechanism into the television franchise allocation process has reduced, but not eliminated, the element of discretion allowed to the regulating authority.

In any case, what may appear to be a constraining regulation may in fact benefit existing firms within an industry by raising entry costs to a prohibitive level. In the pharmaceutical industry, 'the research-based firms have attempted to secure a stricter enforcement of rules on product safety, in order to frustrate potential competition from rival generic manufacturers' (Hancher, 1990, p. 16).

Much of the academic debate about regulatory agencies has been influenced by an American literature which has argued that such agencies are 'captured' by the industries they seek to regulate. While there may be individual examples of agency 'capture', this does not mean that all, or even the majority of regulatory agencies, behave in this way. 'Contrary to what conventional capture-analysis would appear to assume, the French and British pharmaceutical industries have in practice been confronted with the prospect of more rather than less government infringement of their commercial freedom, and they are constrained to react accordingly' (Hancher, 1990, p. 16). The agencies regulating the privatised public utilities cannot be said to have been 'captured'; rather the contrary. It seems helpful to characterise the relation between regulator and regulated as 'a more subtle, complex one ... based on interdependence' (Hancher, 1990, p. 8).

Regulations are, of course, often weakly enforced. Enforcement resources are often limited in relation to the scale of the task, and the emphasis is often on compliance through a process of persuasion. Peacock (1984, p. 115) comments that 'A framework of negotiated compliance, rather than strict enforcement of performance standards, is the dominant characteristic of regulatory policy in the UK.' However, the British emphasis on such approaches as 'reasonably practical means' is being eroded by the increasing involvement of the EC, with its emphasis on uniform emission standards, in environmental regulation. The distinctiveness of the British approach to regulation is gradually disappearing, with the UK finding itself 'under continual pressure to bring [its] system of pollution control more in line with that of the other members of the European Community' (Vogel, 1986, p. 104).

In 1991 John Major proposed the establishment of a National Environment Agency which would combine the regulation of waste disposal by county councils with the work carried out by the Pollution Inspectorate and part of the National Rivers Authority. Her Majesty's Pollution Inspectorate was itself formed in 1987 to merge the previous separate inspectorates for emissions to air, land and water. The intention is to create a 'one-stop shop' enabling industry to have pollution control dealt with by one set of inspectors implementing standardised regulation. From industry's point of view, this would have the advantage of cutting out overlap and duplication. In the chemical industry, for example, companies have sometimes found one inspector saying that emissions must be released to the atmosphere and another insisting that they be dealt with inside the building.

Regulatory agencies for public utilities

All the public utilities which have been privatised are subject to supervision by a new family of regulatory agencies: the Office of Gas Supply (Ofgas) for the gas industry; the Office of Telecommunications (Oftel) for the telecommunications industry; the Office of Electricity Regulation (Offer); and the Office of Water Services (Ofwat) for water supply. The former British Airports Authority, now BAA, is regulated by the Civil Aviation Authority.

The National Consumer Council has expressed doubts whether bodies such as Oftel and Ofgas really qualify as regulatory organisations:

> Their powers are primarily administrative, checking that the regulated industry is conforming to a set of conditions which they have no part in setting. They lack the United States public utility commissions' legislative powers to make rules, their judicial powers in deciding ... tariff cases, have no role at all in investment decisions, and even lack most of the significant executive powers ... The real *regulatory powers* lie, if anywhere, with the Monopolies and Mergers Commission. (National Consumer Council, 1989, p. 19)

Nevertheless, some of the leading companies in Britain are subject to a different operating environment from other companies, in which their decisions on key commercial questions are open to challenge and may be modified or overturned. One privatised utility noted in interview in 1992 that regulation was making the company more bureaucratic. There was a closer inspection of procedure, and a tendency to equalise procedures such as discounts which the regulator might insist should be repeated elsewhere. In many respects, the regulators seem to have taken on the task of giving the industries the competitive structures which privatisation did not provide.

In the telecommunications industry, Sir Bryan Carsberg of Oftel was one of the main authors of a major reform plan published in 1991 which aims to promote competition in an industry traditionally dominated by a monopoly supplier. In the electricity industry, Professor Stephen Littlechild at Offer has shaped the creation of the network of contracts and 'pool' purchasing which govern commercial relationships between electricity generators and distributors. Stezler (1988, p. 70) predicts the regulation of these industries will tend to increase rather than decrease, moving closer to the American model. The regulatory system is based on price controls, but issues of price and quality of service cannot be separated, because one way to evade price controls is to cut quality of service. Since privatising BT, which experienced something of a quality crisis in 1987, the 'government has laid noticeably greater emphasis on standards of service for the other utilities it has floated ... Oftel's development also exemplifies why once a regulator becomes involved in an industry there is a logic for regulation to spread wider and deeper' (*Financial Times*, 13 March 1991).

The case of Ofgas disproves arguments that the regulatory agencies would turn out to be toothless watchdogs, outsmarted and outgunned by the huge enterprises they were seeking to regulate. Assumptions that the regulator, James McKinnon, was a semi-retired accountant who would give British Gas little trouble turned out to be misplaced. Instead, through a mixture of determination, threats of court action, and the subtle use of the media to appeal to public opinion, he 'profoundly affected the industry's development since its privatisation in 1986' (*Financial Times*, 25 January 1990). For example, in April 1991 the regulator obtained the reluctant agreement of British Gas to a new price controls which meant that the company could raise its prices by five per cent less than the rate of inflation, rather than the two points which had applied before. The new price formula, which was also linked to quality standards, led to a two per cent cut in domestic gas prices from October 1992, to keep British Gas within the price cap. As the chairman of British Gas commented, 'This is a very tough package' (*Financial Times*, 30 April 1991).

The need for regulatory agencies is in part a reflection of the fact that the privatisation programme placed quick and profitable sales of unreconstituted companies, as favoured by government financial advisers and the managements of the companies themselves, over competition objectives (Bishop and Kay, pp. 22–3). 'The proliferation of the [regulatory agencies] has, like the privatisation programme itself, evolved in a piecemeal fashion and has not been governed by a set of clearly defined objectives' (Veljanovski, 1987, p. 175). There is still no general policy framework guiding what the regulatory agencies should be doing. Each regulator has had to evolve his own strategy, although this has necessarily led to a more detailed examination of the way in which each regulated utility works. As far as business–government relations are concerned:

The key point is that privatisation and liberalisation have not meant the removal of the state from industrial activity. They have removed the state from its role as producer and are transforming it into the 'protective state', whose main function is to ensure that businesses play by the agreed rules of the game. (Ibid, p. 170)

Government as a customer

Government is a major customer of a number of industries, especially construction, pharmaceuticals and the defence industries. In many of these sectors, entry costs for new companies are high, and may be increased by government standards that companies have to meet before becoming recognised suppliers. Efforts have been made to increase the number of smaller companies supplying government, but it has been estimated that small firms take only 25 per cent of the market represented by £16,000 million of government spending each year on stores and services (Burns, 1984, p. 38). For many large companies, particularly in the defence sector, government is their principal customer. Dunleavy argues that in such areas as military procurement and the civil nuclear industry, 'the industry's affairs are negotiated privately by the main firms' (1982, pp. 190–1) rather than by representative organisations. The Society of British Aerospace Companies has argued that the prime contractor system is the most effective way of managing large defence contracts, while the Defence Manufacturers Association, representing smaller firms that are largely subcontractors, is concerned about a tendency for major contractors to undertake more of the work themselves (Defence Committee, 1982, pp. xxv–xxxvi).

The situation of a monopsonist facing an oligopolistic (or in some cases a monopolistic) seller is fraught with dangers. The employment of former civil servants or military officers by firms substantially dependent on defence contracts is a practice which has attracted criticism from time to time. More generally, a fear that is often expressed is that government's dependence on a small group of suppliers with a monopoly or near-monopoly of specialist expertise will lead to it being exploited by profit-maximising enterprises. The Thatcher Government tried to place more emphasis on competition in the defence sector, but there are limits to what can be achieved. The challenge for the industry in the 1990s is, of course, that of coping with the decline in business that is likely to result from the changed strategic situation following the end of the Cold War. Given that the ratio of defence procurement (net of imports) to manufacturing GDP was 12.3 per cent by 1984 (Kaldor, Sharp and Walker, 1986, p. 34), this is a problem which has implications beyond the defence industries sector.

In the pharmaceutical industry, government has operated a Pharmaceutical Prices Regulation Scheme (PPRS) in conjunction with the Association of British Pharmaceutical Industries (ABPI). In effect, this is a profit regulation scheme. The seventh PPRS 'remains legally non-binding, but its substantive terms are much more detailed than those of any of its predecessors' (Hancher, 1990, p. 206). The negotiating role of the ABPI is 'considerably strengthened' (ibid., p. 207). Although in some respects this gives the ABPI an important mediating role, 'The history of the PPRS would seem to be one of frustrated and incomplete development of private interest government' (Sargent, 1985, p. 125). Hancher's more recent research emphasises the fragile and informal character of the agreements in the industry (Hancher, 1990, pp. 216–21). She also shows how American transnationals were able to exert effective political pressure over the transfer pricing issue (ibid., p. 209).

Government's relations with industry as a customer do lead to the creation of special bargaining or institutional arrangements such as the PPRS or the National Defence Industries Council in the defence industries. Although this creates special roles for associations, particularly in pharmaceuticals, direct contacts with the leading contractors are very important.

European Commission

Any contemporary discussion of government and business cannot be confined to domestic institutions, but must take account of the European Commission or, more strictly, of 'Commission services', the civil servants who serve the College of Commissioners. These civil servants are organised into directorates-general (twenty-three in 1991) which are divided into directorates, which in turn are usually subdivided into divisions. Despite public perceptions that the Commission is a huge bureaucracy, a policy and executive staff of ten thousand (Nugent, 1991, p. 65) is in fact rather small in relation to the range of tasks that the Commission has to undertake.

All of the Commission's directorates-general, except those concerned with its internal administration, are of some interest to business, but some are of greater significance than others. These include DG 1 (External Affairs) which deals with external economic relations; DG III which covers the internal market and industrial affairs; and DG V which is responsible for employment, industrial relations and social affairs. DG III in particular is sometimes seen as performing something akin to a sponsorship role for industry. Other directorates-general, because of their missions, are seen as less sympathetic to the business point of view, notably DG IV (Competition) and DG XI (Environment).

One of the characteristics that differentiates the Brussels bureaucracy from that in London is its relative openness. This is in part a reflection of a different bureaucratic style which lacks the British preoccupation with secrecy, but also arises from the Commission's need to build external support for its policy proposals. The need to secure information for policy design; consent for policy clearance; and cooperation for policy information is even more pressing for the European Commission than it is for the British civil service.

4 Banks and the Financial Sector

The economic strength and political influence of the financial services sector is a distinctive feature of British business which merits separate treatment. The financial sector is often referred to as the 'City', but although this is a convenient shorthand, it has always been something of a misnomer, and has become even more so as financial institutions have moved away from the 'square mile' in search of dealing rooms which give them the space to cope with round-the-clock international trading. Although the British financial sector has been distinguished for centuries by its international orientation, 'Perhaps for the first time it is now possible to speak of a *single* world financial market' (Coggan, 1989, p. 9). Financial globalisation has been a major driving force behind economic globalisation, and has been accompanied by the growth of 'financial engineering', the creation of customised products for both borrower and investor. Financial globalisation has been made possible by developments in information technology which have been facilitated what has, in effect, now become twenty-four hour international financial trading. As one of the three great financial centres of the world, along with Tokyo and New York, London is at the centre of these developments. For example, by 1989, according to the Bank for International Settlements, monthly turnover on the foreign exchange market was $3,740 billion in the UK, compared with $2,580 billion in the US, and $2,300 billion in Japan.

Changes in the international financial markets have prompted major readjustments in the organisation of domestic markets, with many of the traditional institutional barriers becoming blurred or disappearing. For example, a leading building society, Abbey National, has become a retail bank. These changes can be traced back to the end of sterling convertibility in 1958, the subsequent rise of the London Eurodollar market, and the exposure of traditional financial institutions to competition from foreign (especially American) banks. Changes introduced by the Heath Government had far-reaching consequences, replacing a system of credit rationed administratively by one influenced by price, and greatly increasing competition in the banking sector (Moran, 1984b). October 1986 saw the so-called 'Big Bang' which liberalised the securities market through the ending of minimum commissions and the traditional distinction between brokers and jobbers. The 'Big Bang' initiated a frenetic period of often ill-considered expansion and acquisition in the City, exemplified by the emergence of the 'yuppie' who was able to indulge in considerable conspicuous consumption. The stock exchange crash of October 1987 cooled this fever, and by the end of the decade, sudden redundancies were a familiar occurrence in the City. Some Lloyds 'names' were finding that they were incurring substantial losses, and the Building Societies Commission was having to find merger partners for building societies to prevent their collapse. Taken together with the BCCI affair, and the tangled collapse of the Maxwell companies, the impression given was of a financial system in which there were substantial opportunities for ill-thought out initiatives, sharp practice, and fraud.

The financial sector is made up of an 'institutional structure of short term markets (or exchanges) in commodities, securities, money and services' (Ingham, 1984, p. 60). The banks (the retail banks, the merchant or investment banks and, of course, the Bank of England itself) have played a crucial role in the system of financial intermediation. Other key actors have included the Stock Exchange, providing the focus of the securities market; the various commodity markets and exchanges; Lloyds and the insurance market; the insurance companies and pension funds; unit trusts and investment trusts: and the building societies. The accountancy profession is an important component of the financial sector, not least because of the influence it exerts within manufacturing industry, where an accountancy qualification offers one route to a seat on the board. Accountants specialising in receivership found their services increasingly in demand as the recession deepened at the beginning of the 1990s. There has been a growing intergration of financial services and the commercial bar, with the growth of regulation and litigation pushing barristers up the corporate hierarchy. It should be remembered that Edinburgh is a leading international financial centre in its own right, with major strengths in life assurance and pension fund management.

One consequence of the 'Big Bang' was the emergence of large financial conglomerates performing a wide range of functions. For example, clearing banks acquired merchant banks and stockbrokers. However, partly because of a clash of cultures, and partly because of a simultaneous expansion of capacity beyond what the market could sustain, these arrangements often failed to work well. One clearing bank, the Midland, faced serious difficulties at the beginning of the 1990s. It would certainly be unwise to herald the development of conglomerates as representing the final establishment of 'finance capital', itself a problematic term (see Ingham, 1984, pp. 32–6).

What must be emphasised is that the emergence of enterprises straddling traditional boundaries in the financial sector has not produced a new political unity of purpose. As Moran (1986a, p. 29) notes:

> To state a truism: the City is not a united interest; the financial services industry is less united still. Hostility, suspicion and competition divide sector from sector and firm from firm. Deregulation, structural change and uncertainty about the results of the 'Big Bang' have intensified this traditional culture of alien suspicion.

Later in the chapter some of these sectoral divisions within the financial sector will be examined in greater detail. However it is first necessary to examine the argument that the financial sector exerts a greater influence in Britain than industry; that manufacturing has been subordinate in political terms to finance. In economic terms, what is often remarked upon is the absence of a relationship; large British firms generally raise the greater part of their investment capital from retained profits. It should be noted that arguments about the hegemony of the financial sector have an 'efficiency' as well as a 'power' dimension: the two types of argument tend to overlap. The 'efficiency' arguments focus on what is seen as the contribution of the nature of the financial sector, and its relationship with manufacturing industry, to relative economic decline. Among the arguments advanced are the lack of a close relationship between banks and industry; the dominant role of institutional shareholders interested in short-term portfolio management rather than the longer run viability of an enterprise; and the absence of adequate funding arrangements for smaller concerns.

These 'efficiency' arguments are not the focus of this particular study, although they unavoidably creep into the analysis. However, three brief comments may be made. First, a close relationship between

industry and finance is not necessarily desirable. It can lead to the
easier translation of a financial crisis into an industrial crisis or vice-
versa, and it assumes that financial institutions actually have some
worthwhile advice to transmit to industry. Second, the gap between
industry and finance is often exaggerated, as is their closeness in other
countries (see Grant, Paterson and Whitston, 1988, pp. 115–32). Third,
there is a persistent view that a principal cause of Britain's economic
problems is a lack of investment. This overlooks the argument that the
real problem is the relatively poor rate of return on investments made,
which largely results from well-documented deficiencies in the organisation of production in the workplace. 'In retrospect, post-war
Britain's relatively slow growth compared with France or Germany
appears to be due primarily to poor productivity performance rather
than low investment in physical capital' (Crafts, 1991, p. 88). That is
not to say that the organisation of the financial sector is irrelevant to
explanations of poor industrial performance. Relatively low levels of
private sector investment in research and development in Britain can be
explained in terms of the substantially higher cost of capital for long-
term research and development projects in Britain compared to
Germany, and an active hostile takeover market which encourages
managers to focus on current earnings (Crafts, 1991, p. 94).

Finance and industry

In analysing the relationship between finance and industry, a rather
sceptical view will be taken of the argument that there is a an easily
identifiable divide between finance and industry in Britain. In so far as
such a division does exist, it does not often manifest itself in overt
conflict, although tensions did increase against the background of the
recession at the beginning of the 1990s. A CBI report published in 1990
criticised the short-term attitude towards manufacturing among British
financial institutions and called for steps to redress the 'imbalance of
power' between banks and smaller manufacturing businesses.

Institutional domination by finance in the sense of 'victory' in open
political struggles is not common. For example, it is difficult for the
financial sector to overturn new taxation measures announced by the
Chancellor in his Budget speech. There is, however, evidence of
ideological domination in the sense of the shaping of policy debate by
the 'internationalist' assumptions of the leading parts of the financial

sector. As Judge notes, in one of the most balanced and thoughtful recent reviews of these questions, internationalism 'was not simply because of the capture of the state machine by financial capital, but simply because the definition of the interests of the state had become so rooted in an international perspective' (Judge, 1990, p. 19). It was not a simple question of industrial interests being systematically dis- criminated against. Sometimes its preferences were coterminous with those of finance. 'In fact for long periods of Britain's industrial history the interests of financial and industrial capital progressed along parallel, not divergent tracks' (ibid., 1990, p. 19). When those interests did diverge, the failure was often one of the political capacity of manufacturing industry which 'articulated no coherent view in contradistinction to that of the City–Treasury–Bank nexus' (ibid., 1990, p. 18).

The division between finance and industry has conventionally been presented as having historical origins in the way in which the industrial revolution was financed by individual entrepreneurs, compounded by the subsequent development of the City as an international financial centre and its consequent preoccupation with finding a profitable outlet for British capital abroad. However, Ingham argues that too great an emphasis on overseas investment can distract attention from the finan- cial sector's commercial activities. He notes, 'Since the 1830s ... the City's earnings from the foreign exchange and money markets, freight and commodity broking, and — spectacularly in recent years — insur- ance have exceeded the income from overseas investment' (Ingham, 1984, pp. 35–6). However, it should be added that the commercial ser- vices provided in London are heavily oriented to international markets.

As Ingham points out, many of the writers on this subject have failed to take 'the basic step of closely examining the nature of the City's activities' (ibid., p. 33). One consequence is a tendency to present the financial sector as more monolithic than it actually is and to ignore the fact that some parts of the City may be closer to industry than others. This is particularly true of the clearing banks who do not wish to accumulate bad debts through the collapse of significant numbers of their industrial customers, although this may lead them to treat their smaller commercial customers more harshly.

Analysts have overlooked the significance of the development of a professional corporate treasurer function within large firms. A survey by the Association of Corporate Treasurers reported in 1985 found that fifty per cent of the treasury departments surveyed had been in existence for less than ten years (*The Accountant*, 7 March 1985). One of the most important tasks of the treasurer is to manage a company's relationship with its suppliers of financial services. The development of a professional treasury function has given companies a more sophistic- ated appreciation of the rapidly-changing range of financial services available to them. More generally, corporate treasurers may be seen as a means of bringing the financial and industrial sectors in Britain closer together. The Governor of the Bank of England commented in 1983:

> By the nature of their job, corporate treasurers embody the link between industry and finance, and they are therefore especially well placed to increase the degree of understanding between the two ... I see a key role here for corporate treasurers, on the one hand in explaining financial constraints and opportunities to their own companies; and, on the other, in explaining to financial institutions the objectives and policies of their own companies and in specifying the precise financing requirements which they entail. (*The Treasurer*, December 1983, p. 9)

Radical analysts are prepared to admit that 'the gap between industrial and financial capital in Britain has diminished significantly of late, and that the City banks and large industrial concerns are now closely interrelated' (Coates, David, 1989, p. 26). Although they would acknowledge that the relationship between City and industry has changed to some extent, radical observers regard what they see as the dominance of finance capital as a fundamental pathology of the British economic system. It is seen as leading to enormous concentrations of power in the hands of the financial institutions, but, more importantly, it is argued that the financial sector has been able to impose policies which are in its interests on government, but which damage the economy as a whole:

> City interests prevailed over industrial ones in the opposition to free trade after 1906, in the decision to return to the gold standard in 1925, and in the way in which the 1931 financial crisis was handled. City interests benefitted disproportionately from the retreat from planning after 1948, and from the way in which successive post-war governments strove to maintain a world role for Britain based on the use of sterling as a reserve currency, on the liberalisation of capital markets, and on the maintenance of the sterling area. (Coates, David, 1984, p. 62)

Coates admits that the City has not always had its own way. For example, for most of the postwar period, real interest rates have been negative. Tolliday reminds us that in the interwar period, the Governor of the Bank of England, Montagu Norman, 'had a clear shared interest with the government in industrial regeneration since it was felt by many in the Bank that continuing industrial decline imperilled the stability of the Gold Standard and Britain's world financial power' (Tolliday, 1984, p. 59). Moreover, much of the autonomy, and hence the power, of the financial sector has depended on its ability to exercise a largely unsupervised self-regulation. The rapid pace of change in financial markets in the 1980s, combined with a number of financial scandals in the 1970s and 1980s, created pressures for greater regulation of the financial sector, even if the proposals adopted did not go as far as many critics of existing arrangements wanted.

Even if they are reluctant to accept that 'The traditional British division between City and industry is being closed' (Moran, 1983, p. 67), advocates of the view that there is a major divide between finance and industry have to contend with the difficulty presented by the observation that open conflict between finance capital and industrial capital is spasmodic. It should be remembered that industrialists sit as non-executive directors on the boards of financial institutions, and financiers are to be found on the boards of many industrial companies. Indeed, Useem argues that 'the interlocking directorate forms a national transcorporate network overarching all sectors of business' (Useem, 1984, p. 53). In particular, the experience of multiple directors 'even transects the industry/City divide' (Useem and McCormack, 1981, p. 384). It is also worth recalling that companies which are interested in growing through takeovers have a particular interest in cultivating good relations with the financial sector. Not all companies, however, welcome what they see as the growing intrusion of the financial sector into their affairs. One company interviewed in 1991 complained about the growing role of business analysts from stockbroking firms. They made judgements about companies which influence their share price, their ability to raise capital, and their vulnerability to takeover.

In terms of political representation, the financial sector and manufacturing industry have been coming closer together in recent years, with increasing numbers of financial firms and institutions (even the Stock Exchange) joining the CBI. Most of this increase in financial sector membership occurred in the late 1970s. It is doubtful whether the financial institutions joining the CBI did so because they now saw it as their main spokesman; rather they wanted to give their support to a revitalised organisation battling with a Labour Government. The chairs of key CBI committees continue to be drawn very largely from manufacturing industry. Nevertheless, Leys suggests that the recruitment of so many non-manufacturing members may have diluted the organisation's commitment to manufacturing industry:

> ... the fact that non-manufacturing companies supply nearly 30 per cent of the organisation's membership and funds acts as a significant restraint on its representation of manufacturing interests. This restraint was operative in 1980 when many commercial and all financial companies were benefiting from high interest and exchange rates. (Leys, 1985, p. 14)

There were signs of increasing concern within the CBI in the early 1990s about its ability to provide a distinctive voice for manufacturing industry, reflected in moves to form a National Manufacturing Council within the CBI. In the past, such differences had come to the surface more in private than in public. They are still overriden to some extent by a recognition that what unites industrialists and financiers is more important than what divides them.

Longstreth (1979, p. 188) has argues that the real divide is not between finance and industry, but between finance and multinationals — with a common interest in the export of capital — and domestic industry (Longstreth, 1979, p. 188). This is an interesting modification of the usual broad-brush distinction between finance capital and industrial capital. However, as Ingham points out, Longstreth fails to identify the boundaries of what he regards as a dominant 'fraction' of capital. Nor is it clear from Longstreth's analysis whether the two interests must necessarily be opposed, or whether this just happens to be the case in Britain (Ingham, 1984, pp. 29–30).

The political influence of the financial sector

Although one must not exaggerate the division between finance and industry, there is a distinctive financial sector, and it is able to exert considerable political influence. In part, this is achieved by informal links between financial interests and the Conservative Party, channelled through individual MPs with City links through such mechanisms as

the Conservative backbench finance committee. The Governor of the
Bank of England has traditionally acted as the City's representative to
government, whilst in the 1970s and 1980s the trade associations of the
financial sector have undergone a process of revitalisation and pro-
fessionalisation, while banks have developed their own government
relations operations.

Perhaps the real key to the influence of the financial sector resides in
its 'exceptionalism'. By 'exceptionalism' is meant the long-standing
freedom of the financial sector from extensive government intervention
and the way in which issues which might be awkward to it have not
appeared on the political agenda. For example, the Eurocurrency market developed in London with far less regulation than in the United
States. More generally, Moran notes that the City's power has rested
not on a crude capacity to influence overt policy, but on ability to
convert matters vital to its interests into non-decisions: 'they were not
matters thought to be the concern of bureaucratic politics in Whitehall
or partisan politics in Westminster' (Moran, 1983, p. 54). This privileged treatment cannot be explained simply in terms of City 'hegemony'. As Ingham emphasises (1984, p. 37), 'During the twentieth
century, the policies which the City had advocated have also been
favoured by the Treasury and Bank because of their favourable impact
on their own *independent practices* and *institutional power*.'

The influence of the financial sector can only properly be understood
in terms of the broader acceptance of particular orthodoxies by policy
actors outside the financial sector. For much of the postwar period,
British industry was handicapped by an excessively high exchange rate
for the pound (it was further decimated by the pound's appreciation in
value between 1978 and 1981). When the Labour Government came
into office in 1964, it quickly rejected the option of devaluation. Given
the size of its majority, that was not a surprising decision. However, in
the summer of 1966, with a substantial mandate from the electorate, it
chose deflation rather than devaluation, a decision which can be seen as
the start of the erosion of the postwar commitment to full employment.
It was finally forced into devaluation in 1967.

This unhappy sequence of events was not simply the result of
incompetence by Labour politicians (indeed, if they lacked anything, it
was courage rather than competence). They were acting on the advice
given to them by their senior civil servants, and those civil servants
were reflecting established wisdom in the Treasury and the City (even
though it was challenged by many economist). (But for a critique of

this analysis, see Stones 1988.) Blank convincingly argues that the postwar conduct of British economic policy was dominated by the defence of sterling prompted by the foreign policy goal of trying to maintain Britain's status as a world power. He comments (1978, pp. 120–1):

> Rather than searching for the influence of one department, the City, or the bank, it is more useful and accurate to think in terms of an 'overseas' or 'sterling' lobby within the government and administration. This lobby shared the belief that Britain's international position and responsibilities constituted the primary policy objectives and that the international role of sterling was vital to this position.

When the position of the financial sector is threatened, it has a number of sanctions at its disposal. One of the most potent is the gilt-edged 'strike', a coordinated refusal to buy government stock. Moreover, the attention given by the media to such indicators as the sterling exchange rate or movements in the FT Stock Exchange Index also allows City 'opinion' to exert a subtle influence on policy-making. 'In these instances it is not the actual ownership (or even possession) of assets by City organisations which is important but rather their privileged access to the 'mood' of the markets' (Ingham, 1984, p. 230).

The analysis of City–state relations presented in the first edition of this book has been criticised by Stones (1988). His fundamental objection is 'that the relations between certain business sectors or fractions of capital and the state should not be expected to exhibit some sort of unity or homogeneity in every policy area or in a given policy area over time' (Stones, 1988, p. 1). 'In particular Grant imposes a unity on City–State relations where ... no unity exists' (ibid., p. 34).

The City is, of course, a much less homogeneous entity than it once was, and this was recognised in the first edition. The City often loses direct political battles with government. However, it is still possible to make some general statements about relationships between the financial sector and government. Stones considers that 'Overall policy is the result of a fractured and fragmented set of processes' (ibid., p. 2). There is an implicit postmodernist view of the world here which may not fit as well with key, deeply institutionally-embedded economic relationships as it might, for example, with explanations of cultural change. Where Stones is correct is in pointing to the fact that government was slow to appreciate the wider implications for economic policy objectives of matters that were seen as 'technical' questions which could largely be left to the City (ibid., p. 33). This has changed, but although the systems of regulation within which the City now operates are often quite costly to operate, their effectiveness in an era of financial globalisation remains open to question.

Stones dismisses the idea of a common normative outlook between the Labour Party and the City as 'fanciful' (ibid., p. 36). Labour's values are different from those of the City, but the policies of a Labour government, and even of a Labour opposition, often converge with those of the City because of the underlying structural imperatives. The Labour Party was assiduously courting the City in the run up to the 1992 General Election. A senior clearing bank employee interviewed in 1991 viewed the prospect of a Labour Government with equanimity:

> The idea of a National Investment Bank may well be forgotten. We expect more intervention and less self-regulation. But we have no major concerns.

The Bank–Treasury relationship

The Bank of England–Treasury relationship has been the fulcrum of contracts between the financial sector and government. Until the 1970s, financial interests largely relied on the Bank to express their views to government. The Bank thus has a dual role as government's representative in the City (the Treasury's 'East End branch' as it is sometimes jokingly called), and as a voice for financial (particularly banking) interests within government. The Governor in office in 1970, Sir Leslie O'Brien, made it clear in evidence to the Select Committee on Nationalised Industries that he was not undiscriminating advocate of the financial sector's interests. He filtered their advocacy (Select Committee on Nationalised Industries, 1970, pp. 273–5).

Since the 1970s, the role of the Governor as a general representative of financial interests has diminished in significance. Denis Healey as chancellor made a point of developing his own personal contacts with financial institutions, something which upset the Governor at the time (Healey, 1990, p. 375). Sector specific trade associations have become far better organised and more significant intermediaries in government–financial sector relations than was previously the case. Increasing government intervention in the financial sector, exemplified by the growing role of the Department of Trade and Industry in financial matters, brought to the surface tensions between the Bank of England's representative and public roles. As Moran (1983, p. 61) explains:

◊ The Bank remains, rather in the manner of a conventional sponsoring department, an important means of expressing City interests in government ♠. But no significant City interest now feels it necessary to approach central government only through the Bank of England; and the powerful clearing banks, who a couple of decades ago, would not have ventured into Whitehall except in its company, now look upon it as just one way among many of influencing public policy.

Later work by Moran emphasises the extent to which the Bank has been transformed from a City institution to a governing institution that regulates the City. 'In brief, the Bank that emerges after the First World War as a guardian of the City elite against a potentially democratic state had now itself become, to some degree, an institution of that state' (Moran, 1991, p. 67). The Bank was concerned to retain Britain's prominence as an international financial centre, which was not the same thing as protecting the interests of particular firms, especially the more backward ones. Moran shows how the Bank has become increasingly guided by its own full-time professional staff, for whom economic analysis is an important as informal contracts in the market.

That is not to say that the Bank–government relationship is no longer a significant one; indeed, one of the constraints on the Bank is 'the need to respond to the demands of bureaucratic politics in Whitehall' (Moran, 1991, p. 67). Apart from the high-level contacts between the Governor of the Bank and the Chancellor and, on occasion, the Prime Minister, Bank of England staff are extensively represented on various government advisory committees. The bank plays an important role in the management of the money markets, the foreign exchange markets, and the placement of gilt-edged stock. The latter task is of particular political significance and offers a good illustration of the sharing of tasks between the Treasury and the Bank. The legal authority to make issues is in the hands of the Treasury. In practice, the Treasury and the Bank work closely together, with the Bank 'aiming to provide the monetary conditions desired by political decision. There is informal and frequent contact between the Head of the Gilt-Edged Division and the Treasury Under-Secretary in charge of the Home Finance Division by telephone, in writing and in meetings' (Wormell, 1985, p. 22). In

addition to these daily meetings, there is a monthly cycle of consultation based on each month's money stock data, which is discussed
by the Bank and the Treasury. One of the issues discussed will be the
implications for interest rates.

The Chancellor of the Exchequer receives a daily report on the gilt-
edged market. Developments in the market are also carefully assessed
in the financial press. This will include discussion of the impact of any
political events, e.g., an unfavourable by-election result for the government which might influence assessments of political risk. Although the
market is clearly influenced by the attempts of players in it to maximise
their own returns, it is also very sensitive to political developments,
and, on occasion, may be a means of signalling an adverse City response to such developments. It should be remembered that issues are
continually maturing. These have to be redeemed in cash creating a
need for new stocks to be sold.

A reluctance on the part of the City to buy gilts can thus have a
considerable impact on government decisions. In May 1978, the then
Labour administration faced what appeared to be a crisis. As a member
of the cabinet at the time recalls, 'The City was in a jumpy mood and
we were not selling Gilts' (Barnett, 1982, p. 146). The Chancellor
advocated measures to control the money supply and an increase in the
National Insurance Surcharge. No immediate statement was issued, and
there were worries about how the markets would react. Attempts by the
opposition to build up a crisis atmosphere were unsuccessful, 'and we
later heard that the mood in the City had improved, with £450 million
of Gilts being sold in an hour' (Barnett, 1982, p. 147). This particular
episode was thus handled successfully from the Government's point of
view, but it illustrates the extent to which governments have to heed
developments in the gilt-edged market.

Sectoral financial associations

Sectoral associations in the financial sector have in the past often been
little more than gentlemanly clubs performing a restricted range of
functions, or, at best, running a cartel. However, in the 1970s and 1980s
there has been a noticeable improvement in the professionalism and
sophistication of such bodies. A number of factors have contributed to
this trend, including the replacement of specialised, often family-con-
trolled, businesses by large financial conglomerates; a series of failures

in the old mechanisms of representation; the limitations of the Bank of England as a representative of financial interests; and the new pressures generated by EC membership (see Moran, 1983). Thus, 'The Committee of London Clearing Bankers ... has in recent years been transformed from a trade association operating restrictive practices into a highly efficient lobbyist in Whitehall' (Moran, 1984b, p. 12). In 1985, an enlarged group called the Committee of London and Scottish Bankers was formed. This grouping represented the Bank of Scotland, Barclays, Lloyds, Midland, National Westminster, Royal Bank of Scotland, and Standard Chartered. The US bank, Citibank, which is a clearing bank, is not included because it does not meet the full membership requirement of being a publicly-quoted, British-owned recognised bank operating branch networks in the UK.

The other principal banking organisation, the British Bankers' Association (BBA) 'was roused from a dormant state in 1972 to lobby for the wider interests of all bankers, especially in Brussels' (ibid., p.12). The lobbying functions of the clearing bankers' committee have now been absorbed by the BBA which has thus emerged as the principal representative organisation for bankers There has been some criticism of its domestic effectiveness, for example in relation to the local authority swaps affair which was estimated to cost the banks £550 million but where the Environment Secretary, Michael Heseltine, could not be persuaded to take any remedial action in relation to the banks' difficulties. This was claimed to be 'yet another disaster for the UK banking lobby. The trade groups representing UK banking interests [the Merchant Bank and Security Houses Association as well as the BBA] already have an impressive record of failure in their Whitehall battles' (*Financial Times*, 5 May 1991). Moreover, the increasing reliance of banks on their own government relations operations places limits on the role of the BBA, even though it is chaired by the chairman of one of the banks. A government relations manager of one of the clearing banks commented in interview in 1991:

> We use the BBA for sectoral matters. Each bank tries to do it own thing. Because of the cartel problems, we see a competitive advantage in doing work ourselves... if a formal view is required on a piece of legislation, or a code of conduct, then it is done through the BBA.

In the area of insurance, the formation of the Association of British Insurers (ABI) in 1985 gives insurance companies operating in Britain a potentially more effective representative body. Before its formation, there were more than ten insurance associations. There were associations covering life assurance, as well as others such as the Accident Offices' Association and the Fire Offices' Committee which reflected the days when insurance companies operated a tariff system for their general insurance business. This heterogeneous structure made it difficult to present a common industry front to government, Parliament and the media. The process of rationalisation took several years and was not without its difficulties. The Associated Scottish Life Offices has been maintained as a separate association of the chief executives of the Scottish life companies based in Edinburgh. However, it is clear that the ABI, with its integrated secretariat, provides a much more streamlined structure for the representation of the British insurance industry.

The one exception to this general picture of an enhanced importance for sector associations is the Building Societies Association (BSA) which has faced a more difficult operating environment over the last few years. It has lost its cartel function, and the close relationship it had with government over mortgage interest rates in the 1970s, although the Halifax Building Society admitted in 1991 that it had decided to offer borrowers lower repayments the next time interest rates were reduced in part as a response to political pressures. Changes in the structure of the industry following the 1986 Building Societies Act mean that 'It is, on occasions, more difficult for the Association to exercise the representative function for the whole membership when, for example, some building societies have significant estate agent subsidiaries, some own insurance companies, some are involved in the provision of cheque book services and so on' (Building Societies Association Annual Report 1990, p. 5).

The deregulation of financial markets, and the emergence of a more competitive mortgage market, called the traditional role of the BSA into question. The conversion of the second largest building society, the Abbey National, into a retail bank prompted a major reorganisation of the BSA. A Council of Mortgage Lenders, serviced by the BSA, was established with the support of other trade associations such as the Association of British Insurers. All building societies are automatically members of the Council of Mortgage Lenders, but it also covers the newer lenders. At the 1992 Conference of the BSA, there were complaints from smaller societies that the BSA was dominated by larger societies and that they were unable to secure adequate representation. It was argued that the interests of the twenty largest soci-eties had diverged from those of the smallest sixty-five, with the smaller societies being pressured into mergers (*Financial Times*, 7 May 1992). In the longer run, particularly if the special regulatory regime for building societies is replaced by that for banks, further changes in representative arrangements may be necessary.

Conclusions

It is clear that the mechanisms through which the financial sector exerts influence changed in the 1970s and 1980s. Whether such changes represent a shift in the influence of the financial sector is a more difficult question to answer. As has been noted, the financial sector has significant sanctions at its disposal, has a range of formal and informal channels which it can use to influence government and the political process and, above all, has considerable autonomy in the conduct of its affairs. It is in this last area that it is most vulnerable to external pressure, particularly if it is unable to demonstrate that it can put and keep its own house in order.

The debate over the role of the financial sector in Britain has to some extent been obscured by an exaggeration of the divisions of interest between finance and industry (and by the implicit message that a closer relationship would necessarily be beneficial). In so far as industry has been able to exert less political influence (or enjoy less autonomy of operation) than the financial sector, much of the blame lies with industry itself. As Ingham notes, (1984, p. 232) 'Industrial capital's weaknesses should not be seen exclusively (and somewhat tauto-logically) as the corollary of the City's manifest strengths; the former's chronic inability to get its proposals implemented also has quite distinct and independent bases.' In particular, 'industrial capital in Britain has exhibited a very low level of organisation and solidarity' (ibid., p. 233). This is a point that will be returned to throughout the book. The success of a particular CBI campaign, the strength of a particular sectoral association, the effectiveness of an individual government relations division does not amount to an effective identification and articulation of industry's interests as a whole.

Whatever the deficiencies of the financial sector within Britain, they are eclipsed by developments taking place internationally which, of course, profoundly influence the City of London. Thus, relatively weak domestic pressure for regulatory change in Britain were shaped 'into much more formidable [by] the growing global integration of markets' (Moran, 1991, p. 139). More generally, it could be argued that the international financial system is slipping beyond the control of any national government or international institution. A global capital market is emerging. In particular, 'securitisation' has increased whereby lending is channelled through markets in tradeable paper instead of through the banking system. It is open to question whether securitised paper would be generally marketable if several creditors of a single debtor tried to liquidate their holdings at once.

Moran (1986b) takes the relatively optimistic view that, rather than traditional restraints on unscrupulous behaviour being eroded by the progress of capitalist culture, the progress of capitalism raises rather than lowers standards. This is because of the impact of public regulation and the domination of markets by bureaucratically-organised corporations. Public regulation of financial markets may be improving, but institutions such as central banks find it difficult to keep up with the pace of financial innovation. The Cross Report, published by the Bank of International Settlements (BIS) in 1986, argued that with more credit flowing outside normal banking channels, we will see less supervision in the future.

On the national level, 'the intergration of world capital markets implies a set of constraints on national policy-making' (Artis and Ostry, 1986, p. 5). In particular, 'the sensitivity of mobile capital to the prospect of gain or loss is liable to mean that a country whose policy seems unduly adventurous, and in some way prone to inflation, will be heavily punished by the withdrawal of funds, which will result in extensive reserve losses under a fixed exchange-rate regime or in a severe exchange-rate depreciation under a regime of floating exchange rates' (ibid., p. 5). Global financial markets set limits on the autonomy of domestic governments. There was a widely held view in the financial services sector at the beginning of the 1990s that the Labour Partly had not realised just how much British membership of the exchange rate mechanism of the EMS would constrain the range of policy options open to a Labour Government. Equally, the substantial political resistance to full British participation in Economic and Monetary Union, a development generally favoured by the financial services sector, illustrated the limits of the power of the City in areas of policy that become politically contested.

A series of financial scandals, and internal disputes within financial institutions, notably that at Lloyds, has had an impact on the view taken of the financial services sector in the political world, particularly among that key group, Conservative backbenchers. Moran has commented, 'On the whole [the business community's] relations generally with the state have got better. But ... I think the relationship between the City and the state [has] got worse' (transcript of Radio 4 *Analysis* programme, 18 June 1992, p. 6). Many of the conventional assumptions about the role and power of the financial services sector may have to be reviewed in a changed political climate.

5 Large Firms and the Political Process

In the 1980s, political scientists paid increased attention to the role of the firm as a direct actor in the political process. By the end of the decade, it was no longer possible to claim, as Dyson had justifiably done in 1983 (p. 35), 'The politics of the firm has been neglected.' That is not to say that its importance was fully recognised in research. A number of projects, however, made it clear just how important an actor the firm was. Cawson and his colleagues reported (1990, pp. 375–6):

> Our research has led us to the unmistakable conclusion that at the present time the key to unlocking the complexities of industrial politics lies in the corporate strategies of the major firms. Other actors — trade unions, trade associations, even governments — are far less significant as the drivers of change than are the firms.

Direct relationships between firms and government, without the intermediation of a business interest association, have increased in importance in the British political process. One indication of this development is the increasing use by very large firms of specialist government relations divisions to coordinate their interactions with government. The functions and operations of such divisions are extensively discussed in this chapter. Both large firms, and medium-sized firms, have made increasing use of political consultancies, particularly for their contacts with Parliament, and the work of such consultancies is also reviewed here.

The high degree of concentration in the British economy and the persistence of an individualistic enterprise ethic contribute to the development of direct contacts between large firms and government. Another important factor has been the tendency for the industrial policies followed by both Labour and Conservative governments since the launch of the Industrial Strategy in 1975 to emphasise a more 'bottom up' approach which stresses the value of direct contact with firms. As a senior civil servant has commented:

What I now detect is that, as compared with the 1960s, the era of the National Plan which was imposed from the top, and where sectoral implications were carefully worked out with the help of trade associations, in the 1970s there has been a greater realisation that government must also have contact with individual companies, to complement its relations with industry's collective bodies. That principle is now generally accepted and quite a lot of progress has been made. (Mueller, 1985, p. 105)

Firms are increasingly international political actors with, for example, representatives in Brussels. ICI's government relations operation in Washington is larger than that in London. Firms themselves are undergoing an important organisational transformation, as the conventional model of a multinational company, with headquarters, finance and research and development functions being located in the home country, is supplemented by the emergence of the 'stateless company'. Such companies deliberately seek to internationalise their ownership and control by selling shares on stock exchanges across the world, and by drawing their boards of directors and senior management from a wide range of nationalities. Such strategies are seen as an effective response to the phenomenon of economic globalisation.

ABB (Asea Brown Boveri), a company formed from a merger of leading Swiss and Swedish companies is a good example of such a stateless company. It claims to have 'global coordination ... but no national bias' (Taylor, 1991, p.105). The company's chief executive sees clear political advantages in such an arrangement:

Think back 15 years ago when Asea was a Swedish electrical company with 95 per cent of its engineers in Sweden. We could complain about high taxes ... But what could Asea do about it? Not much. Today I can tell the Swedish authorities that they must create a more competitive environment for R & D or our research there will decline. (Quoted in Taylor, 1991, p. 105)

Even when companies are not extensively internationalised, the power balance between firms and governments often favours the

former. Government grants may be welcome supplements to a
company's investment funds, but are unlikely to fundamentally
change its policies. Interventionist government policies may end up
being 'captured' by particular firms to in the pursuit of their own
interests. Cawson, Shepherd and Webber (1989, p. 130) note that the
Ministry of Industry in France was '"captured" by Thomson and
acted at its champion within government ... Such an extreme case of
capture can amount to the regulation of government by the firm.' Of
course, large firms are not usually so dominant. In highly-regulated
industries, 'The relation between regulator and regulated is a more
subtle, complex one and is based on *interdependence*' (Hancher,
1990, p. 8). Even within such a context, less subtle pressures may be
used, as when political pressure from American pharmaceutical
manufacturers secured a satisfactory bargain on an important pricing
issue (Ibid., p. 209). Regulation is a particularly important form of
government intervention directly affecting firms in private enterprise
systems, and its importance is likely to grow in future. Even so, a
survey of the area concludes that 'The importance of the large firm in
the regulatory precess is particularly notable' (Hancher and Moran,
1989b, p. 272). Hancher and Moran's emphasis on the firm as a
reservoir of expertise and an agent of enforcement in the regulatory
process is echoed by the more general conclusions of Cawson and his
colleagues (1990, p. 361):

> Government agencies are unable to exercise detailed controls over
> firms because they lack their personnel resources, marketing know-
> ledge, technical ability, collective memory and strategic orientation.

Although Cawson and his colleagues stress the relative frag-
mentation of government compared with the firm, it is clear that firms
vary considerably not only in the range and character of the markets
they serve, their patterns of ownership, and the technologies they use,
but also in terms of their forms of internal organisation. In particular,
firms vary considerably in their degree of centralisation, and the way in
which control is operated from the centre. In some enterprises,
functions such as personnel, purchasing, marketing etc. are highly
centralised, and only day-to-day production management decisions are
left to the plant level. In other cases, the enterprise is highly decentralised, with considerable autonomy being given to the product
division or subsidiary company.

In a decentralised company, political operations may be conducted at two levels. The corporate centre may lobby on behalf of the company as a whole, either through a government relations division or more personal contacts. The subsidiary units will then work through the appropriate trade association(s). Such a structure can and does lead to different parts of the company pursuing conflicting policies. However, in a relatively centralised company operating units may cherish their political autonomy. One relatively centralised 'top ten' company that was interviewed did not know how many trade associations it belonged to.

Forms of political activity by firms

Very large firms often have their own specialist government relations division. For example, seven of the ten largest companies by turnover in 1991 had such divisions. A survey of the hundred largest corporations by Neil Mitchell (1990, p. 630) found that 42 cent of the responding firms had government relations divisions. Government relations is understood as a specialist function within a firm which seeks to provide strategic coordination of its relations with government and other external actors, and to offer 'in-house' advice on the conduct of such relations. The function may have a number of titles other than 'government relations' such as corporate affairs or public affairs, but it must be distinguished from units or individuals performing a traditional public relations function.

How do companies which do not fall into the very large category handle government relations? Much will depend on the circumstances of the particular company. For example, one such company that was visited in 1991 handled government relations as part of its corporate communications function. This particular company had a long history and was deeply rooted in its community, so it was able to make considerable use of informal networks, including contacts with the local MPs. It was also seeking broader contacts through involvement in the work of the Industry and Parliament Trust, and had been visited by the Labour Party's industry team. Its local links were balanced by its membership of a large conglomerate which included a leading City institution and a newspaper. It was able to call on the resources of the larger group when needed.

The company had recently faced a problem with environmental regulations affecting one of its leading products in the United States which was one of its major markets. To cope with this problem, it had hired lawyers in the Unites States, but had also given considerable assistance to its trade association to set up a special technical section to work on the problem. It was thus able to pursue a sophisticated range of strategies without having a government relations division as such.

Even for very large firms, having a government relations division and being actively involved in business interest associations are not mutually exclusive activities. The evidence suggests that large firms tend *both* to have government relations divisions and to be active in business interest associations. Neil Mitchell notes (ibid., p. 631) that 'Firms with government relations divisions also tend to make use of trade association and CBI contacts somewhat more heavily.' The cost of subscribing to a business interest association for a large firm is so small in relation to turnover that it is hardly worth bothering about as an item on the firm's budget. However, the cost rises when one takes account of the attendance of senior executives at meetings. Estimates made available to the author suggest that large firms may devote between thirteen hundred and seventeen hundred person days a year of the time of senior management to business interest and association activity. Of course, very senior executives are likely to be able to organise their time to use it to the maximum possible effect. Sir John Harvey-Jones recalls how he managed to cope with being chairman of ICI and president of the European chemical industry federation, CEFIC:

> I ran my contribution to the operation on the basis of a one-and-a-half hour meeting each month with three individuals, the director-general of the British federation, the director general of CEFIC . . . and my own ICI man in Brussels who did a lot of the progress chasing. We found . . . that as long as we kept the subjects broad we could communicate adequately for progress on about twenty or thirty different projects that we were running. (Harvey-Jones, 1988, pp. 106–7)

Involvement in an organisation can confer additional benefits to offset the additional costs. A firm that actively participates in an association may become aware more quickly of economic and political developments that affect its operations, will be able to make decisions on the basis of a broader understanding of the economic and political context, and may acquire a better understanding of the strengths and weaknesses of competitors, if only by meeting and observing their senior managers. For junior management, participating in the work of business interest associations can serve as a form of training, introducing the manager to wider decision-making considerations and thus helping to prepare him or her for a corporate role.

Large firms are often able to pursue their own particular interests through business interest associations in a way that they could not do on their own behalf. One of the 'top ten' firms stated in interview that they derived three main benefits from business interest association activity. First, there was a whole series of questions where it was necessary to have an industry view, for example, on international trade matters. Second, although the firm could look after its own interests with the British Government, this was not possible on the European level; it was necessary to have associations for European Community representation. Third, there were a number of consultative bodies in Whitehall dealing with technical matters of great interest to the company: it could not sit on them as Company X, but it could sit on them as Company X, representing Association Y.

A study by Slatter (1983) shows that very few firms solely on government relations divisions for the conduct of their relations with government. Slatter sent a questionnaire to the top hundred industrial companies, plus the major nationalised industries and leading companies in the financial services sector, obtaining an overall response rate of 66 per cent. 44 per cent of responding companies worked only through industry associations, as against 38 per cent who worked through a combination of industry associations and their own government relations divisions, a minority of this category making some use of consultants as well. Only five enterprises worked solely through their government relations divisions and four of these were nationalised industries. Neil Mitchell's study (1990, p. 628) found that 'the number of [top hundred] firms that never contact government directly is 0, rising to 7 per cent that never contact government through trade associations, and 21 per cent that never use the CBI.' It is therefore clear that business interest association activity remains important even to the largest firms.

Government relations divisions

Which companies have a government relations division?

As has been pointed out, size is the best single predictor of whether a company will have a government relations division. This would seem to operate as an explanatory factor in different countries with Australian research providing 'qualified support' for the view that size is a predictor of the existence of a government relations division (Bell and Warhurst, 1992, p. 59). In Britain, all but a few of the 'top ten' companies have a government relations division, but the number falls back to three among the next ten companies by size of turnover, and is one or two in each of the following deciles in *The Times* listing of the top hundred firms. In accounting for why some firms outside the 'giant' category have government relations divisions, the most important explanatory variable is undoubtedly the extent to which they operate in a politicised environment. Neil Mitchell reports (1990, p. 630) that 'there is a moderate, positive, and statistically significant relationship between government involvement and direct political contact.' One factor here is the extent of state involvement in the sector, so that the large privatised companies operating within a regulatory framework generally have government relations divisions. In other sectors, as state involvement has diminished, the activities of various kinds of 'cause' groups has become an important motivation for operating a government relations division.

Companies in the oil and chemical industries are particularly likely to have government relations divisions. Neil Mitchell notes (ibid., p. 629) that 'the clearest clustering ... is with oil firms ... where most of the firms scored the government as heavily involved.' The closely related industries of oil and chemicals are substantially affected by government decisions about taxation and environmental standards, while exploration rights are an issue of concern to oil companies. A government relations executive in the oil industry who was interviewed commented:

In the oil industry, it's not the case that we have a choice, the politics of energy and oil draw us into very close relationships with government. Government has discretionary powers over various aspects of the oil industry. Much of what I do is the result of policies enforced on us by legislation that pulls us into relationships we would not pursue by other means.

The prevalence of government relations divisions in companies with substantial interests in tobacco and alcoholic drinks reflects the extent to which these industries are used by government as sources of tax revenue, and are therefore particularly affected by budget decisions. In addition, the industries have to deal with increasingly effective campaigns to place limits on advertising by them, and, in the case of tobacco, to ban smoking in public places. Companies producing electronics products of various kinds are likely to have government relations divisions because government is often an important customer, and because of the interest of government and the European Community in stimulating 'industries of the future', thus drawing firms and governments into a close relationship. The clearing banks generally operate government relations divisions. The manager of one such division commented in 1991, 'we are always under pressure as money lenders.'

The more internationalised a firm's operations are, the more it may feel that it needs a capability for gathering information about the stability of the regimes in the countries in which the company has invested or is thinking of investing. BP, which has a particularly sophisticated government relations operation, has developed company policies on such issues as the GATT round in a systematic effort to influence the outcome. Of course, no large firm can stand aside completely from the greater internationalisation of politics, particularly the greater complexity introduced into the decision-making environment by Britain's membership of the EC. The work of government relations specialists in Brussels is further discussed in Chapter 9. The balance between a firm's domestic and international activities may have more of an impact on the way in which the government relations is discharged, rather than on whether such a function exists at all.

Industries in which a government relations function is relatively rare in large companies include retailing, food processing and construction. Apart from construction, which has government as a customer, these industries do not have a high political profile. A food industry association official commented in interview in 1991, 'We don't have government relations specialists tripping over each other. We've never really been threatened by anything.' Many construction and food processing companies have been generous donors to the Conservative Party, and continue to rely on personal contacts with politicians.

Why did the function develop when it did?

ICI developed a government relations function as early as the 1950s, but the peak period for the formation of government relations divisions was the 1970s, although some companies set them up in the 1980s. Apart from one firm, 1974 was the earliest reported dated for establishment in Neil Mitchell's study (1990, p. 630). Interviews with firms suggested that many of the reasons for the establishment of a distinct government relations function at a particular time were specific to the individual company — a threat of nationalisation or a Monopolies Commission investigation, a chance conversation between two directors on a long distance flight, the application of the thinking of an American parent company to the British subsidiary.

There were, however, systematic factors operating across companies which encouraged the formation of government relations divisions. Perhaps up to the end of the 1960s it was possible to speak of a socially cohesive Establishment, 'a group of individuals united by common backgrounds and unspoken understandings' (Miller, 1991, p. 51). It had all but disappeared by the 1970s. Matters are occasionally still settled in an informal way, but as one respondent commented, 'The whole area has become more complex, twenty years ago all that a major chairman needed to do was to meet the Chancellor at his club, have a word in his ear and say "This isn't on."' It probably never was quite as simple as that, but the conduct of relationships between business and government has changed over the last thirty years, if only because the London clubs are not the important meeting places they once were. As Miller observes (ibid., p. 51):

> The tight and homogeneous circle that decided things within and outside Government has disappeared. Politicians as a group are more socially diverse than they were, and the traditional concept of a ruling or managerial class has been largely bleached from our national character.

The unstable economic and political situation in Britain in the mid- 1970s convinced a number of companies that they needed an 'in-house' capability that would enable them to understand what was happening and the implications for their firm. As one respondent commented:

> Started not with the Labour Government but with the 1970–74 Conservative Government, comes back to the old myth that a Conservative Government is our government. We got a rude shock in 1970–74, sort of action one might have expected from a Labour Government. Also companies were under pressure because of the economic situation, particularly from 1973 onwards. So much breaking over them, they were angry, upset, many companies reacted against it.

The chairman of ICI in 1991, Denys Henderson, has commented, 'Certainly in the Seventies we all spent an awful lot of time on the government/industry interface. This has to a large extent declined considerably in the last few years' (quoted in Heller, 1987, p. 70). This does not mean that the need for government relations divisions has disappeared. Competition policy, both at the British and EC level, is the setting for decisions which are of crucial commercial importance to an individual company, but do not raise issues which are of the kind which can be considered by a trade association. Takeover attempts are a test of a company's political resources and its ability to mobilise them effectively. One company may want an acquisition to go ahead, the company being taken over may wish to prevent it. In such a situation, having well-developed political knowledge and contacts may be vitally important. Pilkington (which has a government relations division) mounted a much-praised parliamentary defence against a takeover bid from BTR in 1987. Although other factors helped to determine the final successful outcome (Miller, 1991, pp. 61–2), a contrast may be drawn between the parliamentary support that Pilkington was able to mobilise, and Rowntree's unsuccessful effort to fight off a bid by Nestlé. It was noted that 'Rowntree has been slower to mobilise support at Westminster. MPs had been privately critical of the company's efforts at lobbying. For instance, it has only just appointed an adviser on its Westminster and Whitehall activities' (*Financial Times*, 9 May 1988).

Responding to the activities of environmental, consumer and other 'cause' groups is an increasingly important part of the work of government relations divisions. The growing importance of this aspect of government relations work was highlighted by a respondent interviewed in the early 1980s:

When we think of strategies, we have to take that into account. In relations with government departments, if you had government on your side, that was all that mattered seven or ten years ago, now not simply enough, necessary to understand these groups, how you might deal with them — 'deal' in inverted commas — by confrontation or compromise.

Asked in 1991 whether there was a continuing for government relations divisions, a government relations manager in a clearing bank replied that 'there will always be something to do here', emphasising in particular that pressure groups were getting more articulate and

effective. Environmental issues affect a bank, as lending on polluted
land could turn an asset into a liability. An environmental management
unit was being established which, as well as dealing with recycling and
energy conservation, would monitor the environmental practices of
borrowers. This government relations division was also organising a
dialogue with consumer groups on the code of banking practice, but
found third world lobbies that were asking the bank to write off its
Latin American debt more difficult to deal with.

The organisation of the government relations function

The government relations function was not a large one in terms of
staff employed in any of the companies visited. The largest unit was
in a company with a total government relations staff of fourteen
including secretaries, although that was a Europe-wide operation. One
clearing bank had a unit of seven. In many companies, the function is
staffed by just one executive. A not untypical pattern, however,
would be two or three executives in mid-career, placed in a distinct
government relations unit located relatively high up the company's
decision-making structure. In some companies, a spell of two to four
years in the government relations unit is seen as part of the career
development of 'high fliers' who may eventually end up on the main
board.

Companies operating in a highly-regulated environment may have
particularly complex structures for dealing with government relations
unit. In a privatised utility that was visited in 1992, a government
relations unit of four reported to a Director of Corporate Affairs, one
tier below the board. Other corporate affairs departments dealt with
business issues, social policy, and public relations. Four members of
staff dealing with EC matters reported to the Director of Planning.
Regulatory questions are so important to the company that one board
member spends a quarter of his time on such matters. A Director of
Regulatory Affairs has two branches reporting to him; one dealing with
strategic issues, one dealing with day-to-day matters.

Just as being a trade association official has developed into a career,
with skills being seen as transferable from one association to another,
there are some signs of government relations emerging as a distinctive
career. Government relations executives interviewed in the early
1980s were located in more senior posts in other companies in the
early 1990s. Since the early 1980s, some government relations

executives have met in an informal dining group, known as the Caxton Group. Membership is by invitation, and is confined to 'in-house' personnel.

The range of tasks performed

The definition of the government relations function used in this book (p. 87) makes a distinction between tasks relating to the external environment and tasks relating to the company's internal needs. Clearly, there is a close link between the two sets of tasks. For example, monitoring political developments is concerned with the analysis of the external environment for internal purposes. The performance of the strategic coordination function of government relations involves, among other things, ensuring that information and advice provided by a government relations division within a company is related to the more effective handling of the company's external relations. Nevertheless, the internal/external distinction is of some assistance in analysing what government relations divisions do.

As far as external relations are concerned, practice varies from company to company in terms of how much contact with government is actually channelled through the government relations division itself, although it is extremely unlikely that all contacts would be handled through the division. The function of a government relations division is to coordinate the large number of contacts a company has with government at a variety of levels. As one respondent commented, 'we can set things up then back off. We build the bridge, but we don't stand on it' A respondent in a company with a good reputation for effective government relations commented:

We are the eyes and ears of the company, not necessarily its voice. That is quite an important divide to draw. Civil servants particularly, elected politicians to a lesser extent, prefer to talk to people from the coalface ... I find out how the civil service are going to work [on an issue], where the problems are going to be, I aim people in the right direction, make sure they talk to the right people, and express themselves in the right way.

However, another respondent stressed that it was very important that at least some of the work should be done by the division itself and that it should not be confined to a coordinating function, however important it was. One government relations manager commented that a member of the government relations unit would often attend meetings with civil servants as a member of the company team, not necessarily to speak, but to hear what was going on. At a very minimum, most units keep track of contacts between the company and government, so that if an executive or director is meeting a particular politician or civil servant, it is known whether he or she has met anyone from the company before and, if so, for what purpose. Some companies have quite sophisticated 'senior executive calling programmes' to ensure that contact is maintained with ministers, shadow ministers and key civil servants.

Compared with the early 1980s, European Community questions are a more consistently central concern of government relations divisions. Hopefully, no company today would provide an answer that was given in the early 1980s when it was explained that it did not cover the EC as part of its government relations work because 'A large number of directors don't see how we fit into it although we trade with Europe.' It is increasingly common for companies to have a representative in Brussels.

The internal services that government relations divisions provide for their own line managers can be divided into three categories: the dissemination of information through newsletters and briefing papers; 'hand holding' in terms of providing guidance to line managers faced with a task with political implications (e.g., appearing before a Parliamentary committee); and building up the political capabilities of line managers. All these tasks amount to providing a rudimentary political education to line managers who have little understanding or experience of political matters.

The limitations of the government relations function

Since the early 1970s, government relations divisions have been formed in a considerable number of large firms operating in Britain. By the 1990s they were a familiar and established factor in the conduct of relations between business and government. However, one must be careful not to overstate their importance. Such divisions often face two particular limitations: a lack of integration in the decision-making process in many firms; and an absence of control over the firm's involvement in business interest associations.

Integration into the firm's decision-making processes

Before they can contribute effectively to a firm's decision-making processes, most government relations divisions have to overcome a credibility problem within the company. Directors and executives may agree that the political environment has a considerable impact on the firm's profitability, and ultimately its survival. Nevertheless, they may be suspicious of a function which cannot point to a quantifiable result on the bottom line; they may argue that political forecasting is even more unreliable than economic forecasting; and that even if political outcomes can be forecast, there is little that a company can do to influence the course of events. As one house magazine commented in a feature on the company's government relations unit, 'there may still be colleagues who are keen to know how a small team of retired diplomats and young economists contribute to the business of a multi-national insurance group.' It was clear from the interviews that a number of government relations units had experienced or were experiencing difficulties in establishing their credibility within the company, a finding confirmed by subsequent informal discussions with government relations executives at seminars. A number of units appeared to depend on the personal patronage of a board member, which would be lost if he left the board.

A company perceived by civil servants to have a good government relations function explained its success in three ways. First, there was a board-level commitment to good relations with government. The government relations manager reported directly to the chairman. Second, there was a good working relationship between the individual businesses in the company and the central government relations function. This was a relationship based on the establishment of credibility, not the exercise of authority. Third, there was a strong commitment in each business to working with government depart-ments, MPs and MEPs and local authorities.

A number of companies visited were clearly taking the incorporation of political considerations into their corporate planning process more seriously. As one respondent commented. 'Ten years ago the political situation was a footnote to the business analysis, now it is a more fundamental part.' Another respondent remarked, 'Our planning staff are doing the econometric guessing, but we also need an input on social and political guesses.' A privatised firm commented that before privatisation, much of the political justification was undertaken by ministers, but that had now become the responsibility of the company.

Government relations divisions and business interest associations

If government relations divisions are seeking to provide strategic coordination of a firm's political activities, it might be supposed that their responsibility would extend to the firm's participation in business interest associations. In fact, this is generally not the case; most associational activity is dealt with by members of line management. There are a number of reasons why this should be the case. Clearly, the personnel department has a particular interest and expertise in employers' organisation activities. Many trade association activities concern highly technical questions and demand the participation of the relevant expert from the firm's staff. There will be many specialist committees within trade associations (or specialist trade associations) that are the concern of a particular product division or subsidiary company. Given the decentralised character of many British companies, it will be difficult for the government relations division (which is unlikely to have a large staff) to exercise much influence over these activities. Indeed, as one respondent commented, 'No one in company has any idea how many trade associations [this] company belongs to or what their worth is.'

Even if the company decides that it does want to coordinate its business association activities, the internal political costs of doing so may be too great. One respondent commented that subsidiary companies were 'determined to hang on to what they have ... I have to be very careful, I coordinate on occasions.' One firm which has devoted considerable effort to coordinating its business association activities does so through a division which is completely distinct from its government relations function. In another case where a company chairman found that a product division was advocating a policy line in one of its trade associations which was contrary to corporate policy, the chairman decided that the trade association structure required changing rather than the company's own arrangements! (It was subsequently reformed.) What all this suggests is that the political activities of a firm are highly complex, being handled at a number of levels through a variety of channels, with attempts at coordination often being weak.

There was some evidence from interviews at the beginning of the 1990s that at least some firms were developing a clearer idea of which matters could best be handled through trade associations, and those which were better pursued by their own government relations division. Even so, the task of coordinating business association activity remained a difficult one for government relations divisions. One company which tried to coordinate its business association work commented in relation to the managers who were involved in such work, 'Some of them will do their own things, will say that they are the experts. We are lucky if we can get reports out of them.'

Many issues will, of course, be simultaneously pursued through both chapters, but an attempt is made in Table 5.1 to distinguish between those issues which would be handled predominantly on an individual basis, and those which tend to be handled through business associations. For example, the tax dispute between ICI and other leading chemical companies over the so-called 'Mossmorran clause' which disadvantaged ICI and benefited the other companies was clearly a matter which had to be handled individually by each company (Grant, 1991b, pp. 103–4).

Table 5.1 *Methods of handling issues in large firms*

Through firms	*Through associations*
Tax questions which discriminate between firms	General tax policies which do not discriminate between firms
Negotiating government grants	General industrial policy
Customs and trade policy implementation that directly affects company	General trade policy questions, e.g., GATT rounds, anti-dumping policy
Energy concessions for the company	General energy policy questions
Issues relating to individual plant closures	General discussion of overcapacity issues and rationalisation
Direct relations with environmental groups, individual site problems	General health and safety and environmental policies, including transport and waste disposal
Company codes of conduct in relation to consumers	General consumer policies, including labelling

Adapted from Grant and Martinelli, 1991, p. 88.

Political consultants

There has been a considerable increase in recent years in the number of political consultants offering services to firms and business associations. This term is used here to refer to 'someone who is professionally employed to lobby on behalf of clients or who advises clients on how to lobby on their own behalf' (Select Committee on Members' Interests, 1991, p. v). It is difficult to say precisely how many such firms there are, because there are frequent formations, disappearances and mergers, but the best available estimates suggest that there are around thirty with a turnover of around £200,000 to a million and a half pounds a year. Given the intense publicity which this aspect of lobbying has attracted in recent years, it is worth pointing out that 'the total sector turnover is probably only a quarter of that of the largest UK law firm' (Jordan, 1991, p. 22).

Why should firms or associations wish to use a consultancy rather than develop their own expertise in political relations? First, for a medium-sized firm, the likely volume of work may not justify the development of an 'in-house' government relations division. Similarly, a smaller trade association may prefer to subcontract much of its work, especially parliamentary work, to a consultancy. It is also clear that many larger firms and associations also make use of political consultants. Even a government relations manager who was sceptical about the contribution of consultants because 'someone has to handle the input they put in' stated that he used consultants to provide copies of relevant House of Commons papers. Another firm which had its own parliamentary liaison officer within its government relations unit, used consultants not only for monitoring, but also because 'Consultants roam about the outside world, they have more informal contacts, they can duck and weave in a more political way than would be possible for us.'

It is evident that political consultancy has grown considerably as an activity in the 1980s. One explanation is that the Thatcher Government's distaste for vested interests meant that links with the civil service became more fragmented. Business interests lost the point of contact provided by sponsorship divisions. Thus, 'increased attention to parliament was a reflection of manufacturing industry's general belief that its sectoral voices no longer carried the same resonance in Whitehall and a concomitant desire to develop supplementary channels through which these voices could be amplified' (Judge, 1990, p. 221). Privatisation, not just of existing industries, but also of local government and NHS services, provided new business opportunities where it was important to influence the way in which plans were implemented. On the supply side, 'The Government's style, and the size of its majorities, especially after 1983 . . . produced a pool of underemployed, rather independent-minded backbenchers' (Grantham and Seymour-Ure, 1990, p. 46).

Supply can, of course, seek to create its own demand. It has been claimed that MPs have been offered introduction fees, which could range from £4,000 to £10,000, for bringing together clients and consultants (Hollingsworth, 1991, p. 131). It could be that 'some lobbying entrepreneurs are a bigger threat to their clients than they are to the public interest: that their expensive activities are not only ill directed but even counter productive' (Jordan, 1991, p. 14). The greater proportion of lobbying business is directed towards Parliament, although there is an increasing tendency for the more sophisticated companies to approach government departments and the European Community as well.

This concentration on the legislature rather than the executive flies in the face of what is known about the distribution of political power in Britain. As one experienced political consultant comments, 'Parliament is one component of the power structure with the ability to assert itself only when governments have precarious majorities or where a considerable amount of work is done to persuade large numbers of MPs and Peers to oppose or change Government policy' (Miller, 1990, p. 129). Miller argues (1991, pp. 55–6) that this 'Misdirection of effort has been prompted by an exaggerated media interest in Parliament (which is easy to report) compared with what is invariably the real policy making centre of Whitehall which is far less accessible.' Of course, activity directed at Parliament may be another way of influencing government. Parliament does play a role in setting the agenda, and affecting the climate of political opinion which gives some issues a higher priority than others. Particular types of bill such as the hybrid bill for the Channel Tunnel project give backbenchers greater opportunities for influence, and hence offer a more rewarding field for lobbying activity (Hollingsworth, 1991, pp. 124–7). Even so, 'Over concentration on Westminster is less likely to bring rewards than the frequenting of the dull corridors of Whitehall' (Miller, 1991, p. 64).

Should consultants be controlled?

The growth in the numbers and visibility of political consultants has given rise to a debate about wether they should be regulated or controlled. It is evident that 'there are no universally accepted standards of good practice, ethics and discipline, and no industry-wide scheme for improving professional skills' (Select Committee on Members' Interests, 1991, p. x). There have been a number of incidents which have

given rise to concern. The Public Relations Consultants Association
(PRCA) was formed in 1969 in response to widespread concern about a
case in 1968 concerning a public relations consultancy which was
retained by the then military government in Greece. PRCA members are
required to subscribe to a fifteen-point code of consultancy practice
which requires them to publish a list of their clients, state whether they
employ or retain any MPs, peers or councillors, and what their annual
fee income is within a number of bands. Member firms of the PRCA are
not allowed to offer inducements to legislators to favour clients, and are
not permitted to serve some announced client while actually serving an
undisclosed special or private interest. However, a number of successful
lobbying firms are not members of the PRCA. The Select Committee on
Members' Interests reviewed the prospects for self-regulation in the
industry, but concluded (1991, p. xiii):

> We see little hope of obtaining consistently higher professional
> industry until an organisation is created which is fully representative
> of professional lobbying, which commands universal respect and
> which exercises effective professional discipline ... There is no sign,
> as yet, that this is likely to happen.

Parliament itself has hardly regarded the problem as one of urgency.
Parliamentary lobbying was a subsidiary theme of select committee
reports in 1969 and 1974, and a report on the subject was published in
1985. A central theme in this report was that of whether access to the
Palace of Westminster was being abused. Jordan notes that subsequent
evidence from MPs to the Select Committee on Members' Interests
'seemed to dwell on lobbying as a problem for the domestic arrangements of Parliament: there was a sense of intrusion by outsiders into the
club' (Jordan, 1991, p. 33).

Parliament has, of course, to draw a balance between preserving the
right to lobby which is an essential element of any democracy, and
ensuring that that right is not abused through privileged access for those
who can afford to hire a lobbyist. The position is complicated by the
inadequate support facilities available to MPs by international
standards who may therefore appreciate the information that lobbyists
can provide. In its 1991 report, the Select Committee on Members'
Interests concluded that there was no evidence of serious misdeeds, but
that greater openness would be beneficial. Having studied the apparently successful operation of registration in Canada, the committee

recommended the establishment of a register of lobbyists which would initially be confined to political consultants, excluding companies and trade associations. It was thought that the register would provide greater transparency and public accountability, protecting the reputation of the House; would provide an authoritative source of information for MPs; and could, if necessary, provide a basis for future regulation. The Committee subsequently initiated hearings on how such a register might be established. One difficulty with a registration system is that it could be seen to give a badge of Parliamentary approval to a limited number of consultants (Miller, 1991, p. 39). The way in which the system is designed and operated is therefore important.

The Committee left for future consideration the question of MPs being given 'introduction fees' by consultants, and the difficult issue of MPs being consultants to lobbying companies, or owning such companies themselves. The Committee argued that this issue was 'a complex one' (Select Committee on Members' Interests, 1991, p. vii). It is also a crucially important one, as it goes to the heart of the question about the role of MPs as representatives of their constituents and defenders of the public interest. The absence of a comprehensive system of regulation may lead to suspicions that abuses are more frequent than they actually are, discrediting not only consultants, but also the whole political process.

6 Business Associations

As well as being represented by national intersectoral associations such as the Confederation of British Industry (CBI), businesses belong to a considerable variety of associations serving a sector of the economy or a particular locality. The sectoral associations range from associations serving particular products, through subsectoral organisations, to well resourced associations serving, for example, the motor industry or the chemical industry. At the local level, businesses are represented through chambers of commerce and trade. In addition there are associations which represent users of particular products or services (such as major energy users), importers and (less common) exporters.

The overall pattern of business representation in Britain at the sectoral and local level is characterised by high differentiation and low integration of the various associations which claim to speak for business. Even when product and subsector associations are affiliated to a sector-wide association, the relationship between the different levels is often a rather tenuous one. This situation is both a cause and consequence of the political weakness of business identified in Chapter 1.

One particular weakness is the relationship between the CBI and the sector and subsector associations; in many ways, the CBI could better be termed an 'umbrella' rather than a 'peak' association. The CBI organises both business associations and firms, although firms provide by far the greater part of its revenue. A firm can belong to the CBI direct, and bypass its sector association, or it can rely on its sector association's affiliation to maintain contact with the CBI, although many firms are both direct members of the CBI and of their sector associations. An association director commented:

In Germany trade associations pyramid up to the BDI and it is not possible to by pass the second or third tier associations and come directly to the BDI. This produces a very tidy hierarchy of decision taking and commitment. In distinction is the anarchy in the United

Kingdom where [the] CBI is a hybrid organisation . . . Far from giving solidarity this encourages free loading and by-passing of the second and third tier Associations. I am not surprised that we are not more efficient in the British trade association business — I am amazed that we are as efficient as we are in fact taking account of the anarchy which is encouraged by the composition and constitution of the CBI.

Explaining the pattern of business associability

The pattern of business associability at the sectoral and local level in Britain has evolved over a period of two hundred years. The overall pattern of sectoral and local associations is therefore the product of a long drawn-out historical development. For example, a considerable number of the associations studied were founded during the Second World War, often at the behest of government. These organisations survived after their original wartime function had disappeared (Grant, 1991a). A considerable amount of inertia is built into the system of business representation, and associations often continue in existence long after they have outlived their original function and, often, it seems, without acquiring any new one. It will not be possible to examine the historical development of the pattern of business associability here, but a number of useful studies are available (Blank, 1973; Kipping, 1972; Middlemas, 1979; Modern Records Centre, 1992; Reid, 1991; Turner (ed.)1984; Wigham, 1973; Zeitlin, 1991).

Provided that one always bears in mind that the pattern of sectoral and local associations is in the nature of a palimpsest, it is possible to explore the factors affecting the shape and character of the system in two ways. First, one can examine the factors that affect the overall patterning of the system of business associability. Second, one can look at the calculations that the individual firm has to make in deciding whether to join, or remain in membership of, a particular association.

As intermediary bodies, business associations have to retain the support of their menbership and at the same time a credibility with government and other interlocutors such as trade unions. Schmitter and Streeck (1981, p. 50) have formalised the Janus-like character of business associations by introducing a distinction between the 'logic of membership' (the characteristics of members) and the 'logic of influence' (the characteristics of state agencies).

Sources of differentiation between businesses

An examination of the logic of membership draws our attention to variables which differentiate businesses, and therefore make it more difficult for them to combine in organisations with broad domains. It might seem that the most important of these factors would be competition between firms. However, one should not exaggerate the obstacles that competition places in the way of business associability. Firms that are competing vigorously in the market place will not usually see that as a hindrance to cooperation to deal with common problems posed by government or EC measures, or by trade union action. Moreover, in many industries, competition is in practice relatively limited, with firms satisfied with retaining a stable market share. Sensitive commercial data which could be of use to competitors, e.g., data used for calculating competitive performance statistics, can be kept confidential by association staff or even processed by an outside body. In practice, competition is less important as a hindrance to collective action by business than common differentiating factors such as size heterogeneity, product heterogeneity, and technological heterogeneity. Social cohesion is one membership characteristic which could act as a unifying factor, but it seems to have little impact on the contemporary organisation of business interests in Britain.

A line of cleavage which poses persistent problems of organisational design and maintenance for business associations is that between small and large firms. Small firms may serve different markets from large firms, and thus be faced with very different problems. In many industries, they are suppliers to larger firms, a relationship which can give rise to tensions which prevent common organisation, particularly over the slow payment of bills by the larger firms. Small-scale business persons are often attracted to a world view in which they see themselves as the authentic representatives of the virtues of free enterprise (see Scase and Goffee, 1980). It is therefore not surprising that there are a number of national organisations claiming to representing smaller businesses, notably the National Federation for the Self-Employed and Small Businesses. Eight organisations in all are recognised by the Department of Employment as representing the interests of small business (May and McHugh, 1991, p. 16) although it is worth bearing in mind that only a minority of small businesses belong to any representative organisation.

Nevertheless, in many sectors of industry, small businesses are found in the same organisation as larger businesses, so there must be factors that draw them together, as well as influences that pull them apart. One explanation is that larger businesses cross-subsidise the provision of services of various kinds by business associations which are of particular value to smaller firms; the membership of the smaller firms gives the association a more 'representative' character. However, a comparative study by the author and Wolfgang Streeck of the construction industry in Britain and West Germany found that state influences on the market could either exacerbate or reduce tensions between large and small firms (Grant and Streeck, 1985). In other words, the logic of membership is itself conditioned by the logic of influence.

Product heterogeneity can manifest itself in a number of ways, including the use of different raw materials, different production processes, and market segmentation. For example, product heterogeneity is a significant influence on business associability in the food processing industry (see Grant, ed., 1987). The industry uses food as a basic raw material, but that raw material may differ considerably in its origins, the machinery and techniques required for its processing, the packaging of the product, and the product market which it faces.

Particular product interests need not, of course, lead to the formation of distinct associations. They can be catered for by internal differentiation within a sector or subsector association by the formation of product sections, or through serviced affiliates of such associations. Even so, it was not until 1984 that the food processing industry had an organisation that could speak for the sector as a whole (the Food and Drink Federation) and there is still substantial differentiation at the subsector and product level. The Food and Drink Federation had been preceded by the Food and Drink Industries Council, formed at the time that Britain joined the EEC. A shift in the distribution of state functions between national and supranational level, and consequent changes in policy, initiated changes in the system of business associations. Logic of influence factors thus tended to wash out logic of membership factors.

Last but not least, it should be remembered that large firms in Britain are often organised on the basis of product divisions which have a considerable degree of autonomy, including the choice of which business associations to belong to. For example, ICI's agriculture division is closely involved in the work of the British Agrochemicals

Association, its pharmaceuticals division participates in the work of the Association of the British Pharmaceutical Industry, and its paints division is prominent in the Paintmakers' Association. The relative independence of product divisions helps to explain why large firms in Britain are organised in a number of associations specialised by product or market segment, and why they do not press for mergers of related organisations.

State influences on the organisation of business interests

Government interventions to encourage or stimulate the rationalisation of the system of business associations in Britain have been hesitant, sporadic and generally ineffective. The Department of Trade and Industry did second a civil servant to act as secretary of the Devlin Commission on Industrial Representation, set up in the early 1970s by the CBI and the ABCC. However, the report's recommendations for reform proved controversial in business circles, and no significant changes resulted from the report. There have been some government initiatives at the sectoral level. Support was given to the CBI's eventually unsuccessful attempts to reform the chaotic representational arrangements in mechanical engineering through the creation of the British Mechanical Engineering Confederation (see Parker, 1984). The Offshore Supplies Office tried without success to establish a unified trade association for the offshore supplies industry (Jenkin, 1981, pp. 133–5). However, subtle, behind-the-scenes pressure from government can catalyse processes of change that have already been started from within an industry. As one experienced association official commented, 'One way in which association rearrangement does take place is via pressure from Government departments, who find for example that splintering is at times a handicap to their work.' When it existed, the National Economic Development Office displayed an interest in rationalising business associations from time to time and materially assisted the formation of new associations in the retail trade in the 1960s and in the clothing industry in the 1980s.

Commenting on the DTI's attitude towards business associations in 1991, a senior civil servant commented that there was continuing concern within the ministry about the effectiveness of trade associations. He added, 'Trade associations are very difficult to move. They are still on a long list of things we would like to do.' In the early 1990s, the DTI was concentrating its efforts in this area on revitalising the chambers of commerce movement. A civil servant commented, 'We have taken the slightly easier target of chambers of commerce [rather than trade associations]. We could see that by making a contribution we could get a very much better chambers movement.'

There are three main reasons why government appears to have been reluctant to intervene more systematically in the representative arrangements of business. First, government in Britain operates within a largely pluralist paradigm in which business associations are seen essentially as voluntary organisations outside the system of government. The frequent use of the word 'lobby' is instructive in this respect. Second, government policies have been increasingly directed at firms rather than sectors (see Chapter 3). Third, in so far as government has sought a partnership with organisations representing industry, its favoured instruments in the past have been research associations or economic development committees.

Although *direct* state intervention has had little influence on the pattern of business associability, the *indirect* consequences of the way in which government is organised can be considerable. Thus, the unintended consequences of government action are of greater importance than the intended consequences. The state does not pursue some organisational grand design in relation to business associations; rather, the actions of government constitute an 'invisible hand' which guides and shapes (but certainly does not determine) the way which business associations are organised. One indirect influence of government organisation is the relative degree of functional centralisation or decentralisation in terms of the concentration or dispersal of responsibility for a particular industry. As was noted in Chapter 3, each government department tends to act as a focus for a 'policy community' with its own representative associations. Government can structure the market and hence influence the pattern of associative activity. For example, in the pharmaceutical industry, government regulation of the prices of drugs sold to the NHS effectively creates two distinct markets for 'ethical' and 'over the counter' drugs, a divide which is reflected in the existence of two distinct pharmaceutical associations.

The continuing importance of sectoral and product associations

Government may play a role in shaping the contours of business interest organisation, but business associations in Britain remain voluntary organisations that must attract and retain members. For some smaller firms, the principal attraction is the selective incentives which are provided in the form of services. For larger firms, the cost of subscription is such a small proportion of turnover that it is hardly worth the decision costs of considering whether renewal is worthwhile. Costs rise if a firm sends its senior executives to participate in an association's committees, but then so do the benefits.

Firms continue to value sector- and product-based associations which address their own specific commercial interests. This fits in with Olson's observation (1971, p. 143) that the oligopolistic character of much of industry is such that many firms can organise as 'privileged' or 'intermediate' groups. The increasing importance of the EC as a decision-maker means that there are more technical decisions being taken which affect a firm's operations, but which only the very largest firms can afford to scan for themselves, and which can often more effectively be influenced by some form of collective action.

Mitchell's survey of the top hundred industrial firms showed that 68 per cent of the responding firms always or often used direct contacts with government; 46 per cent always or often used trade associations, with only 7 per cent reporting never using them; and only 24 per cent always or often using the CBI, with almost as many (21 per cent) never contacting government through the CBI (Mitchell, Neil, 1990, p. 628). Mitchell notes, 'trade association rather than peak association contact is more common. In other words, the less encompassing the interest organisation, the more frequently it is used' (ibid., p. 631). This finding was confirmed by interviews with firms in 1991 and 1992. One firm commented, 'The CBI is to some extent irrelevant to us. We prefer to work through our trade association. We only really got interested in our trade association as a means of saving our own skins.' Businesses inevitably give a high priority to protecting their own immediate interests.

The CBI: its strengths and weaknesses

The CBI is the most prominent business organisation in Britain, and the only one that can claim to speak for business as a whole. With 2,500 business persons involved in its committees, and an expert staff, it can make an informed response to developments over the complete range of government policy. Yet, 'over two decades since its creation the CBI still disappoints its creators' (Mitchell, 1990, p. 633).

The CBI has a number of inherent structural problems, which tend to be exacerbated when a Conservative Government is in office. The sheer breadth of the interests the CBI seeks to represent sets up a number of potential lines of conflict within the organisation. The elaborate committee structure, including a comprehensive system of regional councils and a special council for smaller businesses, and culminating in a Council of four hundred members, may ensure that all members have a chance to be heard, but it can also lead to lowest common denominator policies. In any case, the regional council system has its limitations. When Anderson interviewed a senior CBI official, he admitted that 'the CBI's regional structure has "varied throughout the years, usually as a function of the availability of cash"' (Anderson, 1991, p. 92).

The CBI is a 'mixed' association which organises both individual firms and trade associations and employers' organisations. Rather than offering the best of both worlds, this may be an unhappy compromise which constrains the organisation's effectiveness. Alternative models of business representation are the Business Round Table type of organisation found in a number of countries which brings together the chief executives of the leading firms, or the German model of an association of associations. The former model brings together the most economically significant and hence politically influential firms in one organisation, while the latter offers the potential of direction and control of the affiliated business associations, increasing the political cohesiveness of business (Coleman and Grant, 1988).

Ever since the CBI sought to transform itself into a *de facto* Confederation of British Business in the late 1970s by significantly increasing the number of members from the financial sector, there has been a potential tension within the organisation between the sometimes divergent interests of manufacturing interests and the City. The reality of such tensions is shown by two CBI investigations in the late 1980s and early 1990s into City-industry relations, against the background of complaints from manufacturing industry about the financial sector's short term outlook. Concern within the CBI that it had not given sufficient priority to the needs of manufacturing led it to agree in 1991 to establish a National Manufacturing Council within the organisation, with a third deputy director-general brought in from a major industrial group (TI) to oversee its work. The *Financial Times* commented in an editorial that the change was 'a bit like setting up a society for the appreciation of the Virgin Mary within the Vatican' (*Financial Times*, 22 October 1991). What the change amounted to was a recognition that the CBI had not done enough to help the manufacturing sector, particularly in the 1980s when the prevailing orthodoxy was that manufacturing had no greater importance in the economy than tradeable services.

Although the CBI was always ready to point out that more than half its member companies employ fewer than two hundred people, such political strength as the organisation has derives from the membership of most of the hundred largest companies which dominate the highly concentrated British economy. While the CBI makes a considerable effort to ensure that the views of its smaller firm members are taken account of, it is difficult for the organisation to deal with issues which bring its larger and smaller firm members into conflict, such as the prompt payment of bills.

The denationalisation of most of the nationalised industries has at least removed the problem of tensions between public and private sector members. One privatised company commented in interview, 'relationships within the CBI are a bit easier now. We were welcomed in the past as very large subscribers, but not regarded as full members, we rarely chaired committees.' However, privatisation has in many respects sharpened conflicts between energy producers and large energy users. CBI member firms in energy-intensive industries were able to persuade the organisation that there should be an Energy Users Committee of the CBI alongside the Energy Committee representing producer interests (Grant, Paterson and Whitston, 1988, p. 109), but this kind of bureaucratic compromise simply reflects the difficulty that the CBI experiences in representing a wide range of business interests. Indeed, leading energy intensive companies have formed themselves into a Major Energy Users Council.

The CBI and the Thatcher Government

Managing relations with a Labour Government is in many ways easier for the CBI than with a Conservative Government, and the relationship with the Thatcher Government posed more difficulties than those with a more orthodox Conservative Government. This is not to say that business prefers the policies of a Labour Government to those of a Conservative Government, although certain aspects of them may be more attractive. Indeed, it was suggested in 1991 that 'There are plenty of people running companies who feel that, in the short-term at least, it would be rather nice to have a Labour government because competition would be rather less, and subsidies rather greater' (*The Independent*, 5 November 1991).

When a Labour Government is in office, it is possible for the CBI to follow a strategy of criticising its policies in public, while extracting concessions from it in private that benefit its members. A Labour Government for its part, because it tends to follow a more interventionist policy, is more dependent on CBI support. In the run up to the 1987 election, Labour Party advisers were concerned to find a way to prevent expansionary policies having inflationary consequences by restraining incomes:

> . . . the group discussed methods of improving the organizational strength of the CBI . . . and in particular its control over the wage setting behavior of the 100 or 200 largest British firms, as a way of precluding these from making concessions to their workforces that would have preempted an increase in employment. (Streeck, 1988, p. 4)

Under the Labour Government of 1974 to 1979, after a difficult start in the initial crisis period of 1974 to the summer of 1975, the CBI enjoyed many policy successes. In particular it 'won tax relief and acceptance of inflation accounting, worth £4bn retrospectively over the period 1973–75' (Middlemas, 1991, pp. 62–3) not least because it was pushing at an open door for much of the time, as many members of the Labour Government welcomed its support in defeating what they saw as misguided policies which the Labour Party had adopted while in opposition. '1974 had opened with what looked like a closure game against the CBI. 1976 revealed it in better array than at any point since its merger ten years before' (ibid., 1991, p. 71).

A Conservative Government poses greater problems. On the one hand, it is more likely to think that it understands what business wants (or, in Mrs Thatcher's case, the medicine it needs). On the other hand, any open criticism of the policies of the Government is likely to create strains within the CBI's ranks, perhaps even prompting resignations. Such problems have surfaced at a number of times within the CBI's history. In 1974 the then director-general, Campbell Adamson, made some widely reported remarks a few days before the February general election which were interpreted as a repudiation of the Heath Government's Industrial Relations Act. A number of leading firms resigned from the CBI or suspended their membership, protesting as much against what they saw as the corporatist tendencies of the CBI's leadership, as against the specific incident.

The Thatcher Government faced the CBI with an especially worrying dilemma. Although they were happy to see trade union power curbed, and public expenditure reduced, they were understandably worried about policies such as an appreciating exchange rate which undermined industrial competitiveness. The Government, for its part, saw the CBI as tainted by the tripartism of the 1970s, a former governing institution which had to be marginalised so that the Government could press ahead with its economic policies without outside interference. Mrs Thatcher refused 'to accept on any grounds that institutions had a right to advise, to be heard, and to receive redress from the state' (Middlemas, 1991, p. 305).

The unexpected death of Sir John Methven, the CBI's director-general, in May 1980, added to the CBI's problems. He enjoyed regular access to the Prime Minister, the Chancellor (Sir Geoffrey Howe) and the Industry Secretary (Sir Keith Joseph) which was not so readily available to his successor, Terence Beckett. Following his appointment, Beckett made a tour of the CBI's regional organisation. Industrial production was falling sharply in a severe recession, and businesses were complaining that they might be forced into receivership by Government policies, especially in particularly hard-hit regions such as the north west and the West Midlands.

Responding to these fears, Beckett made a speech at the 1980 CBI conference at Brighton which promised a 'bare knuckle fight' with the Government. The speech received a standing ovation, but did not go down so well with some CBI members who resigned, thus repeating the 1974 crisis. The CBI's standing was not improved when, the day after the conference, the president and the director-general went to Downing Street to inform the Prime Minister of the worries of industrialists, only to emerge on the pavement empty-handed and declaring that Mrs Thatcher's performance had been 'magnificent'. As one of the industrialists who took his firm out of the CBI commented, 'They went in like Brighton rock and came out like Turkish delight.' Despite the deterioration in relationships, there was no attempt by the CBI to forge an alliance with the dissident moderates who were still in the Cabinet at that time. One of the latter subsequently complained that the CBI 'has become little more than an adjunct of the Conservatives' (Gilmour, 1983, p. 195).

Under the presidency of Sir Campbell Fraser (1982–4) the CBI drew closer to the Conservative Government, too close for the liking of some members. Relations were re-established with government departments on the Government's terms, 'support in public, criticism only in private. This subordinate position lasted through the 1983 election into the prosperity of the mid-1980s' (Middlemas, 1991, p. 354). Even so, tensions between the CBI and the Government continued to surface from time to time. At a meeting of the National Economic Development Council in the summer of 1985, against a background of CBI complaints about high interest rates, the Chancellor tried to stop Sir Terence Beckett from making a highly critical statement calling on the Government to 'untie our shoelaces' and allow British businesses to compete on equal terms with other countries.

During the boom conditions of the late 1980s, the government and the CBI continued to be divided over the question of British membership of the exchange rate mechanism. John Banham, appointed as director-general in 1987, won support for a new strategy intended to move the CBI away from its traditional role as a reactive industry lobbyist. It was envisaged that the CBI would have a 'more positive role as the instigator and co-ordinator of initiatives in tackling the deeper-seated economic and social problems in the inner cities, education and housing' (*The Independent*, 31 October 1987).

The studies undertaken in such areas were, however, overtaken by a new deterioration in the economy which signalled the beginning of an even longer recession than that at the beginning of the 1980s. Following CBI calls for a cut in interest rates in September 1990, John Banham was rebuked by Mrs Thatcher for talking down the British economy. CBI criticism of the Government's handling of the economy provoked new criticism from its members, with Lord Hanson and Lord King being prominent in a group of senior industrialists urging that business rally in support of the Government (*The Independent*, 14 November 1990). Although the CBI found Mr Major a more congenial Prime Minister than Mrs Thatcher, they staged an even more vigorous criticism of the Government's policies for handling the recession in May 1991 after Mr Major had addressed their annual dinner, arguing that the Government was relying on misleading official measures of inflationary pressures (*Financial Times*, 23 May 1991). The new director-general appointed in July 1992, Howard Davies, favoured a less outspokenly critical style for the CBI. He stated that the CBI's task would be to work closely with government to influence the detail of policy-making from the inside. The CBI would pursue its objectives through detailed analysis of policy proposals rather than engaging in wide-ranging public debate (*Financial Times*, 10 April 1992).

The 1980s were not a happy decade for the CBI. The CBI suffered 'from problems of organisation, aims and identity not unlike those of the TUC' (Middlemas, 1991, p. 368). Admittedly, by the start of 1990s, the problems of the TUC were even more acute. Staff numbers had to be cut in 1992 because of a fall in membership. A TUC official was quoted as saying, 'The TUC has adapted much less well than many of the biggest unions to the culture changes of the last decade' (*Financial Times*, 6 April 1992). Labour's defeat in the 1992 election was a further blow for the TUC, with the bigger unions increasingly likely to rely on their own efforts. The possibility of a merger between the TGWU and GMB raised further questions about the need for the TUC's coordinating function. Although the CBI's relationship with the TUC was never an easy one, the strength of the TUC in the 1970s gave the CBI a greater credibility with its own members who saw it as a necessary counterweight to the TUC (Marsh and Grant, 1977).

In the 1980s business persons were divided on how far the Government should be publicly criticised, thus offering succour to a Labour Party viewed at best with cautious suspicion and at worst with outright hostility. Against this background of uncertainty, 'Ministers outmanoeuvred and disarmed the CBI' (Middlemas, 1991, p. 354). There was still a role for the CBI. Its industrial trends and other surveys remained highly respected. It remained capable of mounting a well-argued and supported case on a variety of issues, but the overall impression was of a rather cautious organisation constrained by the need to please as many of its members as possible in its policy pronouncements. A government relations manager of a leading industrial company commented in interview, 'Some CBI committees do a good job. It was very good on the business rate. It provides a good information service for industry.' The CBI's central role should be to remind government of the importance of industry, but it found it difficult to represent manufacturing because there were too many other interested parties in the organisation. He added, 'We've never seen the consensual approach doing much, we do better fighting on our own.'

The CBI's competitors

The membership scope of the CBI is virtually as encompassing as that of the compulsory membership of the Austrian Federal Economic Chamber, but 'the British system is "highly contested"' (Coleman and

Grant, 1988, p. 477). Politicians who do not like the message they are getting from the CBI can turn to other general business organisations. Denis Healey, as Chancellor in the 1974 to 1979 Labour Government, recalls that (1990, p. 382), 'Finding that the CBI was not always the best guide to industrial opinion, since it was heavily weighted towards the big international companies, I made a point of meeting chambers of commerce as well, because they better represented the broad range of small and medium-sized firms.' In the Thatcher years, the CBI's 'subterranean opposition to the government's macroeconomic stance set Ministers looking elsewhere, to the Institute of Directors, or the executives of individual companies for support and confirmation' (Middlemas, 1991, p. 350).

The Institute of Directors

The Institute of Directors (IoD) which organises individual business persons, rather than firms or associations, experienced a significant upsurge in its influence in the 1980s. In the 1970s, its image was largely that of a club for business persons, providing good lunches, cheap executive health checks, and an annual jamboree at the Albert Hall when directors listened to speeches while eating out of up-market lunch-boxes. The attractive selective benefits remain, but under Walter Goldsmith as director general (succeeded in 1984 by the former head of the Prime Minister's policy unit, Sir John Hoskyns), the IoD secured a new reputation as an effective lobbying organisation. Goldsmith claimed, 'A few years ago I think it could justifiably be said that we had not done the homework to back up out policies. That is no longer true' (*Sunday Times*, 29 August 1982).

The IoD's new importance was not only a reflection of a larger staff and a new orientation, but also of its reputation for being a more loyal support of the Thatcher Government than the CBI, trying to talk up the economy when the CBI's prognostications appeared to be doomladen, and always ready to back new initiatives to curb the power of the unions. Government ministers quickly found that what the IoD had to say was more ideologically acceptable than the hesitations and reservations of the CBI, and the IoD is 'widely regarded as a major influence in shaping the Tory employment legislation' (Lewis and Wiles, 1984, p. 75).

With its Thatcherite credentials, and its willingness to mobilise business behind new campaigns, the IoD 'increasingly saw itself as the body truly representing "capital"' (Middlemas, 1991, p. 369). Its director-general in 1991, Mr Peter Morgan, claimed that 'the CBI is "the Civil Service of the business world", doing a good job representing corporate Britain' (*Financial Times*, 6 November 1991). The CBI sometimes seemed to be irritated by the rise of the IoD: 'Ask them how many launderette owners they have as members,' one CBI official is reported to have said (*Sunday Times*, 29 August 1982). The CBI is, however, no dinosaur, while the IoD may turn out to be an exotic species that flourished best in the particular political climate of the 1980s.

The chambers of commerce

The chambers of commerce are the oldest form of intersectoral business representation in Britain. For example, the Birmingham chamber was founded in 1812, and the Association of British Chambers of Commerce (ABCC) was established in 1860 and was for a time the only national representative of general business interests in Britain (Ilersic and Liddle, 1960). However, the chamber of commerce movement was always been handicapped by the lack of public law status and obligatory membership enjoyed by most of its continental European counterparts. In Germany, for example, chambers of commerce have an important role in providing training facilities, monitoring standards of training by employers and setting examinations. In France, chambers are 'empowered to plan, install and manage facilities which are required for the general good of the business community. including airports, bus stations, hotels and tourist centres' (Forster, 1983, p. 91). The French Chambers of Commerce and Industry have 1.5 million businesses in membership compared with 90,000 in the UK, served by 22,000 staff, seven times the UK figure (Association of British Chambers of Commerce, 1990, p. 10).

The ABCC as an organisation has always been relatively under-resourced compared to the individual local chambers, and these have been much stronger in some localities than in others. Major chambers such as London and Birmingham have always been well-resourced, have employed a large and professional staff, and have been effective both in their representational activities and in the provision of services to their members. Some chambers in medium-sized cities have also been very cost-effective, for example, Norwich (Grant, 1983). At the other end of the scale is the type of chamber in London which in an appeal for donations of equipment such as a large teapot, cups and saucers, and a calculator noted that "'the first floor over a small newsagent's shop is not the best of locations for the Commercial Centre of the Borough's Business Activity'" (Stewart, 1984, p. 44).

In the 1980s, the range of functions performed by the chambers tended to widen. A number, for example, have sponsored advisory services for small businesses, often funded from public and private sources. Above all, the Thatcher Government gave the chambers formal responsibilities for vetting the implementation of public policy programmes, most importantly the urban aid programme for inner cities. The July 1981 guidelines to local authorities involved in government-funded urban aid schemes required detailed consultation with the private sector (normally the local chamber of commerce) as a precondition of programme approval. Several satellite offices of the DTI are now located within chambers of commerce. Local authorities were also required to consult business, usually through the chamber of commerce, when setting the level of the local rate. The literature on public–private partnership, and the local authority as an enabling authority, emphasised the possibilities for mutually beneficial cooperation between chambers of commerce and local government (Brooke, 1989).

Sometimes, however, it seemed that the acquisition of new functions and responsibilities by the chambers was running well ahead of the increasingly pressing need for their structural reform. Stewart's study of chambers of commerce, commissioned by the Thatcher Government, showed that the commitment of many chambers to representational work was limited, and that their input to the public policy-making process was weak. Many chambers seemed unable to adopt the broad perspective that participation in public policy requires. Even in the larger chambers, an inherent parochialism tended to direct chamber involvement in inner area programmes towards particular projects that affected members 'rather than upon issues of strategy for the inner areas or the balance of the programme' (Stewart, 1984, p. 47). Stewart concluded that unless some of the constraints on chambers are altered, they are likely to continue to play a modest part in public affairs, and 'any change would require action from central government to increase the formal position and/or resources of Chambers of Commerce since it is unlikely that the Chamber movement could sustain greater local activity at present even if it wanted to' (Stewart, 1984, p. 49).

Some progress has been made. Between 1980 and 1990, chamber staffing increased from 800 to 3,000. The 90,000 businesses in membership in 1990 was nearly double the 1980 figure of 50,000. Turnover increased from £5 to £70 million over the decade. Even so, 'British Chambers generally lack the resources available to invest in a service in a business which would not be likely to make a commercial return . . . for example . . . technology transfer' (Association of British Chambers of Commerce, 1990, p. 11). A report commissioned by the ABCC from Professor Robert Bennett of LSE found that on a ranking of 1–5, where 1 is a chamber with the full range of services and a sufficient proportion of local businesses in membership to claim comprehensive coverage, there were no chambers in the UK that fully made the grade.

Government interest in revitalising the chambers of commerce was signalled in a speech by Lord Young, then Trade and Industry Secretary, in a speech at the ABCC's dinner in 1989 at which he talked of a new era of cooperation between government and the chambers. Their strengths as a chosen instrument of government in the enterprise culture were the very features that were regarded as their weakness in more corporatist times: their individualistic character, breadth of membership, decentralisation, and a high proportion of smaller companies in membership. These ideas were taken forward by Nicholas Ridley in the context of the provision of better business support services, and finally implemented by Peter Lilley. The DTI contributed £150,000 towards an electronic information network to link chambers; made funds available under the Enterprise Initiative for organisation and marketing studies for chambers; and seconded administrative grade civil servants to chambers to help with the rationalisation process (thirty secondments are envisaged over a three year period from 1991), Once they have been reformed, chambers should be eligible for the delivery of more government schemes, enabling them to absorb responsibilities that ministers want to delegate.

The rationalisation scheme adopted by the ABCC following the Bennett Report envisaged around fifty core chambers covering the UK. Each core chamber would have at least 1,000 members, thirty to thirty-five staff, and an income of at least £1 million a year, excluding government training schemes. It was considered that a system based on fifty chambers would enable a chamber to be clear that it was as good as or better than 40 per cent of German chambers, which would still leave 60 per cent of German chambers with superior services. Despite difficulties arising from the recession, by the end of 1991, almost thirty chambers had achieved the standard required. In addition, seven major chambers had joined the ABCC, leaving only two major chambers outside the national organisation.

Most chambers did not want full statutory backing which it was feared might tie them too closely to government policies. Some members saw an analogy with the closed shop. The ABCC did consider a scheme for chambers to become a one-stop registration point, registering all UK businesses with five or more employees. The registration fee would have provided the chambers with a secure income from which to finance an improved range of services, as well as creating a national database of information on smaller British businesses. However, this plan was shelved after complaints that it would increase bureaucracy. The ABCC opted for a limited form of government backing in terms of legal recognition for the name Chamber of Commerce and Industry. Indeed, the ABCC had to reassure its members that chambers would remain independent representative bodies and would not be in the pay of the DTI (Association of British Chambers of Commerce, 1991). Any thorough reform of British business associations, however well-conceived, tends to founder on the attachment of business persons to a voluntary approach which means that firms can opt out of chamber membership. Thus, Professor Bennett has argued, 'businesses fail to act beyond their narrowest interests, and their capabilities as a whole suffer. Arguably that is Britain's key business problem' (*Financial Times*, 4 June 1991).

A further problem is that functions that are handled by one institution in France or Germany are split between chambers of commerce, training and enterprise councils (TECs) and enterprise agencies in Britain, resulting in a confusing overall structure. The chambers of commerce and the TECs are to some extent rivals, although there is as much confusion as direct competition, given that the geographical boundaries of the two types of organisation are not coterminous. Seen from a TEC perspective, each of the chambers operates in a different way and has a different clientele. The chamber movement also finds it difficult to generalise about TECs, but is worried about what it sees as unfair competition and distortion of the market, with examples of TECs developing information services for business and mounting campaigns in Europe. Discussions were held in 1991 between the ABCC and G-10 the committee of TEC chairmen, to try and develop a closer relationship. G10 recognised that 'There was clear potential for conflict in the enterprise side between chambers and Tecs' (*Financial Times*, 7 June 1991).

The formation of G-10, which acquired a permanent secretariat in 1991, adds another organisation to the list of intersectoral business associations in Britain, albeit one with a functional focus. G-10 is a representative committee of TEC chairmen, although it includes in its structure provision for representing the views of TEC chief executives. Its chairman commented that its formalisation was 'a move towards greater independence and an attempt to provide a clear representative body for the TEC movement' (*The Independent*, 5 March 1991). Not all TEC chairmen welcomed its formation, however, as they consider it detracted from the direct personal access they had enjoyed to the Secretary of State for Employment.

Small business associations

Research by May and McHugh 'emphasises the heterogeneity of the small business sector and the lack of a common policy agenda. There are in fact only a very limited number of policies that affect the whole small firms sector in more or less the same way' (May and McHugh, 1992, p. 16). This is reflected in a fragmented system of associations, with many different bodies competing to represent the views of smaller businesses, with all of them taken together representing only a minority of smaller businesses. These problems were compounded by the transfer of government responsibility for small businesses with Lord Young when he moved from Trade and Industry to Employment. This is a function that should have remained with the DTI which is where it returned when Michael Heseltine became President of the Board of Trade.

Smaller businesses make up the bulk of the membership of the CBI and the ABCC. Despite the special arrangements it makes to look after smaller firms through its Smaller Firms Council, and representation on its specialist and regional committees, the CBI is also open to the charge that its main priority is the problems of the larger businesses that provide the bulk of its subscription income. 52 per cent of the members of chambers of commerce have less than twenty employees, and another 40 per cent have between twenty and 199 employees, so 92 per cent of the membership formally count as smaller businesses. The representation of smaller businesses through the chamber of commerce movement will increase further if the target membership of 150,000 businesses by 1994 is achieved. In many ways, however, the emphasis of the chambers is on providing 'crucial areas of service where the business lacks an in-house capacity' (Association of British Chambers of Commerce, 1991, p. 12).

Of the organisations representing only small businesses, the largest is the Federation of Small Businesses (formerly the National Federation of Self Employed and Small Businesses) which has over 50,000 members. Over the years, it has adopted more of an 'insider' strategy, briefing ministers and civil servants, although local branches are used to lobby constituency MPs. Another organisation which adopts an insider strategy is the Association of Independent Businesses (AIB) which has some eight hundred direct members and about 20,000 members who belong to affiliated organisations. It was originally established in 1968 from firms who refused to join the CBI when it was formed, and is seen as being orientated to the 'larger' small firms. The Forum of Private Business, established in 1977 and with 17,400 members in 1990, is a much more high-profile organisation, running campaigns on particular issues which concern smaller businesses. It has been criticised by competing small-firm organisations 'for being "a one-man band" and for arousing government hostility on issues which they are tackling in a more low-key manner' (*Financial Times*, 29 May 1990). The Union of Independent Companies (UIC) is by far the smallest of the associations, having broken away from the AIB in 1978. It has its own niche in the representation of smaller businesses, organising about three hundred small and medium-sized manufacturing companies. 'The UIC has no interest in being a large organisation, strongly emphasising "qualitative" rather than "quantitative" criteria. The quality it claims derives from its strategy of forming its policy by drawing on the best professional expertise' (May and McHugh, 1990, p. 20).

It should be noted that among the minority of small firms who do join business associations, 'the trade association is the most popular choice, but few if any trade associations are structured internally ... to offer significant representation to small firms' (May and McHugh, 1991, p. 16). There are a number of trade associations which confine their membership to smaller firms. These can be significant organisations in sectors which have large numbers of small firms, e.g., engineering (the Engineering Industries Association) or construction (the Federation of Master Builders).

The overall picture is of 'a fragmented array of representative groups lacking the necessary coverage of the small business community to provide them with an authoritative voice' (May and McHugh, 1991,

p. 24). The individualism which is a characteristic of British business persons is particularly noticeable among smaller businesses, and government's willingness to recognise a variety of groups creates little incentive for rationalisation.

Conclusions

Michael Heseltine has expressed his interest in developing a constructive dialogue between government and industry. Government will, however, find itself talking to a complicated mosaic of bodies, considerable overlaps of membership and functions, and in some areas, such as small business, open rivalry. Dore's characterisation of 'a typical British trade association with an ex-brigadier as its secretary, a minor information-distributing and lobbying role and the membership of only half the firms in the industry' (Dore, 1987, p. 200) is a caricature, but it is a caricature with a sufficient grain of truth to make us uncomfortable. There is a considerable body of evidence that well-organised and resourced business associations have made a substantial contribution to the competitiveness of German and Japanese industry (Lynn and McKeown, 1988). The representation of business is too important to be left to business itself. This is not corporatism; it is well-informed common sense.

7 Business and Party Politics

If there are difficulties in the development and expression of business interests through representative associations, then it is possible that other routes may become important for the defence of business interests. One alternative route that suggests itself is through political parties, especially parties apparently favourable to business interests. This chapter will argue that the weaknesses of business political organisation apparent elsewhere are not compensated for by the effective defence of business interests through political parties. Indeed, under Margaret Thatcher's leadership, the British Conservative Party was able to develop its own conception of what was good for business. In some respects, the policies developed did coincide with what was wanted by a broad spectrum of business opinion, but in others they were seen by some business persons as having harmful effects, particularly for manufacturing industry. When economic interest and party doctrine diverged, it was often party doctrine that emerged as more influential on the course of events. 'The ideological hegemony of "Thatcherism" meant that attempts to influence policy, to be successful, had to accept the basic premises of the New Right ideology — yet these were the very premises which large sections of domestically-based manufacturing industry sought to challenge in the first place' (Judge, 1990, p. 221).

The limits of the literature

The relationships between organised (or unorganised) business interests and political parties have been a relatively neglected area of political science research. No doubt this is in part because the study of political parties and the study of interest groups tend to be separate specialisms within political science. (But for an important exception to this general pattern, see Lehmbruch 1979.) Within British political science, the focus of much of the empirical research has tended to be on parties in Parliament, rather than on parties as total organisations characterised by the persistence of unresolved doctrinal battles. There has also been a tendency to study parties as 'closed systems': to focus on such topics as factionalism *within* parties; or the roles of party bureaucracies *within* parties; or the ways in which parties select their candidates and leaders. The debate about the notion of adversarial politics which is sometimes seen as a distinctive property of the British party system was something of a distraction. (For a properly sceptical treatment, see Gamble and Walkland, 1984.) The one writer who has lifted the debate on to a higher plane has been Richard Rose with his discussions of the concept of party government (1974) and the issue of whether party alternation actually makes a difference to the content of government policy (Rose, 1980, 1984).

Despite studies of such subjects as whether Conservative MPs lobby on behalf of industries in their constituencies (Wood, 1987), the relationship between party and interest remains relatively unexplored. One underlying reason is because parties, as vote-seeking organisations, have to transcend particular interests in order to assemble sufficient votes to have a chance of forming a government. There is relatively little mileage in electoral terms in being closely identified with the business interest, especially big business. This is an important consideration for the Conservative Party which is often overlooked by commentators.

In so far as the relationship between political parties and business interests in Britain has been examined, the discussion has tended to focus almost exclusively on donations by business to the Conservative Party. This is a topic which has generated a great deal of heat, many proposals for reform, and relatively little serious analysis. It has also tended to swamp discussion of more important aspects of the relationship between business and political parties. This is not to say that it is unimportant and the question of business donations will be discussed in this chapter. However, it is important to remember that only a minority of businesses give money to the Conservative Party or to organisations identified with it; many companies, including ICI, have a policy of not making political donations.

The general argument that will be advanced in this chapter is that the relationship between business and political parties is often a difficult and awkward one. In referring to a relationship the emphasis is not on the frequency of interaction between business persons and politicians, but on the level of mutual misunderstanding of the different worlds they inhabit. For example, political life is organised around the legislative year; business persons often have to act quickly to take advantage of a window of opportunity for a product. They find it difficult to understand why government is constrained by public accountability, particularly in the use of public money. Government is where everyone's problems come together, and business persons cannot readily appreciate the need for compromise and for symbolic politics when they are used to making a clear choice between alternative courses of action. The Industry and Parliament Trust was formed in 1977 with the specific objective of overcoming misunderstandings between business and the political world, and through its fellowships for politicians and seminars it has done much to overcome the problems arising from the occupational isolation of business persons and politicians.

This chapter will focus on three main aspects of the relationship between business and the political parties. First, there will be a general discussion of the match (or mismatch) between the outlooks of each of the parties and the interests of business. The rather vague term 'outlook' is used deliberately since the term 'doctrine' may be too precise for use in this context and because both major parties are coalitions embracing a wide range of views. In relation to the emergence of 'Thatcherism', it will be argued that it was a newly dominant faction within the Conservative Party that redefined the interests of business; the supposed leaders of business largely followed the political lead they were given. Second, the composition of the political parties will be examined: do business persons play an active role in them at the local and national level? Lastly, the vexed question of business financing of party activity will be reviewed.

The difficult relationship between the Conservative Party and business

The Conservative Party cannot be relied upon to act as the authentic spokesperson of business. This is not surprising when one considers that business firms do not have a vote and that, even counting small business owners, business persons are a relatively small proportion of the electorate. Thus, Mrs Thatcher's Government 'responded more quickly and frequently to stimuli revealed in by- and local elections, or by media inquests than to the "former" governing institutions' (Middlemas, 1991, p. 436). The Conservative Party emphasises that it is the party of free enterprise, but the translation of that commitment into party policy can contain unpleasant surprises for particular sections of business, as happened to manufacturing industry under Mrs Thatcher.

Most business persons are Conservative supporters, but their support is generally passive rather than active. 'By and large, business leaders from the large firms rely on methods other than party channels for exercising political influence' (Jordan and Richardson, 1987, p. 242). Quite apart from the question of the relative effectiveness of different channels of access to decision-makers, business persons often have considerable reservations about the Conservative Party's policies. A survey of board-level executives drawn from the FT top five hundred companies conducted by MORI in March 1992 found that only 49 per cent of those contacted were satisfied with the way that the Conservative Government was running the country. Asked to say who would make the better chancellor, 49 per cent preferred Labour's John Smith against the 39 per cent who preferred the then incumbent, Norman Lamont. Even so, 92 per cent of respondents stated that they would back the Conservatives in the general election, compared with 1 per cent who said that they would back the Labour Party (*Financial Times*, 16 March 1992).

A survey of small business owners, particularly given levels of concern about the Uniform Business Rate, would have no doubt shown more movement away from the Conservative Government. However, the executives surveyed manage the major companies which have a key influence on economic outcomes, and with which any Labour Government needs to have an effective relationship. Business loyalty is often an obstacle to any sustained opposition being mounted within business organisations to Conservative policies. Attempts to mount such a challenge encounter the objection from the more partisan Conservative supporters that business must be loyal to 'our govern-ment'. Even opponents of Mrs Thatcher were worried about the consequences of engaging in open criticism of her. A former ICI chair-man has commented that his reputation 'for being an opponent of the Prime Minister was not something which I actively sought and was, I believe, unhelpful to my company' (Harvey-Jones, 1991, p. 362). The one point at which manufacturing industry did try to mount a critique of the Thatcher policy (or lack of it) for industry was through the 1985 House of Lords report on overseas trade, which included senior industrialists in the committee's membership, and to which many leading industrialists gave evidence. A public affairs manager of an industrial firm interviewed in 1992 commented:

Leading Conservatives rubbished that very good House of Lords report that talked about overseas trade. A very readable and very sound report rubbished by government ministers before they read it.

One of the interesting features of Sir Terence Beckett's 'bare knuckles' speech in 1980 was that he articulated business reservations about the Conservative Party that are usually only heard in private. He warned the CBI conference, 'You had better face the fact that the Conservative Party is a rather narrow alliance.' After asking how many of those in the Parliament or Cabinet had actually run a business he commented, 'They don't all understand you. They think they do, but they don't. They are even suspicious of you, and what is worse they don't take you seriously' (*Financial Times*, 12 November 1980). Despite the deteriorating relationship between the CBI and the Conservative Government, there was no attempt to build an alliance with the dissident moderates in the Cabinet, in part because the CBI approved of some aspects of the Government's policies such as reductions in public expenditure (Middlemas, 1991, p. 242).

For their part, Conservative Party leaders have often felt badly let down by business. Edward Heath as prime minister expressed his frustration at business's failure to invest once, as he saw it, his government had created the economic conditions in which investment could take place. Mrs Thatcher was sceptical about the ability of business to tackle what she saw as labour market rigidities without a clear political lead. Her brand of conviction politics had little time for what were seen as the pleas of vested interests. Mrs Thatcher stated in a television programme in 1984, 'I can give you a check list now of the way in which we have tackled vested interest' (*Weekend World*, 15 January 1984, transcript p. 2/6). By way of contrast, a more traditional Conservative has argued, 'A Tory ... rejects the simple idea that individuals are selfish and good and groups selfish and bad' (Gilmour, 1983, p. 204). John Major is closer to this tradition than Mrs Thatcher.

Part of the problem for the moderates and for business in the 1980s was the extent to which the political agenda was set by 'new right' think tanks such as the Institute of Economic Affairs, the Centre for Policy Studies, and the Adam Smith Institute. Sometimes it seemed when Mrs Thatcher was in office that (to borrow a phrase from another context) any teenage scribbler with new right credentials could write a pamphlet that would be read in Downing Street. Some policy disasters, such as the poll tax, are claimed to have just such an origin. Once Mr Major became prime minister, however, the ascendancy of the think tanks began to wane, a development emphasised by internal disputes in the Institute of Economic Affairs.

The view that what is remarkable about the relationship between business and the Conservative Party is the absence of a proper relationship has been criticised on the grounds that it emphasises formal at the expense of informal relationships:

> Thus there is a general mutual acceptance between elites that means that views of businessmen can be communicated without group intermediation. Some ministers indeed have their private circles of businessmen who can be sounded for their reactions. (Jordan and Richardson, 1987, p. 242)

These informal relationships were of little help for threatened sections of business under Mrs Thatcher. In terms of personal history and doctrinal preferences, she came from outside the traditional elites. She wished to sweep aside the traditional governing relationships which she saw as a root cause of Britain's relative economic decline. It must be emphasised, however, that the difficulties in the relationship between business and the Conservative Party are not confined to the Thatcher period. The role of business in Conservative statecraft, which is essentially about 'the art of winning elections and achieving some necessary degree of governing competence in office' (Bulpitt, 1986, p. 21) has often seemed to be limited to the following components: support the Government publicly and financially; ensure economic success; but do not expect too much help from government in achieving that objective.

It should not be supposed, however, that the problem is simply one of the Conservative Party expecting a great deal in return for very little. It is often difficult for the Conservative Party to get a clear message from business about what it wants. A central theme of this book is that the available mechanisms for articulating a coherent business viewpoint in Britain have serious defects. There is, however, an even more fundamental problem. Even with better mechanisms, deciding what represents the best political strategy for business is not easy. Useem (1984, p. 57) articulates a widely-held viewpoint when he states that 'The overriding and undiminished corporate stress on the growth of profits necessarily dominates the vision of all who enter politics on behalf of the business community.' The creation of conditions in which profits can be protected and maximised must certainly be a central goal of business political activity. However, Useem adds, almost as an afterthought, 'Just how this imperative is translated into specific public policies at a given moment, however, is subject to many interpretations' (ibid.). This is the central, not a secondary problem. Converting the general goal of profit maximisation into a political strategy is a difficult task, given changing conditions, and the range of options available.

The problem of Thatcherism

The Conservative Party is the party closest to business in Britain, but that does not mean that it is a party *of* business, let alone a party *for* business. Indeed, under the fifteen years of Mrs Thatcher's leadership, the gap between what business wanted and what the Conservative Party did often seemed wider than at any time in modern history. Nevertheless, as has been argued, business largely acquiesced in the policies of the Thatcher Government, despite the fact that some of those policies seemed to run counter to the interests of business. One government relations manager interviewed in 1992 commented, 'We have thrown away out industrial base. Industry was relatively spineless in the face of Mrs Thatcher. She walked all over them.' What the Thatcher period represents is an interesting and important special case of the general political weakness of business. A dominant and well-entrenched faction in a political party formulated and applied its own solution to the political problems facing business enterprises. A political strategy for business was evolved outside the organisations of business itself.

In the last decade of the twentieth century, we are too close to the experience of Thatcherism to make a proper and balanced appraisal of its long term impact. It is interesting to speculate about how political analysts in the twenty-first century will look back at the Thatcher period. Will they view it as an interesting aberration, a last attempt to craft a peculiarly British response to the problem of poor British economic performance, before Britain settled into the social partnership embrace of an ever-closer European union? Will they see its electoral success as ultimately leading to changes in the political rules of the game such as proportional representation which undermined the Conservative Party? Or will they see it as having accelerated economic and social changes which enabled the Conservatives to become an electorally dominant party? Will they emphasise the extent to which Mrs Thatcher permanently changed the political landscape of Britain by curbing the power of the trade unions, sweeping away the vestiges of corporatism, and facilitating a fundamental change in the City of London? It is perhaps worth mentioning that in the 1960s there was some discussion by political analysts about whether 'Gaullism' amounted to a coherent political doctrine, one that had some similarities with Thatcherism in terms of its unswerving assertion of a particular interpretation of what constituted national interest. Three decades later it would not seem worth posing the question, even though de Gaulle has an enduring legacy in terms of the institutions of the Fifth Republic.

It is very easy to reify Thatcherism, a trap into which some commentators have fallen. After all, what it really amounted to was little more than three elements: a collection of rather elementary political principles which are capable of being presented in terms of a household economy or the operations of a small business — indeed, the terms 'Robertsism' might be more appropriate so as to refer to the origins of these ideas in Grantham; an unshakeable conviction that the principles are correct, and a willingness to implement them with fervour and determination, combined with considerable tactical skill so that retreats are made when circumstances require it; and a populist instinct for understanding and expressing the aspirations of a considerable body of ordinary people. It was the loss of this last element in the triumphalist final phase of Thatcherism, exemplified by the poll tax, which led Mrs Thatcher's party to ditch her because they feared that she was leading them to electoral oblivion, a violation of the fundamental tenet of Conservative statecraft which prompted them to select a new leader who proved able to deliver a fourth term.

Against the background of Mrs Thatcher's political dominance in the 1980s, it is often forgotten that it took some time for her to win control of her party. After all, throughout the postwar period, it was the 'Tory' or 'one nation', or in the hydrological terminology of the 1980s, the 'wet' tendency that predominated in the Conservative Party. This tendency was not immediately swept aside. The Conservative Party's major 1977 statement on economic strategy, *The Right Approach to the Economy*, reflected a compromise between the Thatcherites and the more traditional sections of the party.

Business was, however, moving into a closer relationship with the Conservative Party, a process facilitated by the role of Lord Watkinson, a former Conservative minister, as CBI president. He was offered the chairmanship of the Conservative Party, but turned it down, 'thinking that it was more important to revive the CBI's spirits and shape its direction. This choice he later regretted' (Middlemas, 1991, p. 195). Working with leading firms on the President's Committee, Sir John Methven as CBI director-general established with the Conservatives 'an informal "Liaison Committee" quite unprecedented in the history of either organisation' (ibid., p. 214). A more informal equivalent of the TUC–Labour liaison committee was thus put in place. However, there was still some distance in the relationship between the CBI and the Conservatives. 'The CBI had not captured the Opposition, nor they it; on both sides, a certain hesitancy about too close an involvement ensured discreet separatism' (ibid., p. 215).

In order to understand the willingness of business to move closer to the Thatcherite Conservative Party, it is important to recall the broader political context. The 1970s were a period of economic and political crisis, culminating in the 'Winter of Discontent' in 1978–9. Mrs Thatcher and her supporters offered a clear, unequivocal set of solutions to that crisis; and, in the absence of any credible alternative, business was largely willing to follow her lead. When the Conservative Government was elected in 1979, many people in business had convinced themselves that it was the last chance to secure a social market system in Britain; the alternative was often portrayed as a slide into a British version of state socialism. In a posthumously-reported interview, the late Sir John Methven described himself as 'a sort of social democrat', but added that 'the situation was now so bad that the shock of Thatcherism might be our last and only chance of survival' (*The Guardian*, 1 May 1980). At the 1979 CBI Conference, the organisation's leadership used such phrases as the 'last call for dinner in the market system' and 'drinking in the last chance saloon'. In retrospect, such fears seem to be exaggerated but they seemed real enough to business persons at the time, and may have helped to reconcile the more doubtful among them to Thatcherism. As Leys (1985, p. 17) argues, a majority of businessmen had come to feel that the survival of capitalism in Britain was at stake:

Consequently short-term business interests, and even the long-term interests of individuals or firms, had to be sacrificed. Even those who were unconvinced by the Thatcherite project saw no realistic political alternative (this was the feeling to which Mrs Thatcher shrewdly appealed with the TINA slogan — 'There Is No Alternative').

When Mrs Thatcher was challenged for the Conservative Party leadership in 1990, the main business response appears to have been to want a quick end to the political uncertainty. The onset of the recession reduced business enthusiasm for the Thatcher Government, which was blamed for 'keeping interest rates too high for too long ... [and] for preventing Britain from joining the ERM at an earlier date' (*Financial Times*, 15 November 1990). Under the Major Government, concern about poor relations with business led the government to start a series of breakfast meetings between cabinet ministers and executives from small and medium-sized companies.

Mr Major was seen to be a more sympathetic listener to business than Mrs Thatcher but he was always caught between his claim to remain faithful to Mrs Thatcher's principles and his attempt to develop a distinctive policy stance of his own, something which he was really only able to do when he won his own mandate. In the run-up to the 1992 Election, the Conservatives had to 'rebuild the party's relations with businessmen closely associated with Mrs Thatcher, the former prime minister, after initially taking a "cavalier approach" to Thatcherite business supporters following Mr Major's election as party leader' (*Financial Times*, 18 March 1992). One significant outcome of the 1992 Election was the role given to Michael Heseltine who had emphasised that the revival of Britain's manufacturing base is the key to its future success and that government has a strategic role to play in the process. 'Such involvement [for government] is not a matter for shame. It is vital to the survival of the British economy' (Heseltine, 1987, p. 97). A more constructive relationship between business and the Conservative Party at last seemed to be a possibility.

The Labour Party: a disappointed suitor

The Labour Party would like to have an effective working relationship in government with business, especially with manufacturing industry.

The effective implementation of its policies require cooperation, or at least acquiescence, from the business community. In the early 1980s, the Labour Party could be relegated to a broom cupboard of nightmare jokes, to be brought out whenever the Conservatives wanted to scare business. The chances of Labour forming a government in the foreseeable future seemed slim. However, under the leadership of Neil Kinnock, Labour was patiently reconstructed as a modern and moderate party which appeared to have a chance of electoral success. Considerable efforts were made to reassure business about the Party's wish to develop an effective partnership relationship with the business community. Policies such as compulsory planning agreements and withdrawal from the EC which had frightened business disappeared from the party's programme.

There is nothing new about the Labour Party trying to develop an effective dialogue with business persons. If anything, it was the early 1980s which were the exception rather than the rule. The Labour Party has realised for most of its history that it can benefit from the friendly support of business persons who are supportive of its policies, but who are also prepared to suggest how the party's intentions could best be translated into measures which would have a practical and beneficial effect at the day-to-day level of business decision-making.

The Labour Party has employed a variety of mechanisms to mobilise the advice and support of such business persons as it has among its supporters. In 1932, the semi-secret XYZ club was formed to bring together Labour sympathisers in the City, economists and a few politicians, with Hugh Gaitskell as secretary. Hugh Dalton linked its activities to party policy-making and 'much of the financial policy in Labour's 1934 document, *For Labour and Peace*, was a product of XYZ deliberations' (Pimlott, 1985, p. 223). The club was revived in 1944 to discuss a paper prepared for the Labour Party's Financial Committee on postwar employment policy (see ibid., p. 395). However, its greatest influence was in the 1930s; although it continued to function after the Second World War, it did so largely 'as a dining club for Gaitskellites' (ibid., p. 223).

During the 1964–70 Labour Government Harold Wilson made use of *ad hoc* contacts with industrialists he trusted for advice. Similarly, at the Department of Economic Affairs, George Brown sought advice at monthly dinners from a group which had at its core individuals such as Frank (later Lord) Kearton of Courtaulds, George (later Lord) Cole of Unilever and John Berkin of Shell. Brown recalls, 'This unpublicised body of industrial advisers had an enormous influence on the apparatus we set up' (Brown, 1972, p. 94).

The formal committee which was re-established in 1972 with the help of individuals such as the late Lord Wilfrid Brown seems to have been more effective than its predecessors. Care was taken to ensure that members were recruited from individuals with a long record of service to the Labour Party. In opposition, the committee offered practical help on the development of policy. When Labour came into office in 1974, its members continued to provide assistance to busy ministers faced with a complex and pressing range of decisions. Its individual members were also, on an informal basis, able to discuss particular problems or pending decisions on behalf of ministers with civil servants, drawing on their first-hand knowledge of business. Eric Varley, as Industry Secretary and James Callaghan, as Prime Minister, working through the 10 Downing Street Policy Unit, are understood to have made use of the availability of help of this kind.

Labour industrialists are invariably on the moderate wing of the party, and it is therefore not surprising that, when the Labour Party split, 30 to 40 per cent of the membership of the 1972 committee joined the SDP, where some of them formed a similar organisation. This loss of members, and the general crisis within the party, meant that the 1972 committee faded into the background for a while. In 1983, it absorbed the Labour Economic Finance and Taxation Association (LEFTA) which had a membership made up largely of accountants and academics. LEFTA had been more involved in the internal politics of the Labour Party and had undergone something of a decline in effectiveness.

The Labour Party Finance and Industry Group is not an affiliated organisation, but is registered with the Party under its revised rules. There would be little point in affiliation for a relatively small group of around one hundred and fifty which, in any case, wanted to keep away from the internal battles in the Party, regarding the conference as a place for the constituencies and the union. Members are drawn from all sectors of business, industry and the City including directors of quoted companies. The Group does not raise funds for the Party, although some of its individual members provide funds. Another organisation which emerged in the late 1980s was Enterprise for Labour, a group of "twenty something" business persons who met for regular 'networking' in a Soho wine bar. Inevitably, the press started to refer to 'Perrier Socialists' and call them 'Yuppies for Kinnock' (*The Independent*, 25 March 1989).

Neil Kinnock was not slow to appreciate the contribution that the Finance and Industry Group could make to the work of the Labour Party, and is understood to have encouraged its activities. One of its roles has been to act as a 'think tank', drawing on the knowledge of its members to produce pamphlets. However, the Labour Party is not short of pamphlet writers and the Group's contribution has been to provide a broader input into party thinking than would have been provided by the trade unions in the past. Members of the Group have also been able to help with campaigning work, and have provided a reservoir of talent on which Labour would have been able to draw if it had been elected in 1992.

Labour's efforts to impress business with the responsibility of its policies, led by John Smith, then the shadow chancellor, appear to have had little effect, other than to convince business persons that Smith would make a better chancellor than his Conservative opponent. The CBI somewhat grudgingly admitted in 1991 that Labour's strategy for industry was 'closer to the real world' than it had been for many years, but said that it retained serious doubts about the party's ability to tackle inflation and control public sector wages (*Financial Times*, 18 April 1991). In the general election of 1992, the CBI mounted a scarcely-veiled attack on Labour's policies. In taking this line, however, they were reflecting opinion in larger businesses. A survey of two hundred top firms, with 105 responding, by stockbrokers James Capel found that 86 per cent of companies in the survey said that a Labour Government would be bad for the economy, and 63 per cent thought it would be bad for their own business (*Independent on Sunday*, 8 March 1992). A MORI telephone survey of executive directors from the FT top five hundred companies conducted in March 1992, found that of the 235 respondents, four-fifths said that a Labour victory would be bad for the country and industry, and five-sixths said that it would hurt their business (*Financial Times*, 16 March 1992). A follow-up survey on the eve of the April 1992 election found that more than a third of those interviewed said that they expected their companies' investment spending to fall if Labour won the election (*Financial Times*, 8 April 1992).

It is difficult to see that Labour could have done much more to win over business opinion. A Labour economic adviser commented, 'The package will work. Labour has changed. The problem is that British industrialists have not changed and they do not want to let it work' (*Financial Times*, 30 March 1992). Memories of past Labour governments still weighed heavily with many business persons. Shadow minister Tony Blair commented, 'Someone of my generation ... can see how sensible some form of social partnership is. But it has to be said that there are those who have been so badly scarred by the past that they cannot learn from it' (*Financial Times*, 27 January 1992).

There were some industrialists who felt that, without being Labour sympathisers, they could work effectively with a Labour Government. One government relations manager commented in interview in March 1992:

A Labour Government is always by definition much more empathetic with manufacturing industry than a Conservative one. I've never known a Conservative Government that had any time for manufacturing industry. A lot of Labour MPs represent the old industrial areas where industries like ours are or were massive employers of labour ... Labour MPs in the main understand ... The Tory predilection is much more for the City, that was emphasised in the Thatcher ethos ... I would expect that with a Labour Government with a working majority, I would have a different conversation with Gordon Brown from those who have fluttered through 1–19 Victoria Street [DTI offices]. I never got anything out of Lilley and his predecessors.

What continued to cause more difficulties for Labour was its relationship with the financial sector. In particular, international financial markets were even more influential in a more internationalised economy in 1992 than they had been when Labour was in office in the 1960s and 1970s. Had a Labour Government taken office in April 1992, given that it was pledged to defend sterling within the ERM, it would probably have been forced to put up interest rates because of a lack of confidence on international markets, thereby undermining its efforts to help manufacturing industry.

The Liberal Democrats: uncertain friends

The Liberal Party is a relatively heterogeneous and decentralised party about which it is difficult to make sustainable generalisations. For example, the Scottish Liberal Party may have different perspectives on an issue from the party as a whole. When the Alliance with the Social

Democrats was in existence, it was possible to see the SDP as the pro-industry wing of the Alliance. The SDP certainly made considerable and quite successful efforts to raise funds from business, and its outlook was closer to that of business (particularly big business) than the Liberals.

The Liberal Democrats see themselves as particularly looking after the needs of the smaller business, but all parties at least purport to be the friends of the small business owner, so there is nothing very distinctive about the Liberal Party in that respect. The Party does place a strong emphasis on competition policy and environmental policy. The former emphasis would not be welcomed in oligopolistic industries, while the latter could raise costs for industry as a whole.

If there is one interest which, in term of practical politics, the Liberal Democrats are particularly identified with, it is the rural interest. This is not surprising when one considers that a considerable proportion of the seats that the Liberal Democrats actually hold (and many of those they might hope to win) are in the rural areas of Britain. After the 1992 Election, the Liberal Democrats held only three of their twenty seats in the large conurbations. This emphasis on rural interests. was very apparent in the Lib–Lab pact of the late 1970s. The defence of rural interests does not actually harm business, but it does relatively little for manufacturing industry.

The CBI tried to develop an arrangement with the Liberals during the Lib–Lab pact, 'but despite the disillusion of David Steel and his colleagues at their inability to force Callaghan to accept a joint programme for 1978–9, there was never any firm substance to it, and it lapsed when the Liberals withdrew their support from Labour' (Middlemas, 1991, p. 539). Asked to comment on what then seemed to be the possibility of a Labour–Liberal Democrat pact after the 1992 election, a government relations manager commented that the political outcome would not be very different from that resulting from an overall majority.

It is worth noting that the informal organisation of government relations managers, the Caxton Group, suspends its meetings during October so that members can attend the party conferences. The Liberal Democrats are usually included on the circuit, although firms that take a stand at the two major conferences may not bother with the Liberal Democrats. It should also be noted that some firms, and not just those with Scottish links, attend the Scottish National Party conference.

Business persons in politics

Most business persons, especially large employers, are too busy to pursue a political career, either as party activists or as MPs. For most of them, becoming a MP would also involve a considerable financial sacrifice. Many employers do not encourage their managers to become actively involved in politics. Indeed, the Industry and Parliament Trust has taken an initiative to change business attitudes towards political service which has not been viewed in a positive light compared, for example, with a Territorial Army commission. The Industry and Parliament Trust has a model corporate policy under discussion. Some firms, such as ICI, have already made considerable efforts to encourage their employees to become MPs. The success of the ICI scheme is reflected in the fact 'that in the 1983 parliament some nine former ICI employees were members of the Commons' (Judge, 1990, p. 231).

Even if a chief executive thinks that political service is a good idea, a local manager may block the process. The Industry and Parliament Trust's discussions show that there is a widespread feeling that political man and woman and industrial man and woman were ultimately incompatible. It was also thought that political service was hindered by the unattractive and complex working practices of Parliament which need to be reformed. This could be particularly important for female managers.

Judge has produced the most extensive and up-to-date analysis of the background of MPs, drawing on data for 1983. He found (Judge, 1990, p. 88):

A total of 217 MPs had ... been active in industry at some stage of their careers before entering parliament. This larger number (i.e. 33 per cent of all MPs) was still below a proportionate representation of the working population (at 38.7 per cent); but was perhaps not as small as many industrialists outside of Westminster appeared to believe it to be.

Judge also notes (ibid., p. 89) that 'one of the characteristics of the Commons has been its ability to reflect, no matter how slowly or unintentionally, the changing composition of British industry.' He points out that the proportionate representation of the information technology industry in the Commons in 1983 was higher than the proportion of the workforce engaged in the industry. However, when the cumulative years of pre-entry experience of MPs are counted, the comparative weakness of industrial experience becomes apparent. Judge observes (ibid., p. 95), 'it becomes apparent that the pre-parliamentary experience of MPs is massively skewed towards the service sector of the economy. The collective experience of the business services, education, public administration, "other public services" and the media outstrip the House's aggregate experience of any industrial sector.'

One experienced Conservative member pointed out to Judge that 'For all that an MP might bring knowledge of industry into the House when he is first elected such knowledge is, if you like, "date stamped" — it can become stale, even outdated as technology advances or the competitive environment changes' (ibid., p. 232). This is why the Industry and Parliament Trust's fellowship scheme is so important. It enables MPs and peers to spend a period of between twenty and twenty-five days with a firm (spread out over a year), with the experience ranging from board meetings to shop-floor visits. Companies appreciate the value of having someone with the skills of a politician, but without an axe to grind, working their way through the company, and the experience often leads the business side to change their appreciation of politicians as individuals. Since 1986 the programme for politicians has been complemented by a successful parliamentary study programme for industrialists.

Business funding of the Conservative Party

In the whole area of relations between business and politics, few issues arouse more political passion than the question of donations by business to party funds. These donations are almost entirely made to the Conservative Party or organisations which channel funds to it. In 1990–91, only one donation could be traced that had been made to another political party, £2,000 given by the Littlewoods Organisation to the Liberal Democrats (*Labour Research*, 1991, p. 7).

There are two problems which arise in any attempt to analyse the extent of political donations. First, company donations to the Conservative Party tend to rise substantially in election years. Should one take as the base year for any analysis a non-election year or an election year? Secondly, information on company donations arises from Section 19(1) of the 1967 Companies Act which requires companies to

publish in their directors' reports donations of more than £200 for a
political purpose. What constitutes a political purpose is specified in
Section 19(3). However, 'This definition does not appear to be comprehensive enough to catch "conduit" organisations which . . . collect
funds from companies and pass them on in whole or in part to the
Conservative Party' (Constitutional Reform Centre, 1985, pp. 7–8).

Nevertheless, it must be emphasised that only a minority of
businesses give donations to the Conservative Party. A comprehensive
survey of political donations by *Labour Research* covering 1990–91
found that out of 3,000 stock exchange and 2,400 UK private
companies surveyed, only 282 made donations to political organisations. As Mitchell and Bretting note (1992, p. 1), 'If corporate
officials perceive a business advantage in a particular party's election
victory, they would only contribute in the unlikely circumstance that
they calculated the election result would turn on their firm's individual
contribution ... There is a free rider incentive not to contribute.'
Mitchell and Bretting investigate the question of whether the real
incentive for making a political donation is to improve one's chances of
appearing in the honours list. Examining the 1979–90 period, they
found that only fourteen per cent of the non-donating firms had officials
who received honours, but that the figure rose to thirty-six per cent for
donating firms. Other factors may, of course, influence the award of
honours. However, 'Even when we control for public and charitable
service and firm size, the relationship between donations and honors . . .
remains' (Mitchell and Bretting, 1991, p. 13).

Pinto-Duschinsky has shown (1985, p. 330) that Conservative
Central Office income in real terms in the 1980s was 10 to 20 per cent
lower than in the 1950s and 1960s. As far as company donations are
concerned, there does seem to have been a trend for the Conservative
Party to become increasingly reliant on a smaller number of companies
which pay an increasing share of the total amount donated. *Labour
Research* figures show that in 1990–91, the top thirty-five corporate
donations accounted for half the money going to the party from that
source. As corporate cash has dried up, the Conservative Party has
increasingly turned to donations by wealthy individuals. Such donations include £2 million from John Latsis, a Greek shopping billionaire,
and £100,000 from Li Ka-Shing, reputedly the richest business person
in Hong Kong, after a private dinner with John Major (*The
Independent*, 6 October 1991). A network of patrons' clubs with a
recommended minimum subscription of £100 a year, but many

members giving more, has been estimated to raise half a million pounds a year for the party, perhaps more in election years (Tether, 1991).

The long-term trend towards a decline in business financial support for the Conservative Party may be related to gradual changes in the structure of companies operating in Britain. There has been an increase in the number of foreign-owned companies and a decrease in the number of family-dominated companies confined to one industrial sector. One point that is well-established in the literature is that British branches of multinational corporations are relatively unlikely to make political donations (Pinto-Duschinsky, 1981, p. 232; Constitutional Reform Centre, 1985, p. 18). This finding is confirmed by Mitchell and Bretting's statistical analysis which found that 'Subsidiaries of foreign firms are, as the literature suggests, less likely to contribute to the Conservative Party' (Mitchell and Bretting, 1991, p. 15).

It is also evident that companies in certain industrial sectors are particularly likely to make donations to the Conservative Party. Ross (1983, p. 37) notes that 'Three sectors of the British economy (finance and property companies; food, drink and tobacco firms; construction companies) have been steadily accounting for a larger and larger proportion of Conservative Party donations.' The two largest donors in 1990–91 were food and drink firms, with United Biscuits donating £112,000 and Allied Lyons £110,000 (*Labour Research*, 1991, p. 7). Mitchell and Bretting's statistical analysis 'suggests that firms with traditional historical links to the Conservative Party (firms in the construction and food and drink industries), consistent with earlier research, are more likely to donate' (Mitchell and Bretting, 1991, p. 15).

Some firms may stop donating because they do not like particular decisions taken by a Conservative government. Following its privatisation in 1987, British Airways was among the top twenty corporate donors to the Conservative Party. However, in 1991 it announced that it was stopping donations to the Conservative Party, the chairman, Lord King, referring to a series of government rulings which were seen to have affected the company's future profitability. In particular, he referred to the government decision 'to confiscate four of our slots each week at Tokyo's Narita airport and open up our Heathrow base to all comers' (*Financial Times*, 17 July 1991). Commentators observed that government policy had seem to become less well-disposed to British Airways after Mr Major replaced Mrs Thatcher as prime minister. 'Since her departure the speed at which BA has fallen from grace in government circles has been remarkable' (*The Independent*, 17 July

1991). It was noted that 'While Lord King was a close friend of the former prime minister, he is no more than an acquaintance of Mr John Major' (*Financial Times*, 17 July 1991). If nothing else, this episode shows that political donations do not shield a company from government determination to pursue its policy objectives, in this case opening up competition in air transport. For a company, although perhaps not for an individual, political donations are a bad buy, and those companies that have a policy of not making donations such as ICI and Pilkingtons are being sensible.

The significance of business donations

It is not easy to assess the significance of the contributions that business makes to party finances because of the difficulty of obtaining reliable figures about party funds at the constituency level. The Constitutional Reform Centre estimated in its report that over 55 to 60 per cent of central Conservative Party funds are provided by companies (Constitutional Reform Centre, 1985, p. 10). However, it should be remembered that the greater part of the Party's funds are raised and spent at the constituency level through individual subscriptions, donations and the various time-honoured (and some new) means of fund-raising. In 1981–82, the income of Conservative constituency associations totalled £8 million, twice the level of central income (see Pinto-Duschinsky, 1985, pp. 330 and 331). It is difficult to say what proportion of total party income is provided by business donations because relatively little is known about such donations at constituency level. If one was to make an informed guess on the basis of the available evidence, perhaps between a fifth and a quarter of total Conservative Party income comes from corporate business donations in a non-election year, but this figure could rise to over a third in an election year.

The Labour Party is, of course, substantially dependent on institutional finance from the trade unions. There is concern about the extent to which both major parties are dependent on institutional funding. A study sponsored by (but not representing a view of) the Hansard Society (1981, p. 45) noted that the growing dependence of the two major parties on institutional funding 'is not only unhealthy in itself, but can lead to a dangerous polarisation of political attitudes, and so distort democratic choice.'

What is often overlooked in this debate about this perceived problem is that British political parties have relatively few individual members in relation to their electoral support and charge them relatively little for membership compared with, say, German parties. For example, Labour's individual membership, at three per cent of Labour's total vote among the electorate in 1983 'was the lowest proportion of any social democratic party in Western Europe' (Butler and Kavanagh, 1984, p. 46). Subsequent campaigns to recruit members have not improved the overall position. An insufficient income from individual members leads to a greater dependence on institutional funding. Many commentators have concluded that the only solution is to provide state funding for political parties. Indeed, such an option might prove more acceptable to the Conservative Party than it has done in the past, given the costs of modern campaigning, and reports that the Party has financial difficulties. However, such funds might further reduce the incentive to parties to attract more individual members. Indeed, the debate on how such state funds might be provided distracts attention from the more fundamental question of why it is that British political parties have become less successful at attracting and retaining individual members. This trend runs counter to the growth in membership of various cause groups, so that the Royal Society for the Protection of Birds now has more members than the Labour Party.

It is often argued that the present funding arrangements tie the political parties too closely to particular interests, particularly business in the case of the Conservative Party. The Hansard report argues that the existing financial relationships between the parties and their institutional supporters accentuate social differences, entrenching class conflict (Hansard Society, 1981, p. 30). However, it should be remembered that there is nothing illegitimate about the expression and organisation of interests in politics: political activity is in large part about articulating and attempting to reconcile divergent interests. It is not surprising that interests should be linked to major political parties. Indeed, they give a solid ballast to parties, a link to the realities of political life which parties might otherwise lack.

Conclusions

This chapter has examined the various ways in which business and political parties relate to one another in Britain, but should not obscure the extent to which the business and political worlds are largely separate ones. Even the Conservative Party's relationship with business is more problematic and tenuous than is often assumed. Despite their overwhelming electoral support for the Conservatives, only 49 per cent of the business leaders interviewed by MORI in 1992 were satisfied with the way the Major Government was running the country (*Financial Times*, 16 March 1992). Although no direct evidence is available, one may speculate with a degree of confidence that business persons spend more time working for business interest associations than they do for political parties. They are naturally preoccupied with the immediate issues affecting their businesses and a trade association can often be more help in those areas than a political party. Government relations managers make the annual round of the party conferences, but seem to view it as a necessary ritual, rather than a core part of their activities. One explained in interview that the conferences were often the first chance to meet MPs after the summer break. Political parties are vote-seeking organisms; business persons do not have many votes; and parties may often be more interested in reassuring groups critical of business such as environmentalists. Business persons cannot ignore political parties, but they cannot rely on them as a principal means of safeguarding their interests.

8 Business Associations and Public Policy

Business interest associations should not only be viewed as 'lobbies', or as providers of services to their members, important though these functions are. Business associations are also capable of contributing to the implementation of public policy. 'Public policy' is seen as covering a task or activity designed to achieve certain objectives which government regards as its duty to discharge, or to arrange for its discharge by others within a framework laid down by government.

In Chapter 3, it was pointed out that business can assist in the task of governance in three principal ways: policy design, policy clearance and policy implementation. Some of this assistance is provided by large firms interacting directly with government, but associations have certain advantages as a mechanism for policy implementation, especially in industries where there is a wide spread of firms of different sizes. Even in industries dominated by a few large firms, government may prefer to work through associations to avoid charges of favouritism.

Although government policies such as aid for high technology projects are often operated by direct contact with firms, without any intermediation by an association, this chapter focusses on the contribution of business associations to policy implementation. The implementation of policies by associations acting as private interest governments, or the provision of associative systems of self-regulation, are more extensive practices than is generally realised. However, as Boddewyn (1985, p. 42) notes, 'the correspondence between the two concepts [of self-regulation and private interest government] is not complete.' For example, codes of practice relating to advertising developed by associations in the pharmaceutical industry first emerged as attempts to retain public confidence and to prevent legislative action; government involvement came later. This type of self-regulation, at

147

least in its original form, is close to what Boddewyn calls 'pure self-regulation'. The system of self-regulation in the financial services industry discussed later in the chapter is more like 'mandated self-regulation' which occurs when 'An industry is ordered or designated by the government to develop, use and enforce norms' (ibid., p. 34). As such, it is closer to private interest government which has been defined as 'an attempt to make associative, self-interested collective action contribute to the achievement of public policy objectives' (Streeck and Schmitter, 1985, p. 17).

The privatisation of public policy

The delegation of public policy functions to business interest associations is not confined to an interventionist state, but can also be associated with a state that is seeking to reduce the scope of its functions, so that public provision is replaced by state-sponsored private provision. Such a retreating state may be faced with situations where there are compelling reasons that lead it to assume new responsibilities, but these again may be discharged through self-regulation by business interests. The process as a whole may be characterised as the privatisation of public policy.

It must be emphasised that such a process of the privatisation of public policy cannot be adequately conceptualised through the revival of old liberal paradigms of the non-interventionist state. The privatised state does intervene in a wide range of areas of economic activity, even if it does so hesitantly, reluctantly and indirectly. (For a discussion, see Bonnett, 1985.) Such interventions can be said 'to entail a blurring of the line of division, crucial to liberal political theory, between the state and civil society' (Goldthorpe, 1984, p. 324). What is public and what is private is often unclear, and the problems of legitimacy and the 'public interest' which such a situation poses are often avoided rather than being confronted and resolved. The underlying confusion is intensified by the fact that one is talking about a variety of *ad hoc* arrangements operating in particular sectors of the economy with no common underlying rationale except an admission, rarely made explicit, that there are some activities that cannot adequately be performed either by the market or the state.

Thus, a number of examples of the assumption of public policy functions by business interest associations may be found in the area of foreign trade where international agreements sometimes prevent government from acting directly. As sectoral trade agreements based on quotas or other allocation mechanisms grew in the late 1970s and 1980s, so trade associations have acquired an important role in the negotiation of such agreements acting in effect, if not officially, on behalf of the British Government. For example, restrictions on the Japanese share of the British car market have been negotiated between the Society of Motor Manufacturers and Traders and its Japanese counterpart.

While business association involvement in public policy implementation has developed in response to specific needs and particular circumstances, creating a patchwork quilt of arrangements about which it is difficult to generalise, there was a strategic thrust to delegation under the Thatcher Government. 'The neo-liberal restoration of the *market* aims essentially at the liberation of *individual self-interests* from bureaucratic-regulatory constraints' (Streeck and Schmitter, 1985, p. 16). The Major Government places a greater emphasis on attempting to guarantee specified quality levels in the delivery of services to consumers. This can be achieved by government regulatory agencies as in the case of privatised utilities; through organisations operating within a legislative framework as in the case of financial services regulation; or through voluntary self-regulation operated by a trade association. As one moves away from the government regulatory agency model, the risk of 'capture' of the regulatory function by the regulated increases, and government's capability to monitor the performance of the regulatory function diminishes. Trade associations are unable to exercise any control over those firms not in membership. On the other hand, self-regulation does not cost public money, and may find it easier to win the cooperation of those being regulated without the use of large inspectorates.

In this chapter, four sets of examples of the discharge of public policy functions by business associations are discussed in order to amplify and explore the general points made in this introductory section. The private security industry offers an example of self-regulation by a trade association. The regulatory framework for the financial services industry, which has been under increasing criticism, is based on the concept of self-regulation, but with compulsory participation. The dairy sector offers an example of long-standing involvement by business associations in public policy where the stability of the arrangements is being disrupted by external pressure. Training policy represents a conscious attempt by government to 'give leadership of the training system to employers, where it belongs' (Cm. 540, p. 43).

Self-regulation in the security industry

The provision of security guarding services has been a growth sector in the UK economy. The British Security Industry Association (BSIA) has developed a system of self-regulation, backed up by an inspectorate and a disciplinary procedure. Membership of the Guard and Patrol Section of the BSIA is open to firms who can satisfy Association rules relating to financial probity, insurance, the good standing of the owners and employees of the company, security screening and training. Separate from, although linked to the BSIA through some of its members, is the Manned Services Inspectorate Board. This operates through an inspectorate which had three full-time staff in 1990, and is funded by members of the BSIA. Inspectors make regular, but not spot, checks on the branches of members. A minor fault leads to a re-inspection, but a major fault leads to an appearance before a disciplinary panel which can impose sanctions ranging from a written reprimand, through a fine, to removal from the roll of inspected companies. One company has been removed in recent years.

It is thought that less than one-quarter of the guards working in the industry are employed by BSIA member companies. This does not mean that all other companies are 'cowboys'. The BSIA is 'viewed by some as an exclusive club for the industry leaders with standards too rigorous to cover the whole of the industry' (*Financial Times*, 13 December 1990). One firm resigned from BSIA over the organisation's minimum wage regulations, complaining that BSIA was 'trying to run companies rather than advise them' (*Financial Times*, 13 December 1991). Inspection fees are unavoidably expensive, with the smallest payment to the BSIA and inspectorate in 1990 being £1,600, and the largest over £40,000 (Defence Committee, 1990, p. 103). The BSIA itself, while trying to strengthen its system of self-regulation, favours some form of statutory regulation. Its chief executive has commented, 'In the last year we have been saying we must have regulation and licensing from the government because we are not satisfied that the government is giving adequate support for self-regulation' (*Financial Times*, 13 December 1990). One issue that was extensively discussed when the BSIA appeared before the House of Commons Defence

Committee was the issue of access to the police national computer for screening purposes.

The Government has taken the view that it would prefer the industry to regulate itself because a licensing system would create a new quango which would work against its policies on free market competition. An alternative view, put forward by Bruce George, a Labour MP who has sponsored a number of Private Members' Bills on regulation of the industry with cross-party support, is that competition in the industry has been so intense that the standards of responsible firms have been driven down by operators who provided a poor service. The more general problems of trade association self-regulation revealed by this example include the problem of coverage, with membership being more attractive to firms competing on quality, rather than simply on price; the resistance of some firms to a system of regulation which they see as interference with their commercial autonomy; and the difficulty in providing trade associations with access to state resources, in this case the police national computer.

Statutory self-regulation of financial services

As the so-called 'Big Bang' of October 27, 1986 approached with its abolition of restrictive practices and traditional demarcation lines in the financial sector, there was a widespread recognition that the absence of adequate investor protection could adversely affect the international reputation of London as a financial centre, and hence its ability to attract and retain business. However, the Government was anxious to avoid regulation that would be expensive or hinder the development of new services in response to market opportunities. The Government therefore took the view 'that the regulation of the financial services industry should be no more than the minimum necessary to protect the investor' (Cmnd. 9432, 1985, p. 1). How could these potentially contradictory aims of investor protection and minimum regulation be reconciled?

The answer had been provided in outline for the Government in a report that it had commissioned, the 1984 Gower Report (*Review of Investor Protection*). This envisaged a system of self-regulation within a new statutory framework. In adopting the Gower framework as the basis for the 1986 Financial Services Act, the Government emphasised that self-regulation would be a more effective means of ensuring compliance.

Critics of the Government considered that any concern for effective investor protection was overridden by a sensitivity to the views of the financial sector. Seen from this perspective, the Government's proposals represented an attempt to perpetuate the privileges of the City in a new guise at the expense of effective investor protection. (Sir) Leon Brittan, the then Trade and Industry Secretary, explained that 'Whilst the bill builds on the tradition of self-regulation it ensures that self-regulation has the teeth and statutory backing it needs to be effective' (*Financial Times*, 20 December 1985). However, it is open to question whether the uneasy balance between self-regulation and statutory regulation in the Act is the correct one, given the need to meet the potentially contradictory objectives of investor protection and market freedom.

Under the 1986 Financial Services Act, considerable powers were devolved to a designated agency, the Securities and Investment Board (SIB) which is at the core of the regulatory system. The SIB is accountable to government (originally to the DTI, since 1992 to the Treasury), but is funded by the self-regulatory organisations (SROs) who in turn levy the firms for which they are responsible. The rule books of the SROs have to be approved by the SIB. Originally, there were five SROs: the Securities Association (shares and other securities); the Association of Future Brokers and Dealers (financial and commodity futures); the Investment Management Regulatory Organisation (IMRO) responsible for fund managers; the Life Assurance and Unit Trust Regulatory Organisation (LAUTRO), responsible for those engaged in marketing life insurance and unit trusts; and the Financial Intermediaries, Managers and Brokers Association (FIMBRA), the SRO with the largest membership covering advisers on life insurance and unit trust products. The Securities Association and the Association of Future Brokers and Dealers merged in 1991 to form the Securities and Futures Authority (SFA). There has been discussion about merging LAUTRO with FIMBRA to create a Personal Investment Authority which would also absorb about one third of the members of IMRO, a change about which they were not enthusiastic, throwing the whole scheme into question. IMRO and the SFA could merge to create a single regulator of 'professionals'.

The SIB stated that 'Close cooperation between SROs will be an essential part of the system' (Securities and Investments Board, 1985, p. 9). In practice, 'political in-fighting and jealousies ... have at times spilled over into bad feeling between regulators, though none has been bad-mannered enough to express it publicly' (*Financial Times*, 11

February 1992). There were also tensions between the SIB and the SROs in the winter of 1989–90 after the circulation of a document called *A Look Forward* which was interpreted by the SROs as paving the way for an extension of the SIB's powers, and a change in the delicate balance between regulators and practitioners. For its part, the SIB was concerned that the SROs were sometimes acting more as trade associations than regulators, putting the interests of practitioners before those of investors. The SIB is reported as commenting:

> Points of unease remain on both sides. The SROs differ a good deal in the strengths and weaknesses, in their working methods and their approaches to regulation. Their boards sometimes have to strike a difficult balance between investor interests and the health of the industry, and it is hardly surprising that, on occasion, SIB has felt that the balance might have been struck in another way. (*Financial Times*, 2 December 1989)

The tensions between regulation and representation were illustrated by a dispute at FIMBRA in 1989 when a substantial section of the membership staged a revolt against the leadership centred around a resolution to unseat the chairman. When the system of self-regulation was set up, the problem of practitioners rebelling against the practitioner-based regulators had not really been anticipated. The specific focus of the dispute was a proposal for a compulsory professional indemnity insurance scheme, although there were other discontents such as the cost of running FIMBRA. The insurance scheme was withdrawn, and FIMBRA reached an agreement with industry trade associations on measures to improve relations with its members. The claim that there was a lack of communication between FIMBRA and its members struck 'a ironic note in the City, where FIMBRA has frequently been seen as erring too far on the side of being a trade association rather than a regulator' (*Financial Times*, 30 November 1989). There have been continuing problems about weaknesses in FIMBRA's finances and in 1991 it was given a financial lifeline by a group of life assurance companies which rely on financial advisers to sell their products.

The Maxwell affair and self-regulation

In the first edition of this book, it was noted that the arrangements for financial self-regulation were vulnerable to a failure to cope with a major scandal. The Maxwell affair provided such a test, and the system of self-regulation did not come out of it particularly well. The Chancellor, Norman Lamont, stated that a SIB review of regulators' handling of the Maxwell affair showed grave deficiencies which were a matter of 'serious concern' to the government (*Financial Times*, 10 July 1992). Although stopping short of questioning whether self-regulation should be replaced by a regulatory body modelled on the American Securities and Exchange Commission, the Chancellor instructed the newly appointed SIB chairman, Andrew Large, to conduct a review of the existing system's shortcomings. Depending on how the task is interpreted, this could lead to the most fundamental reappraisal of UK financial regulation since the Gower Report. The chairman of the SFA noted, 'In a sense, we are in the Last-Chance Saloon for self-regulation' (*Financial Times*, 3 July 1992).

IMRO, which is responsible for regulating certain pension funds, delivered a strongly self-critical report to the SIB which the SIB nevertheless felt did not go far enough. For the first time, the SIB considered removing authorisation from one of its regulators. One of the problems with IMRO's approach to its regulatory task was that it was too mechanistic and bureaucratic. IMRO's report into its own affairs stated, 'Monitoring was applied over-literally as regards returns and visits. Procedures were generally followed conscientiously but for much of the time without flair and imagination' (*The Independent*, 10 July 1992). IMRO also seems to have been far too trusting, relying on the good faith and professionalism of those with whom it dealt. SIB commented that it believed 'that IMRO's monitoring failures in this case revealed a more general lack of market awareness and scepticism in dealing with information about transactions and in monitoring returns' (*Financial Times*, 10 July 1992).

There were also shortcomings in SIB's monitoring of IMRO. In 1989 SIB considered building a stronger monitoring unit to supervise the work of the SROs more closely, but did not pursue the idea. 'SIB has taken a carefully considered decision that the exercise of [the] supervisory role should not entail detailed tracking of a recognised body's handling of its relations with its members' (*Financial Times*, 10 July 1992). SIB relied on the way in which the SRO supervised its own work, backed by an annual assessment of each SRO's work, and day-to-day contact with the SRO on policy issues and individual cases. SIB recognised that it needed to reconsider the way in which it carried out its supervisory role in relation to the system of self-regulation.

It may be that the system of self-regulation is evolving towards an approach closer to the American model than the original concept of self-regulation. It has been argued that one of the few elements of self-regulation that remains is related to the fact that those who are regulated have to meet the costs of regulation. The 'growing intrusion of democratic politics into securities regulation' (Moran, 1990, p. 118) has been reinforced by the perception that there are inadequate mechanisms to deal with fraudulent practices in the financial services sector. Moran considers that there is a clear convergence with American arrangements, 'a shift to the kind of corporatism practised in America, with a negotiated corporatist franchise, and a conscious "attribution of public status" to private bodies' (Moran, 1990, p. 116). If one accepts this interpretation, then meso-corporatism survives in some very different settings: the financial services industry and the dairy sector.

The dairy sector

For more than fifty years, the production and pricing of milk and dairy products in Britain has been regulated by state-sponsored and private bodies operating within a general legal framework. This framework has sought to maintain a balance between the interests of the government, the farmer, the dairy processor and the final consumer, although the principal purpose of the arrangements was to remedy the imbalance between dairy farmers and an oligopolistic processing industry. There are a number of complexities in the private interest government arrangements in the dairy sector which cannot be dealt with in the limited space available here. (For a fuller comparative discussion of the industry see Grant, 1991c.) This discussion will focus on the relationship between the Milk Marketing Board (MMB) and the Diary Trade Federation (DTF) representing the independent dairy product manufacturers and retailers, a relationship conducted largely within a body known as the Joint Committee which is discussed further below.

The MMB is, in essence, a state-sponsored cooperative to which all farmers producing significant amounts of milk for sale are legally required to belong. The MMB buys all the milk that farmers can produce (although the level of production is governed by EC quotas). It then sells the milk to processors, either for retail sale in liquid form or for transformation into a variety of dairy products. This apparently straightforward division of responsibilities is complicated by the fact that the MMB's commercial arm, Dairy Crest, is itself the largest producer of dairy products: in particular, it dominates the butter and cheddar cheese markets.

Since 1954 there has been an official body established by statutory instrument known as the Joint Committee which is the negotiating forum for the MMB and the Diary Trade Federation (DTF). The membership of the DTF is conditional in that 'if in the opinion of the Minister that body has ceased to exist or has ceased to represent the views of buyers of milk, such last mentioned members shall be appointed by such other body or bodies as appear to the Minister to represent for the time being the views of the buyers of milk by retail' (Statutory instrument 1979/249). In other words, a particular organisation is designated by government, as the representative of a defined group of businesses, a classic characteristic of meso-level neo-corporatism.

The Joint Committee negotiates the prices of milk for manufacturing and, since the ending of government regulation of retail prices in 1984, for liquid milk. The DTF's involvement in a publicly-sanctioned negotiating arrangement has had implications for its internal organisation. Not only does it need substantial resources to maintain a large and highly-skilled staff, but these resources are provided through a highly unusual subscription collection arrangement. The problem of 'free riding' is minimised by the MMB imposing a levy on all first-hand buyers of milk which it then passes on to the DTF. This arrangement is obligatory rather than compulsory, as the relevant clause can always be struck out of the contract, but in practice it ensures that virtually all dairies contribute to the funds of the DTF.

The arrangements between the MMB and DTF represent an intricate and carefully-balanced political mechanism operating within a framework established by successive governments. However, in the 1980s, the system was coming under new strains. Surpluses of some products, e.g., cheddar cheese, led to prolonged arguments over how prices should be determined, given the MMB's wish to protect farmers, and the manufacturers' desire to secure their market. The imposition of quotas led to overcapacity in the industry and arguments about how this should be eliminated. However, perhaps the most significant underlying tension was resentment from the independent dairy companies about what they saw as unfair competition from Dairy Crest. A report commissioned by the Ministry of Agriculture (the Touche Ross report) concluded that Dairy Crest had performed less well than an independent company would be expected to and that its strategy had been influenced by the interests of the milk producers which MMB represents. The report cleared the MMB of charges that it has used Dairy Crest directly to assist its negotiating position with independent dairies, but argued that the private companies had been weakened in Joint Committee negotiations over prices by the fact that Dairy Crest had not been represented on their side.

Even the most carefully constructed formula for dealing with commercial issues which involves a complex mixture of the public and the private may be disturbed by external factors which are beyond the direct control of the participants. At the beginning of the 1990s, the arrangements in the dairy sector came under a number of pressures for fundamental change, leading to proposals given the shorthand title of 'New World'. The MMB was one statutory monopoly that had survived Mrs Thatcher's period in office, but the agriculture minister, John Gummer, took the view that the 'present milk marketing arrangements were not in the best interests of consumers or producers and did nothing to help the industry meet the challenge of the single market' (*Financial Times*, 1 August 1990). A more important source of pressure for change came, however, from the European Commission. The Commission stated in a reasoned opinion that the MMB does not hold the statutory right to buy and sell low fat milk. This was a commodity unheard of when the MMB was established in 1933, but was expected to account for 50 per cent of liquid milk sales by 1994. The Commission referred the issue to the European Court of Justice where it was expected to win. This would mean the end of the present milk marketing system. Although John Gummer rejected the Commission's reasoned opinion on the matter, he made it clear that this was to give the MMB's chance to negotiate reforms with the DTF.

The proposed reforms have two main aspects. Over a period of some years, the MMB would be transformed into a voluntary cooperative. Although farmers could, for example, negotiate direct with supermarkets to supply milk, it is expected that 80 per cent of farmers would stay within the scheme. This forecast reflects the conservative instincts of farmers, and the lack of protection even quite large-scale farmers would have outside the cooperative. Under the new scheme, the MMB would still purchase all milk, pool milk returns, and keep its processing company. The processors named this voluntary monopoly the 'son of milk board'. They would prefer a number of voluntary cooperatives, with the MMB retaining no more than twenty-five per cent of the market. They would also like Dairy Crest to be floated on the stock market.

The other aspect of the reforms, which was supposed to be introduced from September 1992, is a change in the way in which milk for manufacturing is sold. Liquid milk, which is the premium market, would still have been sold separately. Under the old arrangements for selling milk for manufacturing, the price paid by the processor depended on the use to which the milk was to be put. There were eighteen price bands, with butter in 1990/91 being the cheapest at 16.4p per litre, compared with 19.1p for chocolate crumb (and 23.9p for the liquid market). The curious nature of these arrangements can be illustrated by considering a mechanism whereby the same quality of steel received a higher price if it was to be used for a Jaguar rather a Metro (with, of course, surplus cars being sold into intervention). Pricing milk for butter and skimmed milk powder was subject to the CATFI (common approach to financial information) system which guaranteed a return on capital, though the actual percentage was subject to joint negotiation, and compensated processors for keeping factories available to cope with seasonal production peaks. 'Simplified, that means it is a profitable to run a butter factory at half capacity as it is to produce yogurt at maximum efficiency' (*Farmers Weekly*, 24 January 1992).

Negotiations to end these arrangements between the MMB and the DTF were protracted, but were finally ended when the DTF gave way on its insistence on a guarantee to existing customers of 75 per cent of their milk supply when the MMB stated that unless the reforms were implemented the offer of a £70 million rationalisation subsidy from the MMB would be withdrawn (*Farmers Weekly*, 3 July 1992). Under the new system, price categories were to be based on the level of service required rather than the end use of the milk. Four types of contract were to be offered differing in level of service and security of supply, and there would also have been a spot market. However, the first two rounds of a price-balancing exercise conducted in August 1992 were so imbalanced that it was impossible to clear the market of milk. The higher the price, the more contracts were oversubscribed, demand exceeding supply by 20 per cent in the case of the top price band. This paradoxical outcome can be explained by the fact that the UK is not self-sufficient in milk with production restricted by quotas, and by dairy companies wanting to reduce their unit costs, although there were also allegations of overbidding by some dairy companies because they realised that they would have to pay substantially more for their milk under the new system (*Farmers Weekly*, 28 August 1992). Whatever the explanation, the immediate outcome was that end-use pricing remained in place, with arbitration between the MMB and DTF likely to be necessary to maintain an orderly milk market.

Securing change has thus been very difficult, even in the manufacturing milk market, where the processors attached considerable importance to continuity of supply. The MMB seems likely to remain as the dominant supplier of milk, and will continue to function as both a participant in the industry and its regulator. Although ownership of Dairy Crest will be transferred to farmers, it will remain intact. Such change as has been secured is the result of pressure from the European Commission, rather than from a British Government which has emphasised privatisation and deregulation. Statutorily-based private interest government arrangements involving suppliers and producers can be very resistant to change.

Training policy

In the introduction to this chapter, it was pointed out that policy functions formerly performed by government or by quasi-governmental bodies could be transferred to business interest associations by a retreating state seeking to reduce government responsibilities. Simple abolition may not be an option because there may be a need to supply some form of collective provision of a particular function or, at a minimum, a mechanism whereby subsidies can be transferred to firms.

Training policy in the 1980s offers a good example of public policy functions being transferred to private interest governments designed to be responsive to business. When the Thatcher Government came into office, the implementation of training policy was very much influenced by the tripartite models favoured in the 1970s. The body supervising training policy, the Manpower Services Commission (MSC), had a government-appointed chairman and representatives from the CBI, TUC, local authorities and educational interests. At the sectoral level, there was a series of statutory training boards with representatives from the employers and the unions in the particular industry (nominally appointed by the responsible minister as individuals). Employer attitudes towards these boards were mixed. In some industries they were regarded as a superfluous, bureaucratic addition to training work already being done at the level of the firm. In other industries, there was concern that training activity by individual firms would not meet the needs of the industry as a whole.

Although the process of change took most of the decade to complete, what had emerged by the beginning of the 1990s was the replacement of tripartism by a system based on a mixture of greater ministerial control over the strategic direction of training policy combined with a devolution of responsibility to local bodies with a strong employer influence. The first bodies to go were the statutory training boards. Sixteen boards were dissolved under the 1982 Industrial Training Act and were replaced by non-statutory training organisations (NSTOs). These were employers' associations, or special 'training councils' set up by employers' associations, or bodies set up by groups of employers' associations to coordinate their training activities. In most industries one statutory training board was replaced by a number of NSTOs. (For a discussion of examples, see Rainbird and Grant, 1985.) Although the Government expressed the hope that there would be opportunities for the trade unions to take part in the new arrangements, in practice their participation was much more limited than in the statutory boards.

One of the main shortcomings of the NSTOs was that, in accordance with the traditions of British employers' associations, they were generally reluctant to exert an influence over their member companies. The general philosophy accepted by NSTOs was that training was most appropriately done at the level of the firm, and that their role was to act as a facilitator and perhaps as a catalyst. This limited conception of their scope of action was particularly apparent in two important areas. First, most of the NSTOs appeared reluctant to develop codes of conduct for their members. Second, when the funds allocated to them by the MSC for particular training programmes exceeded the amount requested by member firms, they did not discriminate between their member firms on the basis of any conception of merit. The funds were shared out on the basis of some simple empirical formula such as 'first come, first served', or of a sum being made available proportionate to the amount originally requested. Such behaviour is perfectly consistent with the self-image of the associations as member benefit associations rather than agents of public policy. A number of associations stressed in discussions that they saw the provision of training grants and other training aids as an extension of their traditional range of services to members, rather than being part of some major new development in associative activity.

One might therefore ask whether the associations really were discharging public policy functions, or whether they were simply providing government-funded selective benefits to their members. In a strategic political sense, there is no doubt that the NSTOs were used by the Government as a smokescreen to defend itself against charges that it was falling back on a pure market solution. Such a position would be difficult to defend when most training experts agreed that training efforts by firms, even if they met the immediate needs of that firm, would be unlikely to meet the long run needs of the nation as a whole for a supply of highly-trained labour. However, in a deeper sense, the NSTOs were an attempt by the Thatcher Government to cope with the contradiction between its attachment to market ideology, and the fact that the application of such a policy in the area of training would undoubtedly lead to shortages of skilled labour or, perhaps even more important, a deterioration in the rate of acquisition of new skills. Whatever the rationale for their creation, they were not a conspicuous success as mechanisms for the implementation of training policy at the sectoral level. A study by the Institute of Manpower Studies graded each organisation according to its effectiveness in ensuring an adequate supply of properly trained and competent manpower in its particular industry. It was found that of the 102 designated NSTOs, only fifty-six were considered 'effective' (*Financial Times*, 5 March 1988).

As far as the Manpower Services Commission, renamed the Training Commission, was concerned, the tripartite character of its operations declined in the 1980s, and it was increasingly used as an arm of central government policy. TUC opposition to the introduction of Employment Training gave the Government the opportunity to abolish the Training Commission and to transform it into a Training Agency within the Department of Employment, later the department's Training, Enterprise and Employment Division (TEED). All but two of the remaining statutory training boards were also abolished at the end of the decade and replaced by NSTOs.

The Government's proposals for a new system of training were set out in its 1988 White Paper, *Employment for the 1990s*. The White Paper led to the establishment of a new system of training and enterprise councils (TECs) in England and Wales (local enterprise companies in Scotland) which were intended to place '"ownership" of the training and enterprise system where it belongs — with employers'

(Cm. 540, p. 40). The difficulty with this approach was that a succession of studies had shown that employers were unwilling to train to the level and extent required by an advanced internationally-competitive economy. For example, a study by Coopers and Lybrand for the Manpower Services Commission found that employers attached a low importance to training; it was seen as an overhead rather than an investment; and that training was not seen as an important contributor to competitiveness. The report concluded, 'if Britain's performance on training is to be improved ... this can only be achieved by a major change in employer attitudes to training' (Coopers and Lybrand, 1985, p. 5). Indeed, the white paper recognised that skill shortages were a result of employers taking a short-term view in the recession of the early 1980s and cutting back on training (Cm. 540, p. 28). Even so, it was insisted that 'At least two-thirds of TEC members should be employers at top management level drawn from the private sector.'

Apart from the limitations of an employer based system, the TECs were launched in 1991 as the economy was slipping into recession. Public expenditure constraints have prevented the TECs from delivering all that was expected of them. The TECs have complained of excessive monitoring of their activities from government, although some accountability for the use of public funds amounting to over £2 billion a year is unavoidable. A Department of Employment internal review concluded that relations between the government and the TECs were unsustainable without further reform (*Financial Times*, 9 October 1991). The permanent secretary of the Department of Employment was reported in 1992 as describing TECs as 'fragile' and that the enthusiasm of the people who run them had been 'dented' (*The Independent*, 2 June 1992). The new CBI director-general, Howard Davies, expressed deep anxieties in the business community over 'whether the government really sees training and enterprise councils as a long-term investment in the workforce, or as a way of administering quasi-benefit programmes' (*Financial Times*, 1 July 1992). Although there were some hopes that the new Employment Secretary, Gillian Shephard, might be able to develop a better dialogue with the TECs, the fundamental problems of public expenditure restraints, and the divisions and variations in quality between the eighty-two TECs, remained unresolved.

Training has often been seen as a functional area of policy in which neo-corporatist policies might be appropriate, given the need for cooperation between employers and labour, and the requirement for the injection of government funds. A limited consensus was attainable at the sectoral level, but 'this did not translate either to the level of the firm or the level of trans-sectoral needs. The meso-level focus of the policy tended to entrench rather than overcome sectoral interests' (Vickerstaff, 1985, p. 62). The replacement of this approach by an uneasy alliance of business and government has not, however, worked well either, even if one makes allowance for the difficult circumstances in which it was introduced. Reliance on the market mechanism to provide training is generally agreed to be unlikely to work; neo-corporatist arrangements have been tried and have not worked well; but the new 'company state' model of TECs has inherent tensions, and at times has seemed in danger of collapse. TEED is much criticised for its bureaucratic approach, so handing policy back to the state is not an attractive option. Given that training policy has experienced considerable institutional instability over the last thirty years, the least bad solution might be to build on the TEC structure by providing them with more funds through levying companies that do not train. This has always been a controversial proposal, but a survey in 1992 found it supported by 36.7 per cent of the private sector executives questioned (*Financial Times*, 25 March 1992). Whatever the eventual outcome, the case of training points to some of the difficulties of using private interest governments for the implementation of public policy.

Models of business involvement in public policy implementation

Lehmbruch (1984, pp. 61–2) make a useful distinction between 'corporatist concertation' and 'sectoral corporatism' which can be used as a basis for developing models of business involvement in the implementation of public policy. 'Corporatist concertation', as discussed by Lehmbruch, involves a plurality of organisations, and the coordination of their actions with government in relation to the requirements of the national economy. Two particular forms of concertation were observed in this chapter, providing a basis for the subdivision of the category. One is 'commercial' concertation where normal market operations are replaced by state setting of key prices, state sponsorship of organisations, and state provision of a forum for reconciling differences of interest. The arrangements in the dairy sector offer a good example.

The other case might be termed 'allocative' concertation where government sets up a tripartite body to supervise and executive public policy within a defined area, and to provide desired 'goods' or prevent unwanted 'bads'. Examples of the former can be found in the MSC and the statutory training boards, and of the latter in the Health and Safety Commission. Business takes part in such arrangements, if only to counterbalance the influence of the unions. However, these traditional forms of concertation were eroded under the Thatcher Government with its attachment to the privatisation of public policy.

The other model, which has been increasing in importance in Britain in the 1980s, is 'sectoral corporatism', defined by Lehmbruch in terms of a privileged access to government of single organised interests limited to specific sectors of the economy. The reconciliation of potentially opposed interests is supplanted by advantageous treaties with particular interests. The arrangements made by the Thatcher Government for self-regulation of the financial services sector fit into this definition very well. Financial services businesses generally prefer limited forms of regulation embodied in the SROs. These are seen as an acceptable alternative to more direct and demanding forms of intervention. However, the very weakness which makes such arrangements acceptable makes them less useful as forms for involving business in the formulation and implementation of public policy. When one privatises public policy, one may end up with something that is neither public nor policy.

None of the models for the private implementation of public policy discussed in this chapter works particularly well, especially when viewed from the perspective of the citizen or consumer. The arrangements in the dairy sector are often seen as a producers' cartel which have forced up milk prices above continental European levels and discouraged product innovation. Regulation in the financial services sector could be seen as too producer-friendly by consumers. Many of the fundamental deficiencies of training provision remain unresolved. One must not expect too much of models of associative action, yet there clearly is a sphere of activity which cannot readily be assigned either to the market or the state (but which is, of course, much larger than that covered by business associations, including, for example, charities). This third sphere of activity, even if confined to the more limited area of the involvement of business interests, lacks coherence and consistency, reflecting the varying origins and purposes of the different arrangements, and the absence of any legitimising philosophy of private interest government. In contrast, the market and the state continue to provide robust paradigms which shape much political thought and practice. As Willmott reminds us (1985, p. 65), 'in the context of advanced capitalist societies, at least, the market and the state may well continue to be the dominant institutions'.

9 Business Interests and the European Community

One of the difficulties with the literature on Britain's membership of the European Community is that much of it is written by academics who are not only favourably disposed to the process of European integration, but if possible would like to see it accelerated. As a consequence, there is a tendency to see the integration process as an inevitable one in which the nation-state is displaced by the Community on the one hand, and new forms of regional government on the other. The outcome of the Danish referendum on the Maastricht treaty was a healthy corrective to those who see the nation-state as an outdated political formation, but many of the theoretical perspectives on European integration impel analysts in a direction which tends to lead to federalist conclusions. Implicit neo-functionalist perspectives emphasise the role of interest groups as catalysts in the integration process. Hence, there is sometimes a tendency to exaggerate the extent to which interest group activity has been 'Europeanised', and to downplay the continuing importance of attempts to influence the Community through national channels of access.

Some recent analyses have emphasised the impact that the Single European Act has had on interest group organisation at the Community level. This has led to some renewed interest in corporatist models of relationships between interest groups and institutions at the EC level (Greenwood and Ronit, 1991). The question of the relative value of different models of the decision-making process will be returned to in the concluding section of this chapter, although it should be noted that much of the debate in this area hinges on ultimately unrewarding definitional problems. Viewed as events without any theoretical presuppositions intervening, the Single European Act, and the internal market project were important developments, although the momentum behind them was checked by the difficulties encountered in the ratification of the Maastricht treaty. Although the Single European Act gave the Community new areas of competence in, for example, environmental policy and technology policy, and extended the use of qualified majority voting, the member states remain important decision-makers, not least because they are largely responsible for the implementation and enforcement of policy. Groups can seek to achieve at least some of their aims by influencing the national stance taken in the Council of Ministers, or by shaping the way in which Community directives are implemented in practice at member state level.

Much recent research on interest groups has emphasised the way in which the state shapes patterns of interest group activity. As G. Wilson notes (1990, p. 105):

> States . . . within limits create and shape both interest groups and interest group systems. . . . Even when states do not, or cannot act consciously to shape interest group systems, however, the character of the state still exerts a profound influence on the nature of the interest group system.

Hence, it is important to consider just what sort of organism the EC is. It is clearly more than just another international organisation. 'The Community is based on a treaty which is more than a conventional interstate treaty. It is a constitutive treaty which, in the act of creating a new body politic, alters the constitutions of partners to it' (Forsyth, 1981, p. 184). Nevertheless, it falls short of being a state. It does not meet the traditional criterion of control of the legitimate means of coercion within a given territory. After reviewing various alternatives, Schmitter concludes (1991, p. 29) 'that the eventual European Community will be a unique form of political domination.' Whatever eventual form the Community takes, it does have the ability to take authoritative decisions, whereas an international organisation has to obtain specific assent from its members to any new general binding rule. Against that, the EC's own means of implementation and enforcement are limited and heavily reliant on the member states. In its current form, it may be seen as a confederation or union of states. Forsyth notes (1981, p. 185) that 'the Community institution which has held the final power of legislative decision has been — in the more usual confederal fashion — the Council of Ministers, in which are gathered the representatives of the member states.'

As a quasi-state, the European Community has given more systematic attention to the role of interest groups in the policy process than most long-established nation-states. There are a number of reasons for this orientation. First, because the European Community is not, as is commonly supposed, a huge bureaucracy, but a relatively small group of high-level administrators (under four thousand) trying to cope with a wide range of subjects, the expertise that can be provided by interest groups can help to move forward a policy process which can easily become overwhelmed by the volume of work that has to be done. Second, the Community has encouraged the formation of EC-wide organisations, in part because they mean that the Commission does not have to deal with twelve national viewpoints, but also because they may adopt a European perspective which will help to facilitate the integration process. Third, the Commission has been strongly influenced by a continental European doctrine of social partnership between business and labour which has its intellectual origins in Catholic social thought, as taken up by the postwar Christian Democratic parties, but which also appeals to social democrats. This long-standing interest in social partnership was reinforced by the Single European Act which provides in what became Article 118b of the revised treaty, 'The Commission shall endeavour to develop the dialogue between management and labour at European level which could, if the two sides consider it desirable, lead to relations based on agreement.'

In some respects, this receptiveness to interest organisations leads to a lobbying atmosphere which is more similar to Washington than that to be found in London. It is no accident that there are now at least twenty US law firms operating in Brussels. The main difference is that there is no central focus of power equivalent to the White House. There are, however, a range of points of access into the decision-making process, particularly since the European Parliament has become more important, while Commission officials are accessible to an extent that is not yet true of British civil servants. There are also considerable opportunities for informal contacts over a drink or a meal. One respondent in Brussels referred to the area in which Community offices and most lobbying organisations are located as 'the village', and although geographical proximity has been temporarily disrupted by the removal of Commission staff from the Berlaymont, the analogy is an appropriate one. One lobbyist emphasised the fact that every significant institution she needed to contact (with the exception of European Parliament sessions at Strasbourg) was within walking distance of her office.

One other feature of the decision-making process in Brussels requires mention. Long periods of inactivity about a draft directive will be followed by a sudden burst of activity. All this may mean is that a Commission official has found time in his busy schedule to turn his or her attention to a particular matter. The intermittent and somewhat unpredictable character of decision-making has two consequences for pressure group activity. First, it means that firms and organisations need to devote part of their activity to maintaining a database tracking what is happening in the decision-making process. Second, it does mean that a presence of some kind in Brussels is increasingly a necessary condition for any firm or business interest wishing to make an effective input into the decision-making process. Nevertheless, there are still large firms and interest organisations in Britain which are not effectively organised to deal with EC questions. A clearing bank corporate affairs manager commented in interview, 'There is a real EC dimension and we are aware of EC directives, but we have done no lobbying so far. We tend to leave lobbying to the Bank of England and the British Bankers Association.'

How business seeks to influence the EC

Operating at the national level

An important part of any firm or business interest association's strategy will be using its well-established contacts at the national level. The firm or association can approach the ministry it normally deals with in the UK, and seek to persuade the national government to pursue the course of action favoured by business in the Council of Ministers. For example, in 1990 the Vegetable Protein Association (VPA) became concerned about a Commission proposal for a regulation on compositional requirements for meat products. The VPA 'lobbied MAFF with the effect that the UK Government has opposed this proposal at EC Commission Working Group level' (Food and Drink Federation Annual Report 1990, p. 26). The continuing significance of national-level activity by business associations is underlined by the fact that even one of the most effective EC-level business federations, that representing the chemical industry, has a much smaller income than its federations in member states such as Germany.

There are serious risks in such an approach, particularly since the extended use of qualified majority voting. Mazey and Richardson note (1992, p. 94), 'the institutional reforms contained in the Single European Act . . . have significantly reduced the policy-making influence of the

British government in key policy sectors, thereby increasing the need for interest group coalition building at the EC level.' Even where the decision is not taken by qualified majority voting, an industry's position may be sacrificed as part of the complex and exhausting rounds of bargaining which produce decisions in the Council of Min-isters. One respondent referred to the way in which she felt pressure had been put on certain UK snack foods manufacturers as a means of persuading the UK government to give way on the issue of cyclamates (artificial sweetening agents). This respondent nevertheless emphasised the extent to which she thought that the effectiveness of the civil ser-vice approach to EC issues had improved since the Single European Act came into effect, although quite complicated and important issues were being handled at principal level.

The national level is also important because, with a few exceptions in such areas as agricultural policy, trade policy and competition policy, Community directives are implemented and enforced by the national governments and the member states. It should be noted that Community standards may be exceeded by member states, provided that the modification is compatible with the treaties, something which national interest organisations monitor and seek to influence. The precise way in which directives are translated into national legislation, and the mechanisms for their implementation and enforcement, can also be the subject of intensive lobbying by national interest organisations.

The CBI office in Brussels

The continuing importance of the activities of national-level represent-ative organisations is shown by the presence of a CBI office in Brussels. The CBI has maintained an office in Brussels since Britain joined the EC. In the early 1990s, this cost nearly half a million pounds a year to operate, suggesting that the CBI places a considerable value on having a continuous presence in Brussels.

The Brussels offices fulfills a number of roles. First, it seeks to nurture the CBI's contacts in the Commission and the European Parliament so that CBI committees and individual members can be advised on lobbying in Brussels. Second, on some occasions it represents the CBI and its members directly. This may be because no expert from Britain is available in time; or because there is expertise in the office in the subject; or because the Brussels office specialises in understanding how decisions are made by the EC. About 20 per cent of CBI representations to EC institutions are made by the Brussels office, the other 80 per cent being covered by experts from the London office or member companies. Third, the Brussels office provides an important link between the CBI and the Union of Industrial and Employers' Confederations of Europe (UNICE), monitoring and supporting UNICE's activities. Fourth, it provides advice to members on their own lobbying activities at the EC level, 'opening doors' so that CBI members have access to the relevant decision makers at the time that it is needed.

In 1991, the CBI expanded the functions of its Brussels office by forming the British Business Bureau to help sector associations in their Brussels activities. By 1992, there were nine trade associations participating in, and funding, the work of the Business Bureau, enabling the CBI to supplement the additional member of staff taken on to run the Bureau with an assistant. As well as helping the sectoral associations to make the best use of their EC-level associations, the Business Bureau offers its clients three levels of service: information gathering; representation; or a combined service. Quite a number of the associations simply want an information service, and are content to do their own representational work if they have a strong EC-level federation. The Business Bureau can, however, ensure that the views of clients are taken into account at all stages of the decision-making process, and not just the final stage. It thus enables sectoral associations to enhance their representational effectiveness at the EC level.

The activities of individual firms

Individual firms may have their own particular interests to pursue at the EC level (e.g., competition policy issues) and they may also consider that EC-level associations are insufficiently effective. In the consumer electronics industry, 'Government–industry relations have been dominated by bilateral links between major firms and national governments and the EEC, with trade associations playing a relatively minor role, largely as "cover" for the self-interest of the dominant European producers, Philips and Thomson' (Cawson *et al.*, 1990. p. 219). Hence, there is considerable and increasing interest in the government relations divisions of firms having their own presence in Brussels which can both undertake lobbying on the firm's behalf, and also monitor and participate in the activities of EC-level associations. In the case of Germany, all three leading chemical companies, who first appointed EC-level coordinators in 1986, have strengthened their EC-level government relations activities at the beginning of the 1990s. The coordinators originally all operated from their headquarters offices, but BASF have now opened an office in Brussels. This is a significant development in a country which has always emphasised working through associations rather than a company-led approach.

There are some twenty-five British firms with government affairs representatives in Brussels organised into an informal grouping by the Brussels office of the CBI. American firms are also much in evidence. They sometimes face special problems because of conflicts between the US and EC over issues such as GATT on which European subsidiaries may have a different perspective from American subsidiaries. There are also a growing number of representatives of Japanese firms. However, they are less engaged in lobbying than in scrutinising the information produced by the EC and funnelling key documents back to their companies (see *Business Week*, 3 June 1991, p. 22).

A variety of approaches are used by British firms in organising their EC-level operations. A privatised utility had four members of staff working on EC questions, but had no presence in Brussels, although it was debating the issue of opening an office there. There have been cases of companies pulling out of Brussels, or substantially reducing their presence there; maintaining an effective presence is expensive. An American financial services company had had only one person dealing with EC affairs in London until they moved to Brussels in 1988 where they have a vice-president in charge of the office with two executives and an information officer in support, as well as a personal assistant in London liaising with the business units. A consumer goods company which had recently established a government relations function in 1992 had in its Brussels office a senior executive, an assistant (spending forty per cent of his time on environmental questions) and a trainee.

The functions performed by EC-level government relations offices vary from company to company in accordance with its perceived priorities, and within a company over time. For example, the Brussels office may acquire a special briefing and coordinating function if a senior executive of the company becomes president of an EC-level association. Such special circumstances aside, three broad functions performed by company offices in Brussels may be distinguished, although not all these functions are carried out by every office.

First, an important task of all Brussels offices is to provide relevant information and intelligence within the company. One respondent stressed that this involved interpreting developments to prevent misunderstandings by line managers not familiar with the Community's decision-making processes. 'Part of our function is to guard against Euro hype in the company, an exaggerated reaction to events.' An American company that was interviewed compared the role of its Brussels office to that of an embassy of the company to the EC. Small memos on developments at the EC level are distributed within the company, and as much time is spent talking to people within the company as to the Commission. However, the function was not simply one of advising line managers on current developments at Community level. It was emphasised that 'Our ultimate business is one of ideas. We must anticipate trends and developments.' This first function of providing information and helping to develop company policy in response to Community developments is closely related to, but distinct from, what was described by a government relations manager of a food processing company as 'an input into company planning to utilise to the full what the Community has to offer.' He explained:

Is the company utilising what the Community has to offer. Are we benefitting from grants and schemes? Are we using to the maximum what the Community says about food law to break down borders between member states because we want to move goods about. We can utilise European law against member states.

A third function is that of representing company interests with Community institutions, or ensuring that they are represented. One company's Brussels offices defined its role in this respect as 'a liaison office between business units and EC officials.' Sometimes if the company was not happy with the way in which Community policy was developing, it might be necessary to pursue the Council route at an early stage supplemented by lobbying in the twelve national capitals as a last resort. As the European Parliament has become more important, this aspect of company's work has increased. Some respondents felt that they were still not giving enough attention to the European Parliament.

The amount of time that Commission officials can spend on seeing representatives from individual companies is necessarily limited, and much representative work will be done through European-level associations. It is easier to participate in their work from a Brussels base, but apart from the variable quality of such associations, there may be reluctance by national subsidiaries to surrender control of their participation in EC-level trade association work via their national associations.

Indeed, it would be a mistake to take too much away from the national managements, although avoiding duplication of efforts is important. One respondent commented:

> EC relations involve national managements because of the Council of Ministers and the European Parliament. It is not just a matter of sitting here in Brussels, I also have a strong relationship with the national managements. It is a question of ensuring that they are doing as much trade association work as they ought to be doing.

'One of the most striking developments since the mid–1980s has been the explosion in the number of professional lobbyists, financial consultants and law firms operating in Brussels' (Mazey and Richardson, 1992, p. 95). Firms vary in the extent to which they use the services of the various consultancy firms that are available in Brussels. One respondent commented, 'We do use consultants for monitoring, for leg work with the Commission — to phone up and find out what is going on, it is cheaper than us doing it ourselves; we also use them for projects on particular issues.' Another firm emphasised the value of the outside view brought in by consultants, although they used them as expert advisers, not to do lobbying. They were also useful for specific projects for which the staff did not have sufficient time, and where the con-sultants might bring in specific expertise.

Government relations managers in Brussels perform a variety of roles, the mix varying from company to company. Most of them probably spend a minority of their time on lobbying. One commented, 'I get asked a lot of questions from people in the company, it is almost consultancy work.' Another respondent commented, 'There's a fairly constant aspect of keeping lines of communication open to operating units so that they pick up what we come across on the Brussels scene, and we pick up their pieces from a business point of view.' Government affairs managers have to justify their value within the company to line managers and the board. They will also be expected to pursue the company's own particular interests, and to supplement the activities of the various EC-level interest associations.

Organisations representing general business interests

There are a number of organisations operating at the EC level which seek to represent cross-sectoral business interests, but there are three rather different organisations which have a special importance: UNICE; the European Round Table; and the EC Committee of the American Chamber of Commerce. UNICE is a confederation of the equivalents of the CBI in the EC and EFTA countries plus a few other countries such as Turkey, although unlike the CBI it does not represent the service sector. The president is always drawn from one of the EC member states.

UNICE has been perceived in the past as a less than fully effective organisation. It suffered in the general atmosphere of the 'Eurosclerosis' period of the late 1970s and early 1980s when Europe was still suffering the impact of the two oil shocks, and the Community, bogged down in enlargement negotiations, seemed to have lost momentum and a sense of direction. It has been revitalised since 1985 under a new director-general, Zygmunt Tyskiewicz. In 1989 UNICE decided to restructure itself over a two year period in response to the changes in European decision-making resulting from the Single European Act. UNICE decided to create an Advisory and Support Group (USAG) made up of companies which was set up in June 1990. This was seen as having the benefits of building closer links between UNICE and companies (USAG membership is confined to multinationals), and of providing a source of additional finance. With membership set at one million Belgian francs a year (approximately £20,000), there were twenty-one members by 1992. UNICE's staff has been expanded to thirty-five, of whom twenty are senior staff.

Although UNICE is a stronger organisation than it was a decade ago, it cannot be regarded as a potential social partner because it does not have a mandate to negotiate agreements which would be binding on its membership, let alone on those its members represent. Viewed as a lobbying organisation, it still has difficulty in effectively covering all the 'horizontal' areas of interest which concern business in general. For example, company government relations divisions give a high priority to environmental issues, but UNICE was rather belated in responding to the heightened interest in environmental matters. For many years, environmental issues was covered by someone who was also responsible for transport and small firms, and it was only in 1992 that this shortcoming was remedied. UNICE also faces the more general problem of reconciling the divergent interests of the organisations representing the member states, with Britain taking a different position on some social issues from some other member states. A government relations manager of a company which had not joined USAG commented:

UNICE was felt to be useless, a federation of federations, a lowest common denominator. It was too slow to respond to events. To give UNICE credit, competition has revolutionised UNICE. It has admitted a series of members and speeded up decision-making. It can still be hamstrung by national differences — the social dialogue differences between Britain and the rest.

A different approach to the representation of business interests is embodied in the European Round Table. Rather than seeking to represent a wide range of interests on a considerable number of issues, it brings together the chief executives of a selected group of large firms to focus on a limited number of key issues. Set up in 1983 on the lines of the US Business Round Table, it organises around forty-five chief executives with membership by invitation only, with the membership list reading like 'a Who's Who of European industry' (Danton de Rouffignac, 1991, p. 146). Although enjoying a combined turnover of ECU 500 billion (£350 billion), the firms involved are not necessarily the largest in Europe, as not all firms who might have been eligible wanted to take part, and others which are not particularly large by European standards have been included to extend coverage to peripheral member states such as the Republic of Ireland. Plenary sessions are held every six months, and in between the plenaries the work is done by what one respondent described as a 'second eleven' known as associates. There is a steering committee of five and a secretariat is maintained in Brussels. The Round Table has produced a number of influential reports, for example on 'Missing Links' in Europe's transport network.

'The personal involvement of the chairmen and chief executives of Europe's major companies lends considerable credibility to the group which, although it claims to speak only for the interests of its members, represents a uniquely informed body of opinion that the Commission cannot ignore' (Danton de Rouffignac, 1991, p. 148). There are meetings twice a year between Commission president Delors, perhaps five to seven commissioners, and a roughly similar number of members of the Round Table. It has also enjoyed access to heads of government, and is credited with giving a considerable impetus to the internal market programme.

The Round Table has made an impact on important issues facing the EC, but cannot provide the comprehensive coverage offered by UNICE, although some industrialists consider that UNICE should be more selective in its choice of priorities. Although a number of British firms are members, one respondent commented, 'British industry is sceptical of it, it sees it as industrialists playing politics.' One remaining issue for the Round Table is whether it should remain as a group of modest-size representative of the member states, or aim for a couple of hundred members like its US equivalent. There are inherent tensions within any group of European chairman, for example, over takeovers which put members in competition with each other. One respondent suggested that as market barriers come down, and companies lose their hegemony in a particular market, these tensions would increase.

Comparing UNICE and the Round Table, a senior Commission official commented:

> One cannot rely on UNICE to deliver a reliable opinion. The Round Table does more in depth studies, it has influenced Commission proposals. The Round Table offers more solid advice than UNICE. It is smaller, it is able to put forward a consensus view.

A more generous perspective would be that the different roles of UNICE and the Round Table mean that they complement and stimulate each other. One respondent commented, 'Competition has produced better representation by both groups, although they are also envious of Amcham [the EC Committee of the American Chamber of Commerce] which has an even quicker response rate.'

The EC Committee of the American Chamber of Commerce developed originally from the committee structure of the American Chamber of Commerce in Belgium. With the onset of the idea of an internal market, the EC Committee was reorganised in 1985 to better represent the views of its members. Membership has trebled in size from 46 in 1985 to 130 in 1992. Among the members are such well known companies as AT&T, Colgate-Palmolive, Exxon, Ford, General Electric, IBM, Mobil, Texas Instruments and Time-Warner. Members pay an annual subscription of BF290,000 in 1992 (nearly £6,000) providing an annual income (including other sources) of 43.6 million Belgian francs (over three quarters of a million pounds). There was a secretariat of fourteen, plus five support staff, in 1992. The 130 members provide 500 active participants in the EC Committee's work. Meetings with representatives of EC institutions take place on average twice a week. A point is made of holding meetings with the permanent representations of incoming presidencies. The EC committee works closely with the US Mission in Brussels to ensure that 'the interests of multinational business were considered in the development of Community-wide legislation' (Annual Review of EC Committee, 1991, p. 4).

An American company explained in interview why a separate organization for US companies was considered necessary:

> The concern for us has always been the risk of explicit or implicit discrimination or exclusion, either conscious or unconscious. The strong tradition of the dirigiste industrial policy of the six [founding members of the EC] has always sent shivers down the spine of American companies. The interests of third country industries are not always represented by UNICE or the European Round Table. US–EC trade and investment is so large, there are always going to be frictions.

Business interest associations at the EC level

For all the interest and significance of the development of Brussels offices by individual firms, and the important role placed by organizations such as UNICE and the Round Table, the greater part of business interest representation at the EC level is undertaken by associations representing specific industries or even product sectors. The European Chemical Industry Council (CEFIC) has around three times as many staff as all the individual British government relations managers in Brussels combined, and more than twice as many as UNICE. The CEFIC staff is split equally between the 'horizontal' problem-related departments, and the 'vertically'-organized product sector groups. Those staff not dealing with sector groups and affiliated associations are split into two main groups dealing with technical affairs (health, safety, environment, science and technology, etc.) and trade and market affairs (trade issues, single market, energy, etc.). Taking trade affairs as an example of CEFIC's 'horizontal' work, this covers both trade policy issues such as the Uruguay Round and the EC's relationships with the countries of Central and Eastern Europe, and technical trade matters involving EC trade instruments and customs regulations. CEFIC seeks to identify priority areas of activity which are then broken down into issues for its operating committees and task forces to tackle.

Operating from new headquarters linked to the centre of Brussels by metro, in modern offices which house sister associations, with some room for others to move in, CEFIC is a highly effective organisation which is able to deal both with issues affecting the chemical industry as a whole, and to provide a secretariat for groups dealing with issues facing product sectors. Product sector groups may be specific to a chemical, such as chlorine; related to an outlet, such as food additives; or deal with a broadly-based industry, such as flame retardants. Because of the expertise CEFIC can offer both on issues that affect the whole industry, and those affecting particular parts of it, it is able to make a significant impact on the development of EC policy, particularly at an early stage when firm positions have not been taken. This might involve influencing the wording of a draft directive, or helping to secure anti-dumping regulations against imports to the EC, or participating in the debate on the development of trade relations with Eastern Europe.

Product-level associations in any industry can face a heavy workload at particular periods of time, and have relatively little to do at other times. In the early 1990s, IDACE, the European association for infant and dietic foods, was faced with a set of vertical directives for individual dietary sectors; weaning foods, medical foods, slimming foods, foods for intense performance, all of which the Commission hoped to have in place by the end of 1992. Some associations have to interest themselves in some detail in questions relating to the implementation of directives. The Titanium Dioxide Manufacturers Association, a CEFIC Sector Group, has been concerned with the implementation of a directive which relates to the effluents from the industry as the means and techniques required to meet the directive vary according to the specific production conditions of each site.

It is relatively easy for, say, the five producers of methylamines in the EC to identify their common objectives and agree on a policy to pursue them. However, once one moves up from the product to the subsector or sector level, it becomes more difficult to secure agreement among firms from the different member states. For example, in the consumer electronics industry, where Japanese firms have been very successful in the European market, some national associations admit Japanese firms and others do not. The European Association of Consumer Electronics Manufacturers 'is handicapped by a degree of distrust between its member associations' (Cawson *et al.*, 1990, p. 223). Particular difficulties have developed in industries where there are both publicly and privately-owned firms. Britain's privatised electricity supply industry refused to sign a paper prepared by the EC representative organization, Eurelectric, opposing moves to open the EC market to greater competition (*Financial Times*, 10 April 1991). In most cases the EC-level sector associations are federations of federations which means that once the national association has agreed a position on a particular issue, its flexibility in negotiations is limited. Often this leads such associations to produce 'lowest common denominator' policies which meet the concerns of each member association, but do not provide a satisfactory basis for influencing Community policy.

One solution to this problem which has been followed in a few industries has been to form a direct membership association at the EC level with no intervening national level. Such associations have been particularly formed in industries where there are a relatively small number of large multinational companies with production sites in a number of member states and marketing their products on a Europe-wide basis. One of the more recent such associations was the Association of Petrochemicals Producers in Europe (APPE). It was formed as a major group within CEFIC in 1985, partly in response to the overcapacity problem in the European petrochemicals industry, and the possible deterioration of that problem if Middle East petrochemicals products were allowed greater duty-free access to the European market. APPE made a significant impact on the debate about these issues in the late 1980s, one source of its strength being that each of its thirty-two member companies is required to be represented by the most senior executive concerned with petrochemicals production. It therefore relies more than many business associations on the commitment and expertise of its members. Some of its more recent work has been of a more technical study group character, for example, the impact on European petrochemical plants arising from changes in oil refinery operations. A structural overcapacity problem has, however, reappeared which is less easy to deal with than the crisis of the 1980s because there are far fewer European petrochemical plants which are obvious candidates for closure because of their relatively poor competitive performance. APPE can demonstrate the size of the problem; make audiences inside and outside of the industry aware of its nature; and try to ensure that DG IV acts quickly to approve mergers and portfolio swaps designed to reduce the problem.

Certainly, the direct membership formula does not necessarily overcome the problems which result from differences of perspective between member states. From 1972 the automobile industry had a direct membership organisation of European-based car producers at the EC level, the Committee of Common Market Automobile Constructors (CCMC), operating alongside a liaison committee of European motor industry associations (CLCA). However, on such key issue as emission standards, 'the car industry lobby was fragmented along nationalistic and product lines' (Jordan and McLaughlin, 1991, p. 13).

The inability of auto manufacturers to present a common front to the Community led them to propose a merger of the CCMC and CLCA. The CCMC had operated a system of unanimous voting which made it difficult to resolve contentious issues such as Japanese car imports into Europe. It was therefore suggested that the new organisation should have a system of majority voting, but this was unacceptable to Jacques Calvert, the chairman of Renault, who argued that no group chairman should have the right to take part in a majority vote on matters which could jeopardise the life of his company, such as the reduction of EC barriers to Japanese car imports. He also objected to admitting Volvo of Sweden, which is linked to Renault, to the organisation. As a consequence, the other eleven members of CCMC resigned en bloc from the organisation, leaving Mr Calvert as the only member. They then formed a new organisation of fifteen firms, the Association of European Automobile Constructors (ACEA) which was seen very much as an organisation responding to company views rather than those of national trade associations. Under the presidency of the chairman of Renault, the new organisation was active in the summer of 1991 pressing its case with the Commission for restructuring assistance to meet Japanese competition.

Most sectors, however, continue to be represented by federations of federations. Some are better resourced, and enjoy a higher reputation in the Commission, than others. In understanding differences in the effectiveness of EC-level federations, it is necessary to examine both logic of membership and logic of influence factors. The logic of membership refers to the characteristics of the members of an association, so that in the case of a business interest association one would look at such factors as the heterogeneity of the industry in terms of products and methods of production, and the extent to which the Community was treated as a single market, or continued to be divided into a number of national markets. Logic of influence factors refer to the influence on association structure exerted by state actors, with the EC serving as a substitute for the state in the case of Community-wide organisations. (For a fuller explanation of these concepts, see Schmitter and Streeck, 1981.)

The chemical and food processing industries offer a good contrast in terms of both logic of membership and logic of influence factors. On the

logic of membership side, the industries are very different. The distinctive characteristic of the food processing industry is its heterogeneity. It
is split into a number of subsectors in terms of the nature and origins of
the raw materials used, the ways in which they are processed, and the
markets served. There is a broad distinction between first stage sectors
which process farm products, and which are more closely linked to
agriculture, and second stage sectors processing semi-finished products,
which are more like other industrial sectors. The first stage sectors tend
to benefit from the CAP regime because they are often processing
products which can be sold into intervention, while second stage sectors
cannot sell into intervention and in sectors such as confectionery are
processing raw materials obtained from outside the Community which
are affected by the EC's import regime. Harris argues (1989, p. 303)
that the CAP emphasises the split between first and second stage
producers, making it more difficult for the food industry to come to a
united view on many issues.

Although consumers are becoming more cosmopolitan, there are
considerable differences in tastes and methods of food preparation from
one country to another (and even within one country). For example,
there is no EC association for breakfast cereals because they are mainly
eaten in Britain. The industry does have some large firms, particularly
Unilever and Nestlé (although the latter is Swiss-based), but there is a
sharp fall away in size after the French firm BSN and the American-
owned Kraft General Foods. Many firms remain confined to one
subsector (e.g., dairy products) and small and medium-sized firms
remain important in the industry, often confined to regional or even
local markets. The presence of agricultural cooperatives owning
processing plants is a further complicating factor. There is a considerable difference between the structure of the industry in Northern
Europe, which is becoming more concentrated, and that in Southern
Europe, which remains relatively fragmented.

The chemical industry is much more integrated than the food
processing industry in terms of both production methods and markets.
This is reflected in the production process where modern methods of
chemical engineering in capital intensive plants, often linked together
by pipelines, transform feedstocks such as oil into the second stage
derivatives which in turn form the basis for downstream products.
Production is geographically concentrated in a relatively limited number
of locations compared with food processing. Although there are smaller
companies serving particular market niches in the industry, it is

dominated by a relatively small number of multinational companies which tend to treat Europe as a single market. After all, PVC made in Italy is no different from PVC made in Britain, while Italian consumers may prefer locally-made pasta. Unlike many companies in the food industry, these leading companies produce a wide range of products from polyethylene to paints to pharmaceuticals.

On the logic of influence side, the Commission has a considerable interest in the chemical industry because of the environmental, competition and trade policy issues connected with it. As far as the food processing industry is concerned, the Commission has been far more preoccupied with the problems of agriculture and the Common Agricultural Policy than with Europe's largest manufacturing industry in terms of gross output:

> There is . . . a great imbalance of involvement in policy making between agricultural producers (and also primary processors) on the one hand, and secondary processors and consumer interests on the other . . . There is an understaffed food division within DG III, but decisions affecting the food industry have been taken in an ad hoc way by a number of different departments within the Commission. Food industry . . . interests have played an insufficient role in its formulation. (European Parliament, 1989, p. 13)

Harmonisation measures arising from the Single European Act have raised the number and importance of issues arising from Community action which face the industry. The British food and drink industry supports mutual recognition of regulations and standards as the only practical way of developing the internal market, but there are some interests who consider themselves threatened by mutual recognition, and call for a return to compositional or 'recipe' legislation.

Given these differences in the logic of membership and the logic of influence, it is not surprising that the chemical industry organisation, CEFIC, is generally regarded as one of the most effective industry associations operating at the EC level. Swinbank and Harris (1991, p. 215) argue that the EC organisation for the food processing industry, Confédération des Industries Agro-alimentaires (CIAA) has a 'relatively weak organisational structure', reflecting divergent interests in the industry. In their view, 'this inability or unwillingness to present a united front weakens the food industry's case for a [Common Food Policy], and for greater recognition of the industry's needs' (Swinbank and Harris,

1991, p. 216). Whereas CIAA has a small secretariat comparable to that which CEFIC had in the early 1970s, CEFIC had a staff of eighty and a budget of 250 million Belgian francs (approximately £5 million) in 1992. Four thousand company experts are involved at any one time of the year in all its committees and Sector Groups activities.

CEFIC has been particularly effective in reorganising its internal structure to overcome the problems associated with being a federation of federations. These problems were particularly serious in an industry which has a number of large multinational companies whose chief executives may resent too great a role being given to directors of national trade associations. Such directors are frequently perceived as middle-level bureaucrats, although they are often very skilled operators in the maze of EC bureaucratic politics. Under the presidency of Sir John Harvey-Jones (1984–6) a new category of corporate associate membership was created for multinational companies operating on a European scale. An Assembly of Corporate Associate Members was created which elected members to participate in meetings of the body representing national association directors.

In an association in which 75 per cent of the funds are provided by the companies, these changes, although useful, did not solve the fundamental problems. The director of the French national chemical federation, Claude Martin commented:

> It was difficult for everyone in the companies. They felt a bit frustrated. They had to pay, and yet only twice a year were they involved. They launched ideas, but were not the masters of those ideas after that. (*Chemical and Engineering News*, 27 May 1991)

CEFIC responded to these problems by agreeing in 1991 to a new structure which was essentially a bicameral system with an executive board of management. Forty-six multinational companies now have full membership of CEFIC alongside eighteen national federations (EFTA countries are members, along with Hungary, Poland and Turkey as associate members). An Assembly of Federations (AFEM) and an Assembly of Corporate Members (ACOM) each elect nine members to a Board of Directors, which also includes the immediate past, current and future presidents. A five-member executive committee is made up of the presidential members plus one representative from each chamber. CEFIC's ninety-six sector groups dealing with technical issues have generally worked well, but the new arrangements will also ensure that there is top-down management of horizontal issues such as GATT and the Fifth Environmental Programme. Concerns have been expressed that the new structure may not adequately represent smaller companies or smaller countries. Even so, this new hybrid structure represents a model which other EC industry federations may wish to emulate. Indeed, it is understood that it is an option that was discussed within CIAA, but rejected by some of the larger firms.

Each industry has to decide for itself just how important EC-level representation is, and allocate resources accordingly. The construction industry, which is less affected by the EC than most other industries, still bases its organisation in Paris. Even CEFIC lacks the resources it needs to tackle the range of tasks it faces. The head of Dow Europe has commented, 'We are probably not quite yet realistic in giving CEFIC the budget it will need' (*Chemical and Engineering News*, 27 May 1991).

Targets of representation

National business associations place considerable emphasis on per-suading their governments to advance their views in the Council of Ministers. Business seeks to influence national governments at all three stages of the Council's work: working group of experts from the member state capitals; the work of Brussels-based representatives of member state governments in the Committee of Permanent Repres-entatives (COREPER); and the ministerial level (Calingaert, 1992, p. 40). One British business association maintained links with the UK permanent representation in Brussels to check on the advice they were giving to London. 'However, the mission's initiative is largely limited to questions of strategy and tactics because positions are normally established in capitals' (Calingaert, 1992, pp. 40–1). Associations also put some effort into persuading like-minded sister federations in other European countries (particularly the Danish, Dutch and Germans) to lobby their ministers in order to create a blocking minority under qualified majority voting arrangements. This kind of arrangement seems to be on the increase, emphasising the extent to which real power in the EC still lies with national governments, and the limits of what can be achieved by EC-level associations. A few EC-level associations maintain links with the secretariat of the Council of Ministers, principally as a source of information on how matters are progressing. Some associations have been able to develop links with COREPER which reaches agreement on some of the business which has to be considered by the Council of Ministers (so-called 'A' items on the agenda). These contacts are usually between persons in the association and the permanent representation of the same nationality.

In general, however, EC-level associations focus their attention on the Commission. The 'Commission' refers both to the college of commissioners, and their cabinets, and to the 'Commission services', the civil servants who work in the directorates-general of the Commission. 'In many cases business (or at least certain sectors) and the Commission are natural allies, in that both will desire a Community solution to a particular issue' (Calingaert, 1990, p. 38). As one senior EC business association official commented, the Commission can appear rather bureaucratic in its working methods, which is less of a problem for the association officials than for their members: 'we in Brussels are used to that, business managers in London are not.' Large firms can secure direct access to individual commissioners. EC-level business associations often approach the cabinets, or personal staffs, of commissioners, not necessarily the commissioner responsible for the issue. They may seek to persuade another commissioner to oppose a particular proposal when the commissioners meet to make policy decisions. Cabinets are particularly important in the decision-making process in Brussels because the links between directorate-generals are so patchy. Committees and working parties do bring together different directorate-generals, but their working methods are not as well-established as those of inter-departmental committees in Whitehall. As a consequence, there is a tendency for much coordination work to be shifted upwards to cabinet level. Respondents in Brussels interviews generally found cabinets to be approachable and receptive. One business association official in Brussels commented, 'Most of the cabinets are friendly. It is difficult to fix appointments because they are so busy.' A government relations manager remarked, 'we very often talk to cabinet people, they are very accessible. Of course we are trying to defend our company.' Trying to block a proposal at this stage is, however, risky and unreliable, and not a substitute for effective representation at the stage when a proposal is being drafted.

At the level of the directorate-generals, as at the national level, the key to successful lobbying is to prepare a well-argued case drawing on specialist expertise available to the firm or association that does not make claims that cannot be sustained. A lobbyist who follows these rules, and builds up a reputation for providing reliable and balanced information can almost become part of the decision-making process. As one respondent commented, 'The Commission knows lobbyists exist, they know they need lobbyists. The Commission needs the input of lobbyists. You need specialists who have practical experience in industry to come to good legislation.'

One question explored in interviews in Brussels was whether some directorates-general, because of their missions, were better disposed to business representations than others. Earlier research on the relations of the chemical industry with the Community led to the conclusion that 'it was clear that some directorates were less responsive to the views of industry than others' (Grant, Paterson and Whitston, 1988, p. 201). Mazey and Richardson report (1992, p. 102) that 'Several of our respondents perceived differences in policy-making styles of different Directorates-General.' The interviews conducted in 1992 confirmed that association officials and government relations managers outside the chemical sector perceived some differences between directorates-general, although these should not be exaggerated. As one respondent commented:

> It very much depends on people. In DG IV, let's say this guy is easier than that guy . . . UK people are easier to lobby than anyone else. Maybe this is because the UK is more influenced by the US where lobbying is a qualified profession.

DG III, the internal market and industrial affairs division, is often seen as a directorate-general that is particularly aware of the problems of industry. It should not, however, be seen as performing an equivalent of the sponsorship role that the British DTI has regained under Michael Heseltine. Its mission is to complete the internal market rather than to act as a lobby within the Commission for industry. In any case, some respondents thought that it was a less effective within the Commission than was once the case. Viscount Davignon and Lord Cockfield, as commissioners responsible for DG III, carried more weight than Martin Bangemann, and the senior staff levels had also been weakened.

The directorate-general that is often seen as causing the greatest difficulties for business is DG XI, the environment directorate. Some respondents found them easier to deal with others. One complained that his association's relationship with them was 'very poor', but another had a more qualified view:

DG XI are reasonably receptive. In some issues they start off in a very purist way, almost an idealistic way, without much knowledge of what they have to do. They're never averse to communication and information. They are inclined to be a little bit idealistic.

Energy-intensive sectors of industry were particularly concerned by a Commission proposal to impose a carbon/energy tax to stabilise carbon dioxide emissions at 1992 levels by the end of the century. One response by business interests was to develop links with DG XXI, responsible for indirect taxation, to open up discussion about the practical limitations of the proposal.

The European Parliament is given an enhanced role in the decision-making process under the Cooperation Procedure introduced by the Single European Act which applies to many of the measures required to complete the internal market. Instead of just being asked for its advice, as under the traditional consultation procedure, 'The co-operation procedure gives more power to Parliament because there is a second reading of draft proposals and time limits apply' (Andersen, 1992, p. 72). As the European Parliament has become more important, EC-level associations have devoted more attention to making representations there. During plenary sessions, the Parliament building in Strasbourg is full of lobbyists. As one regular visiting lobbyist commented,'Where would the European Parliament be without lobbyists? They would lose their ego.'

In the past, relations with the Parliament were often delegated to consultants, or were just part of one staff member's job in a business association. Much greater emphasis is now being given by associations and government relations managers to influencing the Parliament. The calibre of MEPs is perceived to have increased, and as one government relations manager commented, 'If you have a problem with the Commission, you can influence the Parliament.' The EC Committee of the American Chamber of Commerce notes in its 1991 annual review, 'Greater emphasis was . . . placed on interaction with the Parliament, where the status of the EC committee has been strengthened.' CEFIC appointed a liaison officer with the European Parliament in 1990 to monitor its activities and establish working relations with its members and supporting staff. An agreed list of priority issues has been drawn up, and the liaison officer regularly attends plenary and committee meetings, often accompanied by industry experts. The Parliament itself has become so concerned by the growth of lobbying that it has been discussing registration and a code of conduct. Some respondents, however, felt that they were still not doing enough in relation to the Parliament.

Social partnership

From time to time there is an upsurge of interest among academics in the question of whether the European Community can properly be described as pluralist or corporatist. In many respects, this is not a very useful question, given the elasticity of pluralist models, and the lack of agreement about what constitutes a corporatist arrangement. The importance of social partnership arrangements involving employers and labour has, however, been a recurrent theme in the Community, reflecting the importance of Catholic social thinking (for example, the concept of 'subsidiarity' can be traced back to a German translation of a papal encyclical). A fully corporatist vision would, however, have given a more central role to the Economic and Social Committee of the Community. Representing employers, labour, and other groups such as agriculture and the professions, its purely advisory role means that it has faded into insignificance in Community decision-making. Streeck and Schmitter argue (1991, p. 156), 'Tripartism never really worked in Brussels, and where it was tried, it was always too encapsulated and marginal to come in any way close to a neocorporatist model of governance.'

In the 1970s the Community tried to promote social partnership by organising a series of 'Tripartite Conferences' to discuss macroeconomic and social policies. Business associations were never enthusiastic about these meetings, and they collapsed in 1978 after the European Trade Union Confederation (ETUC) withdrew its support because so little progress was being made. They were revived under the French presidency in 1984 by the then Minister of Employment, Pierre Beregovy, who set up informal discussions between the social partners at the Val Duchesse castle near Brussels. Further meetings were held at Val Duchesse in January and November 1985 between Commission president Delors and other commissioners with UNICE, the ETUC and the European Centre for Public Enterprises (CEEP). At the November 1985 meeting, which was concerned with an employment-creating cooperative growth strategy among other issues, it was agreed to continue discussions. In 1989, a political level steering group was set up to stimulate, channel and extend the social dialogue, with priority being given to education and training and prospects for a European labour market. One unresolved issue, always a problem in tripartite arrangements, was how smaller businesses and retailers could be involved in the dialogue. The European Association of Small and Medium-Sized Craft Enterprises (UEAPME) has been pressing for separate representation, but there is a concern on the business side that this would allow the Commission to divide and rule.

The agreement on social policy arrived at by eleven member states excluding the UK as part of the Maastricht process provided for employers and labour to be consulted jointly before draft directives are issued, and to be allowed nine months after that to reach agreements on details. Any such agreements reached by management and labour at Community level would then be implemented by them through collective bargaining in individual member states as a substitute for EC legislation; or, in the case of the wide range of matters concerning working conditions covered by Article 2 of the agreement, at the joint request of employers and labour through a Council decision on a proposal by the Commission. This provision for the authoritative implementation of decisions reached by the social partners is clearly corporatist in character.

This procedure might be deleted in any successor document to an unratified Maastricht treaty, but what is of interest in any case is the disagreement it provoked within the CBI, illustrating different employer attitudes towards social partnership in the UK compared with other member states. The CBI reluctantly supported the proposal when it found itself in a minority of one. Senior figures at the CBI were nevertheless dismayed that the organisation had signed at all, although an alternative view was that it really had no choice. There was no disagreement about the part of the proposal which gave employers and unions special consultation rights on draft directives, but there was concern at the implication that there might be binding collective agreements. Mr Richard Price, deputy director-general of the CBI commented, 'The CBI has no mandate to negotiate on behalf of its members, and if the agreement requires us to arrive at binding agreements by whatever procedure, we would oppose it' (*Financial Times*, 25 November 1991).

In a general review of organised interests at the EC level, with special reference to the internal market project, Streeck and Schmitter argue that the system of interest representation at the EC level looks more pluralist than corporatist, with the system of interest intermediation being pushed further in a pluralist direction by the 1992 process. They state:

> The evolutionary alternative to neoliberalism as a model for the European political economy is clearly not . . . neocorporatism. More likely appears an American-style pattern of 'disjointed pluralism' or 'competitive federalism' organised over no less than three levels — regions, nation-states, and 'Brussels' . . . Whatever turn the European Community may take after 1992, it will not reverse the tide and reorganise European capitalism in the neocorporatist cast. (Streeck and Schmitter, 1991, p. 159)

This chapter has assumed that the speed and direction of the integration process affects interest group activity at the EC level, rather than interest group activity being a motor of the integration process. Interest groups often set up shop in Brussels when their interests have been seriously affected by a Community decision. For example, the Pharmaceutical Manufacturers Association became the first US trade association to set up a Brussels office after difficulties with the 1988 price and transparency directive affected the pharmaceutical industry.

In the aftermath of the September 1992 crisis which saw turmoil on the foreign exchange markets, and a narrow victory for the Maastricht treaty in the French referendum, further interviews were carried out in Brussels with both new and long-standing informants. One theme that emerged was the relative importance of successfully completing the internal market, and of ensuring that a Community-wide environment regime was constructed rather than allowing member states to take their own environmental measures which hampered trade. Economic and monetary union, although desirable to reduce transaction costs, was of less importance than the single market. There would be a new emphasis on subsidiarity, which would discourage bureaucratic incursions into management prerogatives, and might prevent directives of a kind which had been unhelpful to business in the past. If the Maastricht treaty was not passed, the powers of a European Parliament dominated by social democrats and greens would not be strengthened. There was concern about the seriousness of the rift between Britain and the other member states, particularly Germany. As one respondent summed up, 'There is still a Europe — just. We're still here. It's still a European industry. We shall carry on discussions with the EC institutions that want to hear our members.' The more exaggerated accounts of pressure group transformation at the EC level may come to seem rather dated, but important and enduring changes have occurred in the representation of business interests.

10 Conclusions

In the introduction it was argued that business–government relations in Britain have not been mutually productive. A central theme of this book has been that the economic power of business in Britain is not matched by a capacity for developing a coherent political viewpoint and articulating it to government. Business is capable, through the economic power it is able to exert in product markets, labour markets etc., of exerting a considerable influence over people's everyday lives. Politicians must pay attention to the requirements of business, if they wish to gain re-election as the result of being able to claim that they have managed the economy with a tolerable measure of success. As the politics of production occupies a less central place on the political stage, and as issues related to the politics of collective consumption become more important, politicians also face demands to regulate business in areas such as environmental protection (pollution, packaging etc.) and consumer safety. The central problem then becomes, can a political bargain be constructed with capital which is acceptable to politicians, voters and business persons, and which channels the energies of business without curbing them?

One perspective is that Britain adheres to an Anglo-American model of capitalism which is fundamentally flawed (Crouch and Marquand, 1992). Given that Japan and Germany have been the two most successful economies in the postwar world, inspiration should be sought from their models of business–government relations. There are three difficulties with such an approach. First, the received reading of the Japanese and German cases may have been misleading in some respects. Second, just because something works in Germany or Japan, that does not mean that it would work in a very different context in Britain. Third, it is unrealistic to think in terms of borrowing those parts of the Japanese and German models which we like, and leaving the rest. It can be argued, particularly in the case of Japan, that one has to understand the economy, polity and society as a total system, in which

193

the functioning of one part of the apparatus is dependent on others (van Wolferen, 1989).

Interpreting Japan is very difficult for the person who is not a specialist on Japan, and often seems to be difficult (or perhaps is made to appear so) for those who immerse themselves in the Japanese language, culture and society. One real difficulty is the *honne–tatemae* dichotomy: '*tatemae* or the way things are presented, ostensible motives, formal truth, the facade, pretence, the way things are supposed to be ...; and *honne*, or genuine motives, observed reality, the truth you know or sense' (ibid., p. 235). It is therefore not surprising that interpretations of Japanese success have sometimes tended to reduce a complex set of arrangements to one or two variables. In particular, emphasis has been placed on the role of the Ministry of International Trade and Industry (MITI) in guiding the Japanese economy to its postwar economic success, with MITI seen as having 'a central and dominant role' (Cowling, 1990, p. 204).

This approach is inadequate and misleading in three respects. First, it tends to downplay all the other factors which have contributed to postwar Japanese success: to name just a few, supplies of relatively cheap capital mobilised by the postal savings system; the nature of the primary and secondary education system; the *keiretsu* system of interlinked companies; the existence of a dual economy, with subcontractors offering less secure employment to their workers. Second, it is inadequate even on its own terms. MITI does not dominate the bureaucratic scene in Japan, and there are many other ministries concerned with particular industries (e.g., Posts and Telecommunications, Transport) and much bureaucratic infighting between them. The Ministry of Finance has at least a good claim as MITI to being the ministry which has facilitated the postwar growth of the economy. Third, there are liberal explanations of Japanese success which have as much credence as dirigiste ones. One school of analysts argue that the influence of industrial policy on the Japanese economy 'has been, on balance, marginal or even detrimental' (Eads and Yamamura, 1987, p. 423). At the very least, it is arguable that MITI's decisive role was in the postwar recovery period, and that its influence has declined since. 'Japan is an economy driven by firms not by government' (Porter, 1990, p. 420).

It would be particularly misleading in the case of Japan to suppose that one could borrow one or two elements of the system and graft them on to British arrangements. Looked at as a total package, Japanese arrangements may seem less attractive to Anglo-American eyes (see Fallows, 1990). Defenders of the orthodox reformist wisdom might nevertheless argue that Germany is a proper source of inspiration for Britain. Here it is not a government ministry but the banks that are the heroes of the hour. The uniqueness of the German financial system may sometimes have been overstated (Grant, Paterson and Whitston 1988), but it does offer a set of arrangements which have often played an important role in guiding and reorganising industrial companies without direct government intervention. Germany also offers a working example of the way in which an effective set of business associations can help to foster the competitiveness of both large and small companies. It is, however, one thing to say that it is possible to learn from the operations of German business associations, and quite another to specify how these lessons might be applied in practice.

This point can be illustrated if a comparison is made between the formation of business associations in the former state socialist countries of East-Central Europe and Russia, and the problem of seeking to reform them in Britain. In East-Central Europe, the dramatic break with the past at least offered the possibility of a clean sheet on which a new design could be sketched, even if the outcome is very different from the blueprint. (On developments in Russia see Peregudov, Semenenko and Zudin, 1992.) Indeed, the formation of business interest associations is more than just a mechanism for fostering business–government relations, but an essential element in constructing a civil society. It is thus possible to talk in terms of the design of the system of business interest associations in terms of first principles. There was, for example, in 1992 a vigorous debate in Hungary about the relative merits of American and Austrian models of business representation. If one sought to improve the British system of business associations, one would have to consider not only basic principles, but the complex set of interests and institutional arrangements embedded in the existing system, and how government initiative might stimulate effective change without arousing resentment.

Changes in government–business relations

Is, then, Britain locked into an inherently unsatisfactory set of business–government relationships which cannot be changed? There are actually some grounds for very cautious and modest optimism at the beginning of the 1990s. The events of the 1980s helped by clearing some options out of the way. First, the Labour Party at last seems to have accepted that a socialist solution to Britain's problems is not an option that is going to win electoral support, and that any Labour Government would need to build a constructive partnership with business rather than seeking to place it under state control. One very experienced observer of business–government relations remarked in interview:

> There is a totally different culture today towards business across the board in parties. I don't think that there's this enormous polarisation, there is a much greater awareness that there aren't simple solutions.

Second, the end of neo-Keynesianism, and the associated collapse of neo-corporatism as a real choice on the policy menu, has meant that it is no longer necessary to generally view business associations in terms of their potential capacity as intermediaries. It is therefore possible to look at them much more in terms of their contribution to national competitiveness in areas such as training, quality control and export promotion. A Conservative Government is likely to feel more comfortable with helping to reinvigorate business associations if it can be demonstrated that such a policy would help firms to become more competitive in international markets.

Third, the failure of monetarism, the political collapse of Thatcherism, and the decline in the influence of the more uncompromising versions of neo-liberalism, offers the prospect of a return to a more pragmatic style of politics, although the events surrounding Britain's withdrawal from the ERM gave unreconstructed Thatcherites an opportunity to reassert themselves. In the Thatcher period, there was a sense that business was often too supine to sort out its problems, and needed the solutions provided by a government who knew what business really needed, as distinct from what business said what it wanted. Policies which had business support were often ruled out on the grounds that they did not fit in with prevailing dogma, e.g., Britain's delayed entry to the ERM which then took place at an unpropitious time and at a high rate against the deutschmark. This does not mean that the Major Government will deliver what business wants, but it will listen without too many preconceptions. Michael Heseltine is someone who can be relied on to argue the business case in government if he thinks it is a good one, and who has shown an interest in some of the structural problems of government–business relations in Britain.

Fourth, the Industry and Parliament Trust has continued to work carefully to improve the relationship between business persons and politicians, broadening its activities where it has seen an opportunity to do so. As well as continuing to offer fellowships to MPs, MEPs and Commons officials that offer them a long-term attachment to a company and a practical understanding of its objective, strategies and problems at all its levels of operation, the Trust also provides a parliamentary study programme for industrialists. If nothing else, the Trust's programme helps to overcome the occupational isolation between politicians and business persons which is one of the weaknesses of the business–government relationship in Britain. It is difficult to assess the subtle influence of the long-term work carried out by the Trust, but there is no other body which is making such a constructive contribution to enabling politicians to understand the priorities of business, and business persons the problems of politicians.

The limits of change

There are, however, grounds for pessimism as well as optimism. It is still difficult to get an expert collective viewpoint from business at the national level of the kind that has been provided by the Round Table at the EC level. A remark made by Clement Attlee in 1930 remains applicable today: 'The individualism of the British industrialist, which in the past has been largely responsible for his success, and his conservatism, have made him slower than his foreign rivals to recognise the need for collective action' (Harris, 1982, p. 570). Because business has often been incapable of deciding what it really wants, politicians have often made up their own minds about what is good for business, often with unhappy results. The CBI is one of the most wide-ranging business organisations in advanced industrial countries in terms of its membership base (Coleman and Grant, 1988). That very breadth of membership has, however, sometimes made it difficult for it to speak as authoritatively and unequivocally as events have required.

Second, domestic political arrangements may have decreasing relevance at a time when economic globalisation has been developing at a rapid pace. Indeed, business has recognised as much with its efforts to improve its representational capacity at the EC level. The EC is, however, a regional political structure in a global economy, while

Britain's future relationship with it was very uncertain after the events of September 1992. If the trend for nationally-based multinational companies to internationalise their control structures continues, what political structure exists to provide a regulatory framework for their global activities? This problem is even more acute in the financial system where national regulatory authorities have found it difficult to cope effectively with financial scandals that cut across national boundaries.

Third, four election victories in a row does not create a dominant party system, but Britain has at least the potential to develop into such a system. Once again, there are dangers of 'reading off' from the Italian and Japanese examples which have their own features which are distinctive from Britain. Italy lacks an effective state and is menaced by organised crime, and Japanese politicians have been expected to behave in ways which may be functional to the delicate equilibrium of Japanese society, but have no parallel in Britain. Nevertheless, apart from the more general problem of how effective democratic opposition is ensured, dominant party systems can develop two characteristics which affect business–government relations. First, corrupt relationships can develop between business persons and politicians. What is regarded as a corrupt practice differs from one society to another, and even in adversarial party systems, other cultural characteristics can foster it (e.g., the connection between 'mateship' and corruption in Australia). One should also be careful about drawing a parallel between past experience in one-party local authorities in Northern England, and what might happen at a national level. One could, however, see a set of relationships develop in which particular businesses developed their own contacts with politicians, based, for example, on party donations. In such circumstances, 'A system of privilege is created in which competition among groups is discouraged and participants are urged to accommodate themselves to the dominant system of clientilism' (Atkinson and Coleman, 1989, p. 84).

A second characteristic of a dominant party system would seem to be a close association between particular business interests and factions of the governing party. Although Conservative backbenchers have become more restive and more willing to challenge the party leadership, they have not factionalised in the way that has happened to the ruling parties in Italy and Japan. Suppose, however, that the Conservatives continued in office into the next century. One might then see the party break into factions, some of which related to particular sectors of business, e.g., financial services, smaller firms, large-scale manufacturers. If such a system developed, and it remains simply a possible outcome, business interests would become more fragmented, those interests with the strongest connections being best able to protect themselves.

Another source of difficulty for business–government relations in the future may be increasing environmental constraints placed on business activity. The rigour and range of packaging regulations in Germany offers an illustration of the way in which a government may respond to what it perceives as strongly-held preferences by electors. Attempts by business to point to the cost of particular measures may simply be dismissed as special pleading by an electorate with a broad if ill-defined sympathy for stronger environmental measures.

Constitutional change

In examining the long-run political environment for business, it is necessary to take account of possible future constitutional changes. These are very unlikely in any significant form during the lifetime of the 1992 Parliament, but they have not completely disappeared from the political agenda. For example, a future Labour government dependent on Liberal Democrat and Scottish Nationalist support might feel obliged to introduce constitutional changes in the form of proportional representation and significant legislative devolution to Scotland. Neither of these changes would be welcomed by most business interests.

Proportional representation would make it more difficult to form a stable government, and hence would increase political uncertainty, something which is particularly disliked by business, especially the financial markets. It would increase the chances of a centre-left coalition government taking office which would be less well-disposed to business than a Conservative government. Even if the German system of a mixture of members elected in constituencies and members returned by proportional representation was adopted, the chances of the Greens securing representation in Parliament would be increased. At the very least, other parties would have to pay greater attention to the concerns of likely Green supporters. This could lead to more stringent environmental regulations of the kind adopted in Germany. Such a tough environmental regulatory regime would be particularly difficult for business to cope with in Britain's structurally weaker economy.

Business in Scotland is ambivalent about the question of devolution. Some heads of medium-sized businesses gave support to an organisation called Business Says Yes (to constitutional change) in the run-up to the 1992 election. The CBI in Scotland stated that it accepted that constitutional change in Scotland was inevitable, and that 'the present mechanisms of government could be improved' (*Financial Times*, 21 January 1992). Independence was a dangerous option, however, while the main objection to Labour proposals for devolution was that a Scottish parliament could impose higher income tax in Scotland than in the rest of the UK. Government concern about business opinion in Scotland in the months before the 1992 General Election was emphasised by the revelation that the director of the Institute of Directors in Scotland was called to a meeting at 10 Downing Street with the then head of the prime minister's political unit, Judith Chaplin. She wanted to know how institute members in Scotland had been reacting to the debate on constitutional reform (*The Independent*, 4 February 1992).

Businesses do have some interest in maintaining a separate Scottish sense of identity, if only because it may be a lever for attracting government and EC funds for work on infrastructure. Organisations such as the Glasgow Chamber of Commerce and firms such as Scottish Power and Scottish Hydro Electric were among the supporters of a new Scottish office in Brussels, Scotland Europa, set up in 1992 as a joint venture between the official development body, Scottish Enterprise, and the private sector. It is one thing, however, to seek to increase the flow of EC funds to Scotland, and another to back devolution or independence. A major firm headquartered in Scotland interviewed in 1992 commented that its big concern about devolution was that it might lead to higher taxation there, which would mean that it would have to reduce its head office functions north of the border. There was particular concern in the Scottish financial services sector about the prospect of devolution before the 1992 election. Edinburgh is the second most important centre for fund management in the EC, and the life offices were notably concerned about the impact of any constitutional changes. The existing relationship can suit business interests well because of the ease of personal contact with politicians and civil servants in Edinburgh. The corporate affairs director of a Scotish financial services company commented in interview:

We are closer to the Scottish Office based in Edinburgh than any institution based in London. Edinburgh is much smaller, there are closer contacts, lots of connections which are fairly informal.

Any constitutional changes are unlikely to occur until the late 1990s. Some possible constitutional changes, such as a fixed-term parliament, might be welcomed by business because they would reduce the uncertainty associated with a moveable election date. The combination of proportional representation and Scottish devolution would create a new and uncertain political context for business, and would probably lead to adverse policy changes when viewed from a business perspective.

Living with the company state

Changes in the domestic and the international economy are likely to increase the economic and political displacement of very large firms in Britain. Business–government relations in Britain seem to be very much set in the company state mould, at least for the rest of the 1990s. An analysis of global firms and their relations with states concludes that 'there is a growing possibility for new forms of collaboration between states and firms in the pursuit of shares of world markets' (Stopford and Strange, 1991, p. 204). Multinational companies can no longer be treated as an afterthought in the analysis of international relations. Multinational companies 'are increasingly indispensable allies, whether liked or not' (Stopford and Strange, 1991, p. 211). At a domestic level, given that hopes for some kind of British version of the German associative state have faded, the least unsatisfactory strategic option for the future development of business–government relations in Britain might be to live with the company state by building on its better features.

Such a strategy would require the following steps. First, the formation of government relations divisions in large firms should be encouraged, including the development of operations at the EC level. There is nothing new about government having direct relationships with large firms, but such discussions should take place on a systematic and regular basis. Second, such a strategy requires the formation of a Round Table organisation to represent the largest firms in the economy.

Third, as a quid pro quo for improved access, government should insist that firms act as 'good corporate citizens'. This could involve a package of policies including effective equal opportunity schemes; employee involvement and profit-sharing arrangements; community programmes; environmental objectives; 'best practice' training programmes; and more informative annual reports. Many large companies are already taking action along these lines. A number of major UK companies have joined 'Opportunity 2000', a Business in the Community initiative aimed at increasing the quality and quantity of women's participation in the workforce. One would also expect a 'good corporate citizen' to be involved in the work of the Industry and Parliament Trust. Party donations are best eschewed to avoid the dangers of too close a relationship with the governing party in a quasi-dominant party system.

One of the main objections to such a strategy is that it privileges larger firms at the expense of smaller-scale businesses. That is why business associations should be maintained and reinvigorated to ensure that the concerns of smaller businesses are taken into account. Such associations have always involved an element of cross-subsidisation of smaller firms by larger firms, particularly in the provison of services. Larger firms might be encouraged by government to rationalise and reinvigorate associations, something which has already been success-fully attempted in a number of sectors through large firm involvement. Chambers of commerce have an important role in representing smaller firms, and providing services to them at a local and regional level, and it is believed that the DTI under Michael Heseltine is playing a mediating role between them and the TECs which are seen as potential rivals.

What about the implications of a 'company state' for democracy? The view taken here is that organised interests are an important part of a healthy democracy. Societies which lack such organisations, such as those in East-Central Europe and Russia, need to construct them as part of a process of re-creating civil society. Intermediary organisations are not a threat to freedom, but an essential part of a free society. Brittan argues (1989, pp. 3–4) that the shift to freer markets in Britain has been 'associated with a blitz on intermediate sources of authority between the state and the individual not seen in other countries.' Brittan includes employers' associations in his list of intermediaries, arguing that such centralisation of state power was not needed to eliminate corporatism and is 'incompatible with the dispersion of authority and influence, which is just as much part of a wider liberalism as free markets themselves.' There is thus a broader political case for ensuring that the company state does not go too far, and that intermediary organisations representing a broad spectrum of business opinion are maintained.

Government's role is to ensure that business interests do not prevail over all other considerations. In part, this means ensuring that large companies operate in a responsible way, not necessarily by imposing laws and regulations, but by persuading them that it is in their own interest to do so. Such an approach is most effective when a company develops an internal culture that recognises the importance of its commitments to its own employees and the wider community. ICI and Northern Foods offer good examples of such companies. One cannot, however, rely just on the good intentions of companies to secure public policy objectives. That is why a framework of regulation, and adequate mechanisms of enforcement, are necessary in areas such as equal opportunities, health and safety, privatised utilities and environmental policy. The one area in which further development of regulatory capabilities seems to be necessary is financial services regulation, although that also requires more effective international cooperation between regulators.

The principal roles of government in a company state are therefore those of regulator, and facilitator of best practice. As the economy becomes increasingly internationally integrated, effective political action needs to move to an international level. The European Community is the most advanced of a number of regional political structures developing in the world. It therefore represents the best available, although often flawed, mechanism for cross-national cooperation to regulate business activity, and it has made progress in areas such as competition policy and environmental policy. As the principle of subsidiarity reminds us, however, many problems can still be tackled most effectively at a national or local level, while Britain's future relationship with the Community may be less intense than some other member states, emphasising the importance of national-level initiatives.

There is therefore a need to continue to be concerned about the condition of business–government relations in Britain. The British relationship has many distinctive features which differentiates it from the relationships to be found in other European countries. It is difficult to see prevalent attitudes and existing structures permitting any cooperative solution to Britain's underlying economic problems and their solutions. Britain needs a continuing and informed debate about its government–business relations, not one that anticipates miracle cures based on patent remedies derived from simplified interpretation of German or Japanese experience, but one that recognises that some change is both desirable and possible. A realistic understanding of what is and what is not possible can help to secure feasible changes, a task which has been one of the main purpose of this book. The political climate in the 1990s may encourage a revival of pragmatic realism, permitting a concluding statement of cautious optimism about the prospect for government–business relations in Britain.

Guide to Further Reading

Chapter 1

Leys (1985) is a key article which tackles a number of important issues which arise in the analysis of business and politics in Britain. Smith (1991) provides insights into the ways in which traditional policy communities are challenged by the emergence of new agendas. van Wolferen (1989) offers a thought-provoking account of Japan which challenges much received wisdom.

Chapter 2

Truman (1951) offers a classic pluralist analysis of the role of business in society, whilst Lindblom (1977) offers an important account of the view that business is a privileged interest. Williamson (1989) provides a comprehensive survey of the corporatist debate. Vogel (1989) reminds us that business power may vary significantly from one time-period to another.

Chapter 3

Jordan and Richardson (1987) contains a considerable amount of useful material on government's attitude towards interest groups. Grant, Paterson and Whitston (1988) provides a sectoral analysis of government's relationship with business. Hancher (1990) and Hancher and Moran (1989a, 1989b) offer essential reading on government's role as a regulator.

Chapter 4

Michael Moran is the leading expert on the politics of the financial sector in Britain and all his work is worth reading, especially Moran (1990) and Moran (1991). Ingham (1984) offers a sophisticated and subtle analysis of the economic and political role of the financial sector.

Chapter 5

Alan Cawson has been one of the analysts of government–industry relations who has been most sensitive to the importance of large firms as political actors in their own right, and there is much valuable material in Cawson et al. (1990). Neil Mitchell (1990) provides an informative survey of the political behaviour of large firms. Harvey-Jones (1988, 1991) provides readable accounts of what it is like to be chairman of a major firm. Miller (1990, 1991) provides a consultant's perspective on the political process.

Chapter 6

For the development of the CBI and its predecessors see Blank (1973) and Grant and Marsh (1977). Middlemas (1979, 1986, 1991) provides carefully researched material on the role of organised business interests in British politics. Lynn and McKeown (1988) offer interesting comparative material on business associations in Japan and the United States.

Chapter 7

The literature on business and political parties remains the least well-developed area of those covered in this book. Judge (1990) is a mine of information on the background of MPs, but is well worth reading for the many other insights offered on business–government relations in Britain.

Chapter 8

Streeck and Schmitter (1985) provide a theoretical overview of the potential role of business associations in public policy implementation. On financial services, see Moran (1990); on the dairy industry Grant, (1991c); for contemporary government thinking on the role of business in training, see Cm. 540. Lehmbruch (1984) tackles some of the broader issues in this area.

Chapter 9

Guides on 'how to lobby in the EC' were starting to proliferate, at least before the Danish referendum. Andersen (1992) is one of the better ones. For some of the latest academic research, see Mazey and Richardson (1992). An interesting analysis of the direction being taken by interest representation at the EC level is to be found in Streeck and Schmitter (1991).

Chapter 10

For a comparative review of different national-level forms of business organisation, see Coleman and Grant (1988). Atkinson and Coleman (1989) provide a sophisticated typology of the different kinds of policy networks that may develop between government and business. Stopford and Strange (1991) is the most important book written so far on the global firm in a global economy.

Bibliography

Almond, G. (1983) 'Corporatism, Pluralism and Professional Memory', *World Politics*, 35, pp. 245–60.

Andersen, C. (1992) *Influencing the European Community* (London: Kogan Page).

Anderson, J. J. (1991) 'Business Associations and the Decentralization of Penury: Functional Groups and Territorial Interests', *Governance*, 4, pp. 67–93.

Artis, M. and S. Ostry (1986) *International Economic Policy Coordination* Chatham House Papers 30 (London: Routledge and Kegan Paul).

Ashmore, G. (1988) 'Government and Business: Reducing Red Tape', *Public Money and Management*, 8 (1 & 2), pp. 78–81.

Association of British Chambers of Commerce (1990) *Effective Business Support: a UK Strategy* (London: ABCC).

Association of British Chambers of Commerce (1991) *Effective Business Support: a UK Strategy — Phase Two* (London: ABCC).

Atkinson, M. M. and W. D. Coleman (1989) *The State, Business and Industrial Change in Canada* (Toronto: University of Toronto Press).

Barnett, C. (1986) *The Audit of War* (London: Macmillan)

Barnett, J. (1982) *Inside the Treasury* (London: André Deutsch).

Batstone, E., A. Ferner and M. Terry (1984) *Consent and Efficiency: Labour Relations and Management Strategy in the State Enterprise* (Oxford: Basil Blackwell).

Bell, S. and J. Warhurst (1992) 'Political Activism Among Large Firms', in S. Bell and J. Wanna (eds), *Business – Government Relations in Australia* (Sydney: Harcourt Brace Jovanovich).

Bishop, M. and J. Kay (1988) *Does Privatization Work?* (London: London Business School).

Blank, S. (1973) *Industry and Government in Britain: the Federation of British Industries in Politics* (Farnborough: Saxon House).

_____ (1978) 'Britain: the Politics of Foreign Economic Policy, the Domestic Economy, and the Problem of Pluralistic Stagnation', in P. Katzenstein (ed.), *Between Power and Plenty* (Madison: the University of Wisconsin Press).

Boddewyn, J. J. (1985) 'Advertising Self-Regulation: Organization Structures in Belgium, Canada, France and the United Kingdom', in W. Streeck and P. Schmitter (eds), *Private Interest Government: Beyond Market and State* (London: Sage).

Bonnett, K. (1985) 'Corporatism and Thatcherism: Is There Life After Death?', in A. Cawson (ed.), *Organised Interests and the State: Studies in Meso-Corporatism.* (London: Sage).

Brittan, S. (1989) 'The Thatcher Government's Economic Policy', in D. Kavanagh and A. Seldon (eds), *The Thatcher Effect* (Oxford: Oxford University Press).

Brooke, R. (1989) *Managing the Enabling Authority* (Harlow: Longman).

Brown, G. (1972) *In My Way* (Harmondsworth: Pelican).

Brown, W. A. (1981) 'Comments', in F. Cairncross (ed.), *Changing Perceptions of Economic Policy* (London: Methuen).

Browning, P. (1986) *The Treasury and Economic Policy, 1964–1985* (Harlow: Longman).

Bruce-Gardyne, J. (1986) *Ministers and Mandarins* (London: Sidgwick and Jackson).

Bulpitt, J. (1986) 'The Discipline of the New Democracy: Mrs Thatcher's Domestic Statecraft', *Political Studies*, 24, pp. 19–39.

Burns, P. (1984) 'State Contracts: How to Crack the Market', *The Director*, May 1984, pp. 38–40.

Butler, D. and D. Kavanagh (1984) *The British General Election of 1983* (London: Macmillan).

Cabinet Office (1978) *Industrial Innovation* (London: HMSO).

Calingaert, M. (1992) 'Business–Government Relations', in Committee on Foreign Affairs of the US House of Representatives, *Europe and the United States: Competition and Cooperation in the 1990s* (Washington D.C.: Government Printing Office).

Cawson, A. (1982) *Corporatism and Welfare* (London: Heinemann).

_____ (1985) 'Introduction' in A. Cawson (ed.), *Organised Interests and the State* (London: Sage).

_____ (1986) *Corporatism and Political Theory* (Oxford: Basil Blackwell).

_____ (1988) 'In Defence of the New Testament: a Reply to Andrew Cox, "The Old and New Testaments of Corporatism"' *Political Studies*, 36, pp. 309–15

_____, G. Shepherd, D. Webber (1989) 'Governments, Markets and Regulation in the West European Consumer Electronics Industry', in L. Hancher and M. Moran (eds), *Capitalism, Culture and Economic Regulation* (Oxford: Clarendon Press).

_____, K. Morgan, D. Webber, P. Holmes and A. Stevens (1990) *Hostile Brothers: Competition and Closure in the European Electronics Industry* (Oxford: Clarendon Press).

Cm. 278 (1988) *DTI — the Department for Enterprise* (London: HMSO).

Cm. 540 (1988) *Employment for the 1990s* (London: HMSO).

Cmnd. 9432 (1985) *Financial Services in the United Kingdom: a New Framework for Investor Protection* (London: HMSO).

Cmnd. 9571 (1985) *Lifting the Burden* (London: HMSO).

Coates, David (1984) *The Context of British Politics* (London: Hutchinson).

_____ (1989) 'Britain', in T. Bottomore and R. J. Brym (eds) *The Capitalist Class: an International Study* (London: Harvester Wheatsheaf).

Coates, Dudley (1984) 'Food Law: Brussels, Whitehall and Town Hall' in D. Lewis and H. Wallace (eds), *Policies into Practice* (London: Heinemann).

Coffin, C. (1987) *Working with Whitehall* (London: CBI).

Coggan, P. (1989) *The Money Machine: How the City Works* (Harmondsworth: Penguin).

Coleman, W. D. and W. Grant (1988) 'The Organizational Cohesion and Political Access of Business: a Study of Comprehensive Associations' *European Journal of Political Research*, 16, pp. 467–87.

Constitutional Reform Centre (1985) 'Company Donations to Political Parties: a Suggested Code of Practice' (London: Constitutional Reform Centre).

Coopers and Lybrand associates (1985) *A Challenge to Complacency: Changing Attitudes to Training* (Sheffield: Manpower Services Commission).

Cowling, K. (1982) 'Monopolies and Mergers Policy: a New Perspective', in D. Currie and M. Sawyer (eds), *Socialist Economic Review 1982* (London: Merlin Press).

_____ (1990) 'New Directions for Industrial Policy', in K. Cowling and M. Tomann (eds) *Industrial Policy after 1992* (London: Anglo-German Foundation).

Cox, A. (1988) 'Neo-Corporatism Versus the Corporate State', in A. Cox and N. O'Sullivan (eds) *The Corporate State* (Aldershot: Edward Elgar).

_____ and N. O'Sullivan, 'Preface', in A. Cox and N. O'Sullivan (eds) *The Corporate State* (Aldershot: Edward Elgar).

Cox, G., P. Lowe and M. Winter (1990) 'Agricultural Regulation and the Politics of Milk Production', in C. Crouch and R. Dore (eds) *Corporatism and Accountability* (Oxford: Clarendon Press).

Crafts, N. (1991) 'Reversing Relative Economic Decline? The 1980s in Historical Perspective', *Oxford Review of Economic Policy*, 7, 3, pp. 81–98.

Crouch, C. and D. Marquand (1992) 'Commentary: What kind of Capitalism?', *Political Quarterly*, Vol. 63, pp. 253–7.

Dahl, R. A. (1989) *Democracy and its Critics* (New Haven: Yale University Press).

Danton de Rouffignac, P. (1991) *Presenting Your Case to Europe* (London: Mercury).

Defence Committee (1982) Second Report of the House of Commons Defence Committee 1981–2, *Ministry of Defence Organisation and Procurement* (London: HMSO).

_____ (1990) Sixth Report of the House of Commons Defence Committee 1989–90. *The Physical Security of Military Installations in the UK* (London: HMSO).

Dobson, W. (1991) *Economic Policy Coordination: Requiem or Prologue?* (Washington D.C.: Institute of International Economics).

Dore, R. (1987) *Taking Japan Seriously* (Stanford: Stanford University Press).

Dunleavy, P. (1982) 'Quasi-Governmental Sector Professionalism: Some Implications for Public Policy-Making in Britain', in A. Barker (ed.), *Quangos in Britain*, (London: Macmillan).

_____ (1988) 'Group Identities and Individual Influence: Reconstructing the Theory of Interest Groups', *British Journal of Political Science*, 18, pp. 21–49.

Dyson, K. (1983) 'Cultural, Ideological and Structural Context', in K. Dyson and S. Wilks (eds), *Industrial Crisis* (Oxford: Martin Robertson).

Eads, G. C. and K. Yamamura (1987) 'The Future of Industrial Policy' in K. Yamamura and Y. Yasuba (eds), *The Political Economy of Japan, Volume 1: the Domestic Transformation* (Stanford: Stanford University Press).

Elkin, S. L. (1989) 'The Political Theory of American Business', *Business in the Contemporary World*, 1, pp. 25–37.

European Parliament (1989) 'Report drawn up on behalf of the Committee on Economic Affairs and Industrial Policy on the Food Industry' (Luxembourg: Office for Official Publications of the European Communities).

Fallows, J. (1990) *More Like Us* (Boston: Houghton Mifflin).

Fidler, J. (1981) *The British Business Elite* (London: Routledge and Kegan Paul).

Forster, N. (1983) 'Chambers of Commerce: a Comparative Study of Their Role in the UK and in Other EEC Countries' (London: Industrial Aids Limited).

Forsyth, M. (1981) *Unions of States* (Leicester: Leicester University Press).

Gamble, A. M. and S. A. Walkland (1984) *The British Party System and Economic Policy 1945–83* (Oxford: Oxford University Press).

Garner, R. (1991) 'The Animal Lobby', *Political Quarterly*, 62, pp. 285–91.

Gilmour, Sir I. (1983) *Britain Can Work* (Oxford: Martin Robertson).

Goldthorpe, J. H. (1984) 'The End of Convergence: Corporatist and Dualist Tendencies in Modern Societies', in J. H. Goldthorpe (ed.) *Order and Conflict in Contemporary Capitalism* (Oxford: Oxford University Press).

Grant, W. (1982) 'British Industrial Policy: the Problem and its Perception', *Parliamentary Affairs*, 25, pp. 282–96.

____ (1983) 'Chambers of Commerce in the UK System of Business Interest Representation', University of Warwick, Department of Politics Working Paper No. 32.

____ (1985) 'Introduction' in W. Grant (ed.), *The Political Economy of Corporatism* (London: Macmillan).

____ (1986) 'Why Employer Organisation Matters', University of Warwick Department of Politics Working Paper.

____ (1989) 'The Erosion of Intermediary Institutions', *Political Quarterly*, 60, pp. 10–21.

____ (1991a) 'Continuity and Change in British Business Associations' in W. Grant, J. Nekkers and F. van Waarden (eds), *Organising Business for War* (Oxford: Berg).

____ (1991b) 'DIY: the Government Relations Function of Large Companies', in G. Jordan (ed.), *The Commercial Lobbyists* (Aberdeen: Aberdeen University Press).

____ (1991c) *The Dairy Industry: an International Comparison* (Aldershot: Dartmouth).

____ (ed.) (1987) *Business Interests, Organisational Development and Private Interest Government: an International Comparative Study of the Food Processing Industry* (Berlin: de Gruyter).

____ and D. Marsh (1977) *The CBI* (London: Hodder and Stoughton).

____ and A. Martinelli (1991) 'Political Turbulence, Enterprise Crisis and

Industrial Recovery: ICI and Montedison', in A. Martinelli (ed.), *International Markets and Global Firms* (London: Sage).

____ and S. K. Nath (1984) *The Politics of Economic Policymaking* (Oxford: Basil Blackwell).

____ W. E. Paterson and C. Whitston (1988) *Government and the Chemical Industry* (Oxford: Clarendon Press).

____ and W. Streeck (1985) 'Large Firms and the Representation of Business Interests in the UK and West German Construction Industry', in A. Cawson (ed.), *Organised Interests and the State: Studies in Meso-Corporatism* (London: Sage).

Grantham, C. and C. Seymour-Ure (1990) 'Political Consultants', in M. Rush (ed.), *Parliament and Pressure Politics* (Oxford: Clarendon Press).

Greenwood, J. and Ronit, K. (1991) 'Organised Interests and the Internal Market', Annual Conference of the Political Studies Association, University of Lancaster.

Grove, J. W. (1962) *Government and Industry in Britain* (London: Longmans).

Hall. P. (1986) *Governing the Economy* (Cambridge: Polity).

Ham, A. (1981) *Treasury Rules* (London: Quartet).

Hancher, L. (1990) *Regulating for Competition* (Oxford: Clarendon Press).

____ and M. Moran (1989a) 'Introduction', in L. Hancher and M. Moran (eds), *Capitalism, Culture and Economic Regulation* (Oxford: Clarendon Press.

____ and M. Moran (1989b) 'Organizing Regulatory Space', in L. Hancher and M. Moran (eds), *Capitalism, Culture and Economic Regulation* (Oxford: Clarendon Press).

Hansard Society (1981) 'Paying for Politics: the Report of the Commission Upon the Financing of Political Parties' (London: Hansard Society for Parliamentary Government).

Harris, K. (1982) *Attlee* (London: Weidenfeld and Nicolson).

Harris, S. (1989) 'Agricultural Policy and its Implications for Food Marketing', in C. R. W. Spedding (ed.), *The Human Food Chain* (London: Elsevier).

Harvey-Jones, Sir J. (1988) *Making It Happen* (London: Fontana/Collins).

____ (1991) *Getting It Together* (London: Quality Paperbacks Direct).

Healey, D. (1990) *The Time of My Life* (Harmondsworth: Penguin).

Heller, A. and F. Féher (1988) *The Postmodern Political Condition* (Cambridge: Polity).

Heller, R. (1987) *The State of Industry* (London: Sphere).

Heseltine, M. (1987) *Where There's a Will* (London: Hutchinson)

Hollingsworth, M. (1991) *MPs for Hire* (London: Bloomsbury).

House of Lords (1985) *Report from the Select Committee on Overseas Trade 1984–85, Vol 1, Report* (London: HMSO).

Ilersic, A. and P. Liddle (1960) *The Parliament of Commerce: the Story of the Association of British Chambers of Commerce* (London: Newman Neane).

Industry and Trade Committee (1980) *House of Commons Industry and Trade Committee, Session 1979–80, Department of Industry* (London: HMSO).

Ingham, G. (1984) *Capitalism Divided? The City and Industry in British Social Development* (London: Macmillan).

Jacomb, Sir M. (1985) 'The Role of the Securities and Investments Board', *The Treasurer*, 7, 11, pp. 15–18.

Jenkin, M. (1981) *British Industry and the North Sea* (London: Macmillan).

Jesson, B. (1987) *Behind the Mirror Glass* (Wellington: Penguin).

_____ (1989) *Fragments of Labour: the Story Behind the Labour Government* (Wellington: Penguin).

Jordan, G. (1990a) 'Policy Community Realism versus "New" Institutionalist Amibiguity', *Political Studies*, 38, pp. 470–84.

_____ (1990b) 'The Pluralism of Pluralism: an Anti-Theory', *Political Studies*, 38, pp. 286–301.

_____ (1990c) 'Sub-Governments, Policy Communities and Networks. Refilling the Old Bottles?', *Journal of Theoretical Politics*, 2, pp. 319–38.

_____ (1991) 'The Professional Persuaders', in G. Jordan (ed.), *The Commercial Lobbyists* (Aberdeen: Aberdeen University Press).

_____ and McLaughlin, A. (1991) 'The Logic of Participation in Euro Groups: Some Evidence from the Car Industry', paper presented at the conference on Pressure Groups and Policy-Making in the European Community, European Studies Centre, Nuffield College, Oxford.

_____ and Richardson, J. (1982) 'The British Policy Style or the Logic of Negotiation', in J. Richardson and G. Jordan (eds), *Policy Styles in Western Europe* (London: Allen and Unwin).

_____ (1987) *Government and Pressure Groups in Britain* (Oxford: Clarendon Press).

Judge, D. (1990) *Parliament and Industry* (Aldershot: Dartmouth).

Julius, DeA. (1990) *Global Companies and Public Policy* (London: Pinter).

Kaldor, M., M. Sharp and W. Walker (1986) 'Industrial Competitiveness and Britain's Decline', *Lloyds Bank Review*, No. 162, pp. 31–49.

Katzenstein, P. J. (1984) *Corporatism and Change: Austria, Switzerland and the Politics of Industry* (Ithaca: Cornell University Press).

_____ (1985) *Small States in World Markets* (Ithaca: Cornell University Press).

Kipping, Sir N. (1972) *Summing Up* (London: Hutchinson).

Lehmbruch, G. (1979) 'Liberal Corporatism and Party Government'. in P. Schmitter and G. Lehmbruch (eds), *Trends Towards Corporatist Intermediation* (London: Sage).

_____ (1984) 'Concertation and the Structure of Corporatist Networks', in J. H. Goldthorpe (ed.), *Order and Conflict in Contemporary Capitalism* (Oxford: Oxford University Press).

Lewis, N. (1990) 'Corporatism and Accountability: the Democratic Dilemma', in C. Crouch and R. Dore (eds), *Corporatism and Accountability* (Oxford: Clarendon Press).

_____ and P. Wiles (1984) 'The Post-Corporatist State', *Journal of Law and Society*, 11, pp. 65–90.

Leys, C. (1985) 'Thatcherism and British Manufacturing: a Question of Hegemony', *New Left Review*, no. 151, pp. 5–25.

Linblom, C. (1977) *Politics and Markets* (New York: Basic Books).

Lively, J. (1978) 'Pluralism and Consensus', in P. Birnbaum, J. Lively, G. Parry (eds), *Democracy, Consensus and Social Contract* (London: Sage).

Longstreth, F. (1979) 'The City, Industry and the State', in C. Crouch (ed.), *State and Economy in Contemporary Capitalism* (London: Croom Helm).

Lynn, L. H. and T. J. McKeown (1988) *Trade Associations in America and Japan* (Washington, D. C.: American Enterprise Institute).

MAFF (1984) Ministry of Agriculture, Fisheries and Food, 'Review of Food Legislation: Consultative Document'. (Typescript.)

Marquand, D. (1988) *The Unprincipled Society* (London: Jonathan Cape).

Marsh, D. (1983) 'Interest Group Activity and Structural Power: Lindblom's *Politics and Markets', West European Politics*, 6, pp. 3–13.

_____ and W. Grant (1977) 'Tripartism: Reality or Myth?', *Government and Opposition*, 12, pp. 194–211.

_____ and G. Locksley (1983) 'Capital in Britain: Its Structural Power and Influence over Policy', *West European Politics*, 6, pp. 36–60.

Martinelli, A. and W. Grant (1991) 'Conclusion', in A. Martinelli (ed.) *International Markets and Global Firms* (London: Sage).

_____ and T. Treu (1984), 'Employers Associations in Italy', in J. P. Windmuller and A. Gladstone (eds) *Employers Associations and Industrial Relations: a Comparative Study* (Oxford: Clarendon Press).

May, T. and J. McHugh (1990) 'Policy Making and Small Business in Britain', ESRC Small Business Research Initiative Group.

_____ (1991) 'Government and Small Business in the UK: the Experience of the 1980s', Annual Conference of the Political Studies Association, Lancaster.

_____ (1992) 'Policy Making for Small Business: the Case of the Loan Guarantee Scheme', Political Studies Association Government and Industry Group, Staffordshire Polytechnic.

Mazey, S. and J. Richardson (1992) 'British Pressure Groups: the Challenge of Brussels', *Parliamentary Affairs*, 45, pp. 92–107.

Meier, K. J. (1985) *Regulation* (New York: St. Martin's Press).

Middlemas, K. (1979) *Politics in Industrial Society* (London: André Deutsch).

_____ (1986) *Power, Competition and the State. Volume 1. Britain In Search of Balance, 1940–61* (London: Macmillan).

_____ (1991) *Power, Competition and the State. Volume 3. The End of the Postwar Era: Britain since 1974* (London: Macmillan).

Miller, C. (1990) *Lobbying* (Oxford: Basil Blackwell).

_____ (1991) 'Lobbying: the Development of the Consultation Culture', in G. Jordan (ed.), *The Commercial Lobbyists* (Aberdeen: Aberdeen University Press).

Mitchell, Neil (1990) 'The Decentralization of Business in Britain', *Journal of Politics*, 52, pp. 622–37.

_____ and J. G. Bretting (1991) 'Business and Political Finance in the United Kingdom', Department of Political Science, University of New Mexico.

Mitchell, William (1990) 'Interest Groups: Economic Perspectives and Contradictions', *Journal of Theoretical Politics*, 2, pp. 85–108.

Modern Records Centre (1992) *Employers' and Trade Associations' History* (Coventry: University of Warwick).

Moran, M. (1983) 'Power, Policy and the City of London', in R. King (ed.), *Capital and Politics* (London: Routledge and Kegan Paul).

_____ (1984a) 'Politics, Banks and Markets: an Anglo-American Comparison', *Political Studies*, 32, pp. 173–89.

_____ (1984b) *The Politics of Banking* (London: Macmillan).

_____ (1986a) 'Corporatism Resurrected: Economic Interests and Institutional

Change in the City of London', Number 3 in a series of working papers available from the author at the Department of Government, University of Manchester.

_____ (1986b) 'Investor Protection and the Culture of Capitalism', Number 2 in the author's series of working papers.

_____ (1990) 'Regulating Britain, Regulating America: Corporatism and the Securities Industry', in C. Crouch and R. Dore (eds), *Corporatism and Accountability* (Oxford: Clarendon Press).

_____ (1991) *The Politics of the Financial Services Revolution* (London: Macmillan).

Mueller, A. (1985) 'A Civil Servant's View', in D. Englefield (ed.), *Today's Civil Service* (Harlow: Longman).

National Consumer Council (1989) *In the Absence of Competition* (London: HMSO).

Nettl, J. P. (1965) 'Consensus or Elite Domination: the Case of Business', *Political Studies*, 8, pp. 22–44.

Nielsen, K. (1991) 'Towards a Flexible Future: Theories and Politics', in B. Jessop, H. Kastendiek, K. Nielsen and O. Pedersen (eds), *The Politics of Flexibility* (Aldershot: Edward Elgar).

Nugent, N. (1991) *The Government and Politics of the European Community* (London: Macmillan).

Offe, C. and Wiesenthal, H. (1985) 'Two Logics of Collective Action', in C. Offe (principal author), *Disorganised Capitalism* (Cambridge: Polity Press).

Okimoto, D. I. (1989) *Between MITI and the Market* (Stanford: Stanford University Press).

Olson, M. (1971) *The Logic of Collective Action,* 2nd edition (Cambridge, Mass.: Harvard University Press).

_____ (1982) *The Rise and Decline of Nations* (New Haven: Yale University Press).

Overbeek, H. (1986) 'The Westland Affair: Collision over the Future of British Capitalism', *Caputal and Class*, No. 29, pp. 12–26.

Pahl, R. and J. Winkler, (1975) 'The Coming Corporatism', *Challenge*, March/April, pp. 28–35.

Panitch, L. (1980) 'Recent Theorisations of Corporatism: Reflections on a Growth Industry', *British Journal of Sociology*, 31, pp. 161–87.

Parker, S. (1984) 'Corporatism and Business Interest Associations: the Relationship Between the Confederation of British Industry and its Member Associations with Special Reference to the BRIMEC Experiment', M. A. thesis, University of Warwick.

Peacock, A. (1984) *The Regulation Game* (Oxford: Basil Blackwell).

Peregudov, S., I. Semenenko and A. Zudin, 'Business Associations in the USSR and After: Their Growth and Political Role', PAIS Papers No. 110, Department of Politics and International Studies, University of Warwick.

Pimlott, B. (1985) *Hugh Dalton* (London: Cape).

Pinto-Duschinsky, M. (1981) *British Political Funding 1979–83* (Washington: American Enterprise Institute).

_____ (1985) 'British Political Funding 1979–83', *Parliamentary Affairs*, 38, pp. 328–47.

Pollard, S. (1982) *The Wasting of the British Economy* (London: Croom Helm).

Porter, M. (1990) *The Competitive Advantage of Nations* (London: Macmillan).

Rainbird, H. and W. Grant (1985) *Employers' Associations and Training Policy* (Coventry: University of Warwick Institute for Employment Research).

Reich, R. (1991) 'Who is Them?', *Harvard Business Review*, March/April, pp. 77–88.

Reid, S. (1991) 'Employers' Strategies and Craft Production: the British Shipbuilding Industry 1870–1950', in S. Tolliday and J. Zeitlin (eds), *The Power to Manage* (London: Routledge).

Rhodes, R. A. W. (1986) *The National World of Local Government* (London: Allen and Unwin).

Richardson, J. and Jordan, G. (1979) *Governing Under Pressure* (Oxford: Martin Robertson).

_____ (1990) 'Government and Groups in Britain: Changing Styles', Strathclyde Papers on Government and Politics No. 69.

Rose, R. (1974) *The Problem of Party Government* (London: Macmillan).

_____ (1980) *Do Parties Make a Difference?* (2nd edn 1984) (London: Macmillan).

Ross, J. (1983) *Thatcher and Friends: the Anatomy of the Tory Party* (London: Pluto Press).

Samuels, R. J. (1987) *The Business of the Japanese State* (Ithaca: Cornell University Press).

Sargent, J. (1985) 'The Politics of the Pharmaceutical Price Regulation Scheme', in W. Streeck and P .C. Schmitter (eds) *Private Interest Government: Beyond Market and State* (London: Sage).

Scase, R. and R. Goffee (1980) *The Real World of the Small Business Owner* (London: Croom Helm).

Schmitter, P .C. (1979) 'Still the Century of Corporatism?', in P. C. Schmitter and G. Lehmbruch (eds.), *Trends Towards Corporatist Intermediation* (London: Sage).

_____ (1991) 'The European Community as an Emergent and Novel Form of Political Domination', Centre for Advanced Study in the Social Sciences of the Juan March Institute, Madrid, Working Paper 1991/26.

_____ and W. Streeck (1981) 'The Organisation of Business Interests: a Research Design to Study the Associative Action of Business in the Advanced Industrial Societies of Western Europe' (Berlin: International Institute of Management labour market policy discussion paper).

Securities and Investments Board (1985) 'Regulation of Investment Business: the New Framework' (London: Securities and Investments Board/Marketing of Investments Board Organising Committee).

Select Committee on Members Interests (1991), *Third Report 1990–1, Parliamentary Lobbying* (London: HMSO).

Select Committee on Nationalised Industries (1970) *First Report from the Select Committee on Nationalised Industries 1969–70, Bank of England* (London: HMSO).

Shepherd, D., A. Silberston and R. Strange (1985) *British Manufacturing Investment Overseas* (London: Methuen).

Slatter, R. (1983) 'Managing the Socio-Political Environment in Post-Industrial Society', M. Phil thesis, Oxford Centre for Management Studies.

Smeets, M. (1990) 'Globalisation and the Trade Policy Response', *Journal of World Trade*, 24, pp. 57–63.

Smith, M. J. (1990) *The Politics of Agricultural Support in Britain* (Aldershot: Dartmouth).

_____ (1991) 'From Policy Community to Issue Network: *Salmonella* in Eggs and the New Politics of Food', *Public Administration*, 69, pp. 235–55.

Stezler, I. (1988) 'Britain's Newest Import: America's Regulatory Experience', *Oxford Review of Economic Policy*, Vol. 4, No. 2, pp. 68–79.

Stewart, M. (1984) 'Talking to Local Business: the Involvement of Chambers of Commerce in Local Affairs', Working Paper No. 38, School for Advanced Urban Studies, University of Bristol.

Stones, R. (1988) 'State–Finance Relations in Britain 1964–70: A Relational Approach to Contemporary History', Essex Papers in Politics and Government No. 58.

Stopford, J. and S. Strange (1991) *Global States, Global Firms* (London: Cambridge University Press).

Streeck, W. (1988) 'Interest Heterogeneity and Organizing Capacity: Two Class Logics of Collective Action?', conference on 'Political Institutions and Interest Intermediation' on the occasion of Gerhard Lehmbruch's 60th Birthday, Konstanz.

_____ and P. C. Schmitter (1985) 'Community, Market, State — and Associations? The Prospective Contribution of Interest Governance to Social Order', in W. Streeck and P. C. Schmitter (eds), *Private Interest Government: Beyond Market and State* (London: Sage).

_____ and P. C. Schmitter (1991) 'From National Corporatism to Transnational Pluralism: Organized Interests in the Single European Market', *Journal of Social Policy*, Vol. 19, pp. 133–164.

Swinbank, A. and S. Harris (1991) 'The CAP and the Food Industry', in C. Ritson and D. Harvey (eds) *The Common Agricultural Policy and the World Economy* (Wallingford: C. A. B. International).

Taylor, W. (1991) 'The Logic of Global Business: an Interview with ABB's Percy Barnevik', *Harvard Business Review*, March–April 1991, pp. 91–105.

Tether, P. (1991) 'Patrons' Clubs in the Conservative Party: a Special Kind of Membership', *Political Quarterly*, Vol. 62, pp. 291–3.

Tolliday, S. (1984) 'Tariffs and Steel, 1916–1934: The Politics of Industrial Decline' in J. Turner (ed.), *Businessmen and Politics* (London: Heinemann).

Traxler, F. (1990) 'Interests, Politics and European Integration: Austria's Political System in the Wake of 1992', paper prepared for the World Congress of Sociology, Madrid.

Truman, D. (1951) *The Governmental Process* (New York: Knopf).

Turner, J. (1984) 'The Politics of Business', in J. Turner (ed.), *Businessmen and Politics* (London: Heinemann).

_____ (ed.) (1984) *Businessmen and Politics* (London: Heinemann).

Tylecote, A. (1981) *The Causes of the Present Inflation* (London; Macmillan).

Useem, M. (1984) *The Inner Circle: Large Corporations and the Rise of Business Political Activity in the US and UK* (New York: Oxford University Press).

_____ and A. McCormack (1981) 'The Dominant Segment of the British Business Elite', *Sociology*, 15, pp. 381–406.

Utton, M. (1982) *The Political Economy of Big Business* (Oxford: Martin Robertson).

Veljanovski, C. (1987) *Selling the State* (London: Weidenfeld and Nicolson).

Vickerstaff, S. (1985) 'Industrial Training in Britain: the Dilemmas of a Neo-Corporatist Policy', in A. Cawson (ed.) *Organized Interests and the State* (London: Sage).

Vogel, D. (1986) *National Styles of Regulation; Environmental Policy in GB and the US* (Ithaca: Cornell University Press).

_____ (1989) *Fluctuating Fortunes: the Political Power of Business in America* (New York : Basic Books).

Westergaard, J. and H. Resler (1976) *Class in a Capitalist Society* (Harmondsworth: Penguin).

Wigham, E. (1973) *The Power to Manage* (London: Macmillan).

Wilks, S. (1984) *Industrial Policy and the Motor Industry* (Manchester: Manchester University Press).

Williamson, P. J. (1989) *Corporatism in Perspective* (London: Sage).

Willmott, H. C. (1985) 'Setting Accounting Standards in the UK: the Emergence of Private Accounting Bodies and Their Role in the Regulation of Public Accounting Practice', in W. Streeck and P .C. Schmitter (eds), *Private Interest Government: Beyond Market and State* (London: Sage).

Wilson, G. (1990) *Interest Groups* (Oxford: Basil Blackwell).

Wilson, J. (1990) 'Wilderness Politics in BC: The Business Dominated State and the Containment of Environmentalism', in W. D. Coleman and G. Skogstad (eds) *Policy Communities and Public Policy in Canada*, (Mississauga: Copp Clark Pitman).

Windsor, D. (1989) 'The Theory of Business Politics', paper delivered at the 1989 annual meeting of the American Political Science Association, Atlanta.

Wolferen, K. van (1989) *The Enigma of Japanese Power* (London: Macmillan).

Wood, D. M. (1987) 'The Conservative Member of Parliament as Lobbyist for Constituency Economic Interests', *Political Studies*, 25, pp. 393–409.

Wormell, J. (1985) *The Gilt-Edged Market* (London: Allen and Unwin).

Young, D. (1990) *The Enterprise Years* (London: Headline).

Young, H. and A. Sloman (1984) *But, Chancellor* (London: BBC).

Zeitlin, J. (1991) 'The Internal Politics of Employer Organization: the Engineering Employers' Federation', in S. Tolliday and J. Zeitlin (eds) *The Power to Manage?* (London: Routledge).

Index

NOTTINGHAM UNIVERSITY LIBRARY